Performance-Based
Reporting

Performance-Based Reporting

New Management Tools for Unpredictable Times

HANS V.A. JOHNSSON

and

PER ERIK KIHLSTEDT

WILEY

John Wiley & Sons, Inc.

This book is printed on acid-free paper. ∞

Copyright © 2005 by John Wiley & Sons, Inc. All rights reserved.

Published by John Wiley & Sons, Inc., Hoboken, New Jersey.
Published simultaneously in Canada.

No part of this publication may be reproduced, stored in a retrieval system, or transmitted in any form or by any means, electronic, mechanical, photocopying, recording, scanning, or otherwise, except as permitted under Section 107 or 108 of the 1976 United States Copyright Act, without either the prior written permission of the Publisher, or authorization through payment of the appropriate per-copy fee to the Copyright Clearance Center, Inc., 222 Rosewood Drive, Danvers, MA 01923, 978-750-8400, fax 978-646-8600, or on the web at www.copyright.com. Requests to the Publisher for permission should be addressed to the Permissions Department, John Wiley & Sons, Inc., 111 River Street, Hoboken, NJ 07030, 201-748-6011, fax 201-748-6008.

Limit of Liability/Disclaimer of Warranty: While the publisher and author have used their best efforts in preparing this book, they make no representations or warranties with respect to the accuracy or completeness of the contents of this book and specifically disclaim any implied warranties of merchantability or fitness for a particular purpose. No warranty may be created or extended by sales representatives or written sales materials. The advice and strategies contained herein may not be suitable for your situation. You should consult with a professional where appropriate. Neither the publisher nor author shall be liable for any loss of profit or any other commercial damages, including but not limited to special, incidental, consequential, or other damages.

For general information on our other products and services, or technical support, please contact our Customer Care Department within the United States at 800-762-2974, outside the United States at 317-572-3993 or fax 317-572-4002.

Wiley also publishes its books in a variety of electronic formats. Some content that appears in print may not be available in electronic books.

For more information about Wiley products, visit our web site at *www.wiley.com*.

Library of Congress Cataloging-in-Publication Data:

Johnsson, Hans.
  Performance-based reporting : new management tools for unpredictable times / Hans V.A. Johnsson and Per Erik Kihlstedt.
    p. cm.
  Includes index.
  ISBN-13 978-0471-73543-4 (cloth)
  ISBN-10 0-471-73543-4 (cloth)
  1. Corporation reports. 2. Financial statements. 3. Performance. 4. Management. I. Kihlstedt, Per Erik. II. Title.
  HG4028.B2J64 2005
  657.3—dc22   2005010213

Printed in the United States of America.

10 9 8 7 6 5 4 3 2 1

To Mick and Peggie,
with thanks for many years
of patience and support!

Hans   *Per Erik*

Contents

Preface

NEW MANAGEMENT TOOLS FOR UNPREDICTABLE TIMES

A company is more than its accounting data. The aspects and forces that create the numbers, not the numbers as such, are the factors that should be located, defined, and reported, helping managers reduce risk and maximize opportunities in uncertain times. This book aims to put accounting data where they belong, and help managers keep their focus on leading performance indicators in managing for success.

Accounting was long taken for granted as a reliable basis for business reporting, management, and decision making. The wave of dishonesty in big companies, doubletalk of auditing giants, deceptive consulting methods, and rash initiatives taken by legislators have raised justified questions about the usefulness of traditional reporting. Add to that a gradual realization of the dramatic changes in the business world of the twenty-first century.

This book presents radically different but thoroughly tested, 80-percent accounting-free methods for performance-oriented management, assessment, and reporting. More than 25 years of intense experiments and practical use of business-based alternatives to accounting-based methods back up the proposals. More than 1,500 businesses have been involved in testing and improving various elements of the proposed system. Input from more than 4,000 executives has been part of the development work. The results show beyond reasonable doubt that not only do we need new tools for realistic business planning and management in an unpredictable world. Such tools *exist* and can be put to use now!

The Baseline Approach to reporting and management has successfully gone through the scrutiny of years of real-life applications and adjustments.

Six management situations are covered in Part II:

- Business planning in Chapter 5
- Corporate governance in Chapter 6
- Due diligence in Chapter 7
- Fair and meaningful disclosure in Chapter 8
- Auditing and risk management in Chapter 9
- Bank lending, investment, and financing in Chapter 10

Each of these chapters includes real-life examples and cases. In each of them, we outline the traditional approach and then show the Baseline approach as a realistic alternative.

How can *one* system be helpful in all these different situations of advanced decision-making? One simple explanation is that Baseline addresses precisely the fundamental forces and factors that play decisive roles in creating weaknesses and strengths in any company. The ultimate competitive advantage for any company is maximum "freedom to act." Any limitations to freedom to act, inside the company or in the company's environment, also limit its chances of success in terms of survival, growth, and earnings.

The six segments will review areas where Baseline has been proven to provide qualified support to decision making, consistently leading to a higher success rate. We are convinced you will find them thought provoking. As you go into them, please refer to the diagram of the four bases in Chapter 4, and brush up your familiarity with the Baseline mindset.

Thomas S. Kuhn, scientist and philosopher, launched the idea that science advances in jolts and paradigm shifts, not in small, continuous steps. It is our hope that we are seeing the beginning of such a shift in the history of accounting.

Hans V.A. Johnsson   **Per Erik Kihlstedt**
Sarasota, Florida   Stockholm, Sweden

June, 2005

Performance-Based Reporting

PART ONE

New Reporting Needs
for a New Time

CHAPTER 1

Accounting—Crisis or Crime?

Cost and price, but never value,
are what balance sheets can tell you.[1]

THE ACCOUNTING TRADITION

Then and Now—A Touch of History

The fifteenth century was a remarkable period in history:

- Leonardo da Vinci, the universal genius whose name has been revived beyond belief in the last few years, created great art and made impressive designs and inventions.
- Gutenberg launched a new technique for book printing. His invention changed the world, and made new forms of education, information and opinion-building possible.
- Christopher Columbus and Vasco da Gama made bold exploration trips to unknown lands and cultures and changed our perceptions of the world forever.
- Copernicus defied the official truth and put his life at risk as he stated that the earth circled around the sun, not the other way round.
- In 1494, Luca di Pacioli, math professor and Franciscan monk in Northern Italy, published a summary of the double entry accounting system, which entitled him to be named the father of accounting.

That Was Then—This Is Now!

No matter how much we appreciate da Vinci's contributions, we would not send his drawings to Sikorsky and ask them to build a helicopter from them.

While we recognize Gutenberg's invention, we do not print books today the same way as Gutenberg did.

We think highly of the pioneering spirit of the fifteenth-century explorers, but we do not use navigation instruments from the *Pinta* and *Santa Maria* to guide our space ships.

We respect Copernicus's courage and vision in giving us a new view of the world. Yet, today's astronomers and physicists have added entirely new aspects to how the universe works and looks.

Amazingly, 500+ years later we still use di Pacioli's accounting system to guide companies into the global, postindustrial economy of the twenty-first century.

"Buttons on Coat Sleeves"

Over the centuries, tons of academic discourses, detailed guidelines, and government regulations have been added to di Pacioli's 36 short chapters. Fifteenth-century goose quills, abacus frames, and leather-bound ledgers have been replaced by computers. Yet, the system we use is the same. This, in itself, is a tremendous achievement, which means that di Pacioli beats his famous contemporaries by a long shot!

Is it the same system? On the web site[2] of The Association of Chartered Accountants in the United States, John R. Alexander, founder of Net Gain, concludes a long, well-written article on the history of accounting with the statement: "Perhaps most surprising is how little bookkeeping methods have changed since Pacioli." Alexander also quotes accounting historian Henry Rand Hatfield, writing about bookkeeping techniques, "persisting like buttons on our coat sleeves, long after their significance has disappeared."

From the Only Legitimate Role of Accounting to "The Swiss Army Knife"

While we can understand the driving forces behind such initiatives as Sarbanes-Oxley and Basel II, we suggest that the most serious reporting problems cannot be solved by regulation or legislation. Neither will stricter supervision and harsher punishments of wayward CEOs, CFOs, accountants, or auditors be sufficient, even if such measures have a role to play. The crucial issue is not the rules of accounting. It is the exaggerated role of accounting.

Over the centuries, accounting has increasingly come to be used for applications far beyond what it was ever intended for. These extended uses or misuses of accounting are at the roots of many of the problems plaguing the global business community today. They have been exacerbated by the fundamental changes in how we do business in the twenty-first century.

Accounting started out as a specialized tool with one main function: to monitor business transactions. This role, keeping track of the ongoing transactions of a business, is also one that accounting still performs reasonably well. It is when we allow accounting to go beyond this role that it loses its contact with reality. When we start to assign additional meanings to income statements and balance sheets, beyond their function as corollaries of correct entering of basic data, accounting becomes a fallacy.

In the course of its existence, accounting changed from its simple brief of reporting business transactions. It was made to serve and support almost any function in business and the economy. It was seen as an instrument for "valuation." It was applied to decisions on strategies and tactics, used in forecasting, planning, analysis, investments, bank lending, insurance, company mergers and splits, risk assessment, and almost any other kind of business decision making. National and international legislation, taxation, lending and investment policies, and business and banking codes were built on accounting. Ratios based on accounting data have been used to rank and rate companies, with severe consequences. Accounting has been believed to serve equally well in defining the national economies of the biggest countries in the world as in describing the business health of the street-corner bike shop. It has been used to blow bubbles and spread smoke screens. Even limited questioning of the all-inclusive usefulness of accounting has been seen as worse than heresy by fundamentalists in the accounting community. Accounting gradually turned into an all-purpose tool, a "Swiss Army knife" of the business community.

At one time or another there may have been reasons for some of these added applications. In most cases, those reasons, whatever they were, have now either faded away or disappeared altogether, like once-living animals became fossils when their life pattern did not adapt to a changing environment.

"Use Only as Directed"

When doctors and pharmacists hand over prescription drugs that are supposed to relieve pain or bring a patient back to health again, they are anxious to ensure that the medication must be used only as prescribed. The best medication can be dangerous if taken without appropriate caution. Also, nobody should expect a drug to work wonders for any health problems it was never intended to cure. Using ever-so-good medication for the wrong purposes, with the wrong expectations and in the wrong contexts, involves risks. It can even be fatal. The same is true for many electrical appliances, chemical substances, or sophisticated tools and equipment that we use in farms, factories, and homes. Any substance or equipment can be dangerous, or fatal, if used without appropriate caution. This is why manufacturers add strict guidelines and warnings to their products, often supported by government regulation in one form or another. Accounting is no different. It can be a good tool when used for the purposes it was intended for. Ample experience shows that other uses can be dangerous or even fatal.

A conclusion that is long overdue is: To save what is left of its shattered reputation, accounting should be led back to its only legitimate function, direct registration of business transactions.

Our economy needs and deserves other systems for other applications. Such in-depth functions as support of business decision making and relevant, transparent company reporting must be left to business-focused, before-the-fact systems, not finance-focused after-the-fact systems. We need systems that put relevance above (apparent) precision and that give useful, reliable, and timely information about the fundamentals that move companies today.[3]

Reliability and Relevance

Conventional trust in accounting rests on the assumption that published data are both reliable and relevant. The accounting scandals over the last several years have put the spotlight on some of the overall shortcomings of accounting, in both these regards. The records of the SEC and other supervisory authorities show that published data of a big proportion even of highly respected companies are dubious, at best, and a result of management estimates rather than objective facts.

This chapter will deal mainly with the overall lack of reliability, and the next chapter mainly with the lack of relevance in the light of the dramatically different business situation in the twenty-first century.

"There Are Few Words More Reassuring to Investors Than Accountability"[4]

The fact that accounting, as a tool for decision making, is in a crisis is hardly in doubt. It is moving from a situation of broad trust to a situation of being suspect, linked to some of the most dramatic economic crimes of our time. Is the word "misdemeanor"[5] an acceptable term for a function that contributes to create losses to the tune of billions? A crucial question is: *Does accounting, in the extended way we use it, support accountability, or is it an impediment to transparency and accountability?*

CFO Magazine: "The Failure of Accounting"

We cannot claim authorship of the headline "The Failure of Accounting," although we would have liked to. We quote it from a source that has more authority in these matters than we do: It was first used as the headline of an editorial of no less a publication than *CFO* magazine, as early as December 1994.

We accept that a lot of substance and proof (and guts!) will be required to criticize a system with as much clout and historic support as accounting. Fortunately (for us!), over the years that we have worked on these issues, the harshest aspects of our criticism have been increasingly vindicated. We started out suspecting that the accounting system was less than perfect, but we did not imagine that it was that bad. Only in the last four to five years, the media have supplied more material to support our criticism than anyone could have asked for. We will refer to some of this material on the following pages, but no single volume could ever accommodate all the documentation we have encountered.

The consequences of the failing or misused accounting system have been dramatic. Day-to-day decisions based on or influenced by accounting data have created losses in the range of hundreds of billions of dollars, if they can be measured at all:

- Disastrous mergers and acquisitions that have wiped out billions of shareholder assets
- Bank lending mistakes that have forced enormous write-offs, while neglecting the finance needs of deserving companies
- Misappropriated venture capital financing that destroyed shareholder value
- Misguided advice from financial analysts that has led to huge investor and retirement fund losses
- "Undue negligence" from big banks in the underwriting of bond issues for companies that went bankrupt soon after the issues
- Auditing and risk assessment processes that diverted board, manager, investor, and regulator attention from business issues to financial issues, such as "goodwill"

Case in Point—A History of Bubbles

The history of the world economy is a dramatic sequence of bubbles or drastic value swings, such as tulip bubbles in seventeenth-century Netherlands, the Paris-based Mississippi bubble, the London-based South Sea bubble in the eighteenth century, cross-national gold bubbles over hundreds of years, the big American railroad bubble in the mid-nineteenth century, twentieth-century real estate bubbles in Europe, Japan, and the United States, savings bank failures in the United States, currency bubbles in Russia, Germany, Brazil, Venezuela, and other countries, repeated stock exchange bubbles, IT, bandwidth, and telecom bubbles as well as the Sunbeam, Enron, Worldcom, Parmalat, Global Crossing, and other corporate disasters of our time.

Somewhere behind all these and many other bubbles there seems to be a common denominator: too many people putting too much confidence, for too long, in data provided, rightly or wrongly, by "good old" accounting—data that told a manipulated and incomplete story. In all these, and a number of other "bubble" cases, accounting, for a time, provided an apparent rationale for something that proved to be far from rational. The hot air that inflated the bubbles was the misguided trust that accounting commanded and still commands among accounting fundamentalists. The bubbles were largely accounting bubbles.

Case in Point—Red Flags

A Reuters news release, signed by Christopher Noble and relayed on AOL February 13, 2001, had the alarming headline: "Corporate Accounting Woes Raise Red Flags." The news release summarized "a rash of accounting problems" under investigation or review by the SEC and other financial supervisory bodies. The companies mentioned were not from the back alleys of the business community. They included top-of-the-line companies, such as Lucent, Xerox, Cendant, and Belgium-based Lemout & Hauspie. The alarm bells sounded after several other similar cases had been brought to the attention of the investing world. The article quoted big-scale investors who do not feel that these revelations were the end of the story; rather "they expect more of this to happen, not less."

Unfortunately, as we all know, they have been proven right. "More of this" has indeed happened. We read about new cases practically every day.

Those who still believe in accounting are naturally surprised when red flags go up. For those who have seen the warning signs for a long time, the news is not surprising—only depressing—and challenging, in that they confirm the urgent need for change.

An obvious consequence is that both the general public and the business community all over the world experience a lack of trust in accounting and related disciplines, such as auditing. Accounting has been used extensively over the centuries for purposes far beyond its capacity. It has been seen as a basic element, a pillar stone of the whole economic system, which means that when accounting is hit by this lack of trust, it affects the public trust in the business community in general. The loss of trust is reinforced by the fact that too many banks and other companies have stretched the limits of their reporting practices beyond what has been acceptable by supervisory bodies, such as the SEC and FASB in the United States, and their equivalents in other countries.

Accounting has simply proven to be too easy to adapt to shoddy practices and misleading presentations. By being too accommodating to dubious procedures, accounting, and its once-trusted guard and watchdog, auditing, have fallen from the position of credibility and accountability that the general public and the business community should be able to expect from these professions. Illegal, unethical, or borderline practices may hopefully still be in a minority, but the questions surrounding accounting are too many and too serious to keep the lines of trust as strong and clear as they should be.

THE ETHICS OF ACCOUNTING— ILLEGAL, IMMORAL, OR INDIFFERENT?

"Lies, Damned Lies and Managed Earnings"

Fortune, in its issue of February 19, 2001, quotes an example of "managed earnings," managed in order to present consistent quarter-to-quarter earnings growth from the very icon of management perfection, General Electric. Andy Serwer, the writer of the *Fortune* article, cautiously says: "This kind of earnings management isn't illegal, maybe not even immoral. The concern, rather, is that it is not transparent." For details on this case, Fortune refers its readers to the fortune.com archives, under the telling headline "Lies, Damned Lies and Managed Earnings."

In her Market Watch column in the *New York Times*, September 20, 2001, Gretchen Morgenson writes: "The momentous earnings reported by many companies in recent years may have been *digitally remastered* [our emphasis!] to include a lot of hype, embroidery and fluff."

Case in Point—Sunbeam

One of the early cases of "managed" accounting in the wave of dubious cases in later years is the story of Sunbeam.[6]

According to several reports, Sunbeam, under CEO Al Dunlap, ran a severe case of book-cooking. The income statement was "managed" to an extraordinary extent. Commissions to sales reps were withheld, bills went unpaid, vendors were coerced into accepting part payments. Deep product discounts made retailers buy more than they could sell within a reasonable time frame, long credit terms were granted, customers were pre-billed, meaning that Sunbeam booked items that would have been sold in the future as if the sales were made at present. It was an unusually clear case of accounting used to disguise or confuse real business. As a consequence, Sunbeam lost valuable intangibles, such as a loyal management team and a functioning Human Resources Department. It also destroyed important day-to-day resources, such as its computer systems, to the point that the company could not even bill its customers.

Early in 2001, the SEC sued Al Dunlap. In September 2002, Dunlap agreed with the SEC on paying a fine of $500,000, at that time a record amount for settling an accounting case.

Al Dunlap's efforts to save Sunbeam at all costs may have had noble motives. Even so, the means used to reach such goals offered a lasting example of the shortcomings of accounting, or, rather, the ease with which accounting can be misused.

Case in Point—Xerox

The case of Xerox in the 1970s and 1980s, showing excellent profits as it marched, whistling and humming, toward disaster, is well known in management literature. Accounting-based reporting failed to show that profits did not come from happy, satisfied customers. The earnings were based on repair service of faulty copiers. When competitors came in with copiers that did not need a lot of repair, tired customers took the opportunity to jump to the higher-quality products and left Xerox in the doldrums.

What adds to the injury is that, once a company has fallen from glory, it can be very hard to regain a leading position. This is shown by Xerox's ongoing problems, some of which, although not all, are based on shortcomings in accounting. After pressure from the SEC, these shortcomings, reported to have inflated revenues by no less than $3 billion between 1997 and 2000, were recognized by the company, though without admitting any guilt. The company agreed to restate earnings for 1997–2000 and to review its accounting practices. It also had to pay a $10 million fine. The financial reporting of Xerox was opaque. Business-focused reporting would have been more transparent.

Case in Point—Warnaco

According to reports in respectable business media, Warnaco, a company in the fashion business, seems to have stretched the limits of accounting beyond what is acceptable, even with a very broad-minded approach. Positive earnings reports from ongoing operations fooled many seasoned analysts. The seriousness of the adjustments for "nonrecurring" charges made in the footnotes was shrugged off, even when those charges "recurred" time and again. Regular business costs were booked as nonrecurring charges, insurance reimbursements booked as regular revenues, restructurings, which in our time are ongoing adaptations to constant changes in the business environment, treated as special charges, discrepancies between announcements for the general public and the stricter 10-K reports, pointing to a willingness to use the weaknesses of accounting by stretching the standards.[7]

In June 2001, Warnaco filed for bankruptcy under Chapter 11.

Are These Cases Unique?

Sunbeam, Xerox, and Warnaco are three cases of managed earnings—"digital remastering" of accounting that have come under SEC investigation—although it can be argued that they are not necessarily worse or more dramatic than many others.

It would be somewhat comforting if we could say that these cases are exceptional. Unfortunately, it does not seem so. New cases of questionable or outright deceptive accounting are revealed practically every day. A big number of cases are reported—and even more cases are probably not reported—to supervisory and regulatory bodies in many countries. A complete list of examples would be hard to compile and too long to publish.

While the Sunbeam story may be exceptional in its way, it is far from unique. The SEC has boxes of similar cases in their files. The Enron and Worldcom cases may be exceptional through the amounts and the number of people affected. Another example is Rite Aid, which was reported, in *Fortune,* August 14, 2000, to have overstated its earnings for 1998 and 1999 by a (then!) shocking $1.6 billion!

Cases in Point—Enron

Among the hundreds or thousands of cases, Enron is one of the best examples of how strongly the "valuation," in the sense of the current stock price, of a company reflects market perceptions, "the eye of the beholder," rather than any absolute and intrinsic value criteria. At the peak of Enron's market capitalization in early 2001, confidence in management and company performance ran high, resulting in a stock price above $80. Then came opinions and fears—rather than the reality—of unfavorable trends in natural gas prices and an oversupply of electric power. But more than that, in the eyes of many observers, the cut by two-thirds of the Enron share price in the nine first months of 2001 can be seen as the result of a credibility gap. In addition to a massive management exodus and heavy insider selling, the *New York Times* Market Watch column of Sept. 9 2001, lists a typical range of "indecipherable" accounting practices, "sketchy" disclosures of important relationships, and reporting practices that make it "essentially impossible" to understand Enron's statements. Other commentators depict its financials as "dim on the opaque side." In November 2001, the company acknowledges that there was a reason for the credibility gap: For years it had overstated earnings, underreported debt, and kept serious financial and structural problems hidden from shareholders and other stakeholders. In an SEC filing, it admits that financial statements from 1997 through the first half of 2001 "should not be relied upon."

The company tamely acknowledged the credibility problem and promised, "We are looking at a lot of ways to give our investors more information." Hopefully, it aimed at delivering not only more information, but more relevant information than traditional accounting provides.

In November 2001 the stock dropped below $10 from its $90 peak and ended up being submitted to a takeover bid by Dynegy, a much smaller company. Dynegy later withdrew the bid, leaving Enron to sort out its own problems, eventually through a record-breaking bankruptcy process. The share price finally ended well below $1. The rest is history, a history that will no doubt be amply recorded in books and Harvard-type case stories.

More than anything else, the fall of Enron is a reflection of lost confidence, in the board and management of the company, but also in the accounting system. Its transactions and reporting have received much attention, and rightly so, it seems. But Enron is far from alone. Just as when epidemics break out, the individual case is a signal that should release concerns and countermeasures, before the development gets out of control. Enron and its executives may be to blame, but so is the accounting system itself, for being so malleable as to permit blatant misuses.

A Wide Range of Methods for Misrepresentation

The Sunbeam case presents examples of all kinds of accounting malpractices. It may be exceptional in its apparently complete disregard for all honesty standards. Yet it shows how ineffective conventional accounting is in making consistently trustworthy presentations of reality. The ambition for accounting need not even be to provide "full disclosure," just reasonably honest disclosure.

The methods used to fool readers of company reports are almost as many as the cases. Under euphemisms such as "creative accounting" or "digital remastering" the misrepresentations use many techniques, more or less visible. Some of the practices are even seen as common procedures. The following is not supposed to be a complete listing of deceptive methods, nor should it serve as a training session in accounting fraud. It is only a selection of some of the more frequent practices listed just to show the broad variety of methods to destroy transparency that are available in the accounting toolbox.

Examples of unreliable accounting and reporting practices used by companies, small and big, include for instance:

- Expenses, sales, deliveries, returns shifted forward, backward, highlighted, or swept under the rug
- Expense items labeled "nonrecurring," although coming back, year after year
- Ownership, and the responsibility that should go with it, fiddled away through mazes and confusing "Russian Doll" setups
- Dissolving reserves, with incomplete reporting, inflating the income statement and boosting the bottom line
- Possible, but highly uncertain, future revenues recorded as realities today
- Banks padding their earnings by not making adequate bad loan reserves
- Other companies neglecting or misreporting doubtful accounts, loans, inventories, and reserves
- Avoiding formal consolidation, despite the reality of tangible and obvious management and board links
- Start-up costs, research and development costs, and so on tucked up out of the range of the income statement
- One-time gains allowed to boost regular income statements
- Regular operational losses reported as restructuring or nonrecurring charges
- Earnings per share manipulated by accounting tricks
- Pro forma earnings reporting,[8] providing a second set of data, excluding certain forms of costs, such as "one-time charges"
- EBITDA showing earnings before interest, tax, depreciation and amortization, a picture that presents results or cash flow from operations in a way

that cannot easily be interpreted by outsiders and sometimes not even by insiders

- Insurance policies—"finite insurance" or "financial reinsurance"—that artificially beef up a company's financial statements

- Vendor or customer financing without appropriate disclosure

- Companies changing accounting principles from year to year, making it hard or impossible to see a real pattern

- Ineffective "peer reviews" (one accounting firm reviewing the work of another firm): Few or no big accounting firms have ever issued a negative report after a peer review.

- Options, usually offered to top executives, mentioned in small footnotes in financial statements, not booked as an employee cost item on the income statement, as many advocate. (The technique has been called a stealthy transfer of wealth from the shareholders to corporate management, a sort of negative Robin Hood process.)

- Pensions or warranty liabilities reported "creatively" or not at all[9]

To these shoddy reporting practices should be added the frequent cases of distortion, intended or not, in corporate annual and quarterly reports through graphs and charts that manipulate the impressions that data might provide by eliminating appropriate scales, choosing baselines selectively, and other visual tricks.[10]

The fact that the range of malpractices is so broad, along with the wide range of companies under review, prove our point that "creative accounting" is not an exception. It seems to be so frequent as to put the burden of proof on the overall system of accounting. *Fortune* magazine, on the cover of its issue of June 24, 2002, used "failure," the same strong word as *CFO* magazine had used about accounting a few years earlier. The *Fortune* cover headline suggested that the wide misuse indicated a "System Failure."

Dishonesty Is Not Necessarily Intentional

The problem is not always that CEOs, CFOs, accountants, auditors, bankers, and others involved in these operations want to be dishonest. Many of them work as best they can to do a good, honest job and to follow laws and guidelines. GAAP, as many experts have called to our attention, offer endless possibilities for manipulation, still within the framework of the rules to be observed. A major problem is that the system itself, extended accounting, offers such generous opportunities for fraud, or misinterpretation, to use a kind word, that it creates impossible conflicts with the professional ambitions and conscience of those who are in charge.

> **Case in Point—Conflicts with the "Economic Reality"**
>
> The fact is that, even when accounting follows all rules, regulations, or guidelines, it easily turns out to be misleading, deceptive or, at best, irrelevant. In the cautiously balanced words of well-known financial analyst and investor Robert A. Olstein,[11] accounting creates "deviations between the statements as portrayed by the company and the economic reality." Olstein should know, having run a professional newsletter revealing accounting tricks performed by any number of well regarded, major companies. Accounting data simply do not adequately present a true picture of a company's present position and situation, let alone its outlook for the future.

How Could This Happen in the United States?

The examples discussed above refer mainly to companies based in the United States, which are considered to be as well managed and supervised as companies anywhere in the world. That these scandals happened in spite of comparatively tight regulations adds weight to the seriousness of the global problems we face.

Not that U.S. businessmen should automatically be seen to stand above their colleagues in the rest of the world, in terms of honesty or integrity. A system that is so easy to misuse as accounting invites shenanigans, wherever it is used. But the high frequency of accounting irregularities *even* in the United States is a cause of concern. After all, the United States has perhaps the best business education in the world, with some of the most excellent business schools, and an outstanding record of Nobel economy prizes. It has an independent judiciary system second to none. It has an active supervisory system, with the Securities and Exchange Commission (SEC) as a significant watchdog. It has high-level professional accounting organizations and standard-setting bodies, such as the American Institute of Certified Public Accountants (AICPA) and the Financial Accounting Standard Board (FASB), and now the Public Company Accounting Oversight Board (PCAOB), as well as a widely accepted set of guidelines, GAAP. It is also the country where the Institute of Internal Auditors (IIA) has its headquarters. And yet, even with all this on the plus side, the U.S. accounting system has failed to meet reasonable standards of accountability.

It does not take much imagination to realize that accounting in many other countries may be even more of a problem discipline—if discipline is the right word.

It is sad that accounting, traditionally an instrument that has been an icon and a foundation of the business community, has got so many nails driven into its coffin. The bell tolls not only for a few (okay, quite a few) individual companies, unfortunate enough to have been caught with their hands in the cookie jar. It tolls for a *system* that has permitted companies and other actors on the financial and business scene to deceive and confuse owners, the investing public, and other stakeholders for years.

A CASE FOR CHANGE

The Role of the Accounting Community

A number of pioneers within the accounting community, in research institutes and "think-tanks," in academia, in regulatory bodies, and in some of the leading auditing and consulting companies, have launched voices of concern about the shortcomings of accounting. They have even started to suggest changes in accounting practices to accommodate new needs. Interesting work has been done by the Brookings Institution, the American Enterprise Institute, the Cato Institute, the Stern School of Accounting at New York University, and the Wharton School of Economics, to mention just a few examples. Regulatory bodies, scared by the accounting scandals of the early 2000s, have proposed and enacted changes in accounting and auditing guidelines. However, most of these suggestions from the accounting and regulatory communities, even when they are labeled "radical,"[12] fall far short of what is needed.

This should not surprise anyone. It seems to be a general experience from practically all fields that radically new approaches seldom, if ever, originate within an established profession. Typically, those within a profession, whether it is engineering, law, medicine, philosophy, physics, mathematics, or whatever field, carry a heavy bag of professional traditions, from years of training and practice, sometimes even legislation. When they advocate change, they tend to come up with small steps of evolutionary change.[13] To achieve necessary revolutionary change, outsider input seems to be a necessary part of the process.

Thomas S. Kuhn,[14] scientist and philosopher, suggests an explanation that all scientific progress happens in jolts, in leaps and bounds, not as a step-by-step line of progress, in small steps. Kuhn's "jolts" are unpredicted and often unpredictable, and can be explained only in the aftermath, if at all. It could be that a dramatic change of a similar kind is overdue in the accounting profession.

James Gleick expresses the problem well in his important book, *Chaos:*[15] "A new science arises out of one that has reached a dead end. Often a revolution has an interdisciplinary character—its central discoveries often come from people straying outside the normal bounds of their specialties." Gleick has personal experience of this. He describes how the chaos and complexity concepts came up initially, and how they moved ahead through killing fields of entrenched opposition. Gleick shows how he and other pioneers of the new concepts were blocked from publishing their work in accepted scientific magazines and publications. Only after hard struggles did their ground-breaking ideas come to gain their place in the mainstream of science. When they were accepted, they revolutionized the disciplines of mathematics and physics, along with much of our present thinking, including management. The story about the painful birth process of the new complexity and chaos ideas has its parallels in practically all other disciplines, with pioneers from Copernicus and Galileo to Darwin, Einstein, and Chomsky.

Accounting has clearly come to a dead end in meeting many of the needs of our times. A more critical approach to the role of accounting is long overdue. Given the broad and deep changes at the roots of "the fourth economy,"[16] a "jolt" or a revolution seems to call for interdisciplinary input "from people straying outside the normal bounds of their specialties." After 500 years, it is time to puncture the accounting bubble. But it would be unprecedented if the brunt of such a new approach, no matter how necessary and how obvious it is, were to come from within the accounting fraternity.

A Case for Heresy

We can understand that some people have problems criticizing a system as deeply entrenched as accounting. Fundamentalist thinking has a strong platform in many lines of creed. Questioning an established system, such as accounting, has a ring of heresy to many of those who have been brought up in its doctrines. To them, thoughts of abolishing accounting and accounting-based tools for valuation and decision-making must seem as repugnant as swearing in the church, or as questionable as many other dramatically different ideas, when they were new. Copernicus's first ideas of the earth moving around the sun were as heretical as the thought of a round, not a flat, earth.[17] Charles Darwin's theories of evolution took more than a hundred years to be generally accepted in his own home country (and they are still not fully accepted in public schools in all of the United States). Albert Einstein's theories on relativity took a long time to gain acceptance, even by those gifted enough to understand them. The concepts of complexity and chaos theory are still not quite endorsed everywhere.

It is understandable that many experts are looking for an ostrich method, sticking their heads in the sand rather than attacking the problem. Many have a well-intended wish for the problems to go away, or for an easy fix, say new IFRS or PCAOB guidelines, or new SEC standards, thus saving "good, old accounting." Such wishful thinking should not be allowed to stand in the way of an open debate about the appropriate role of accounting. The simplest and most basic reason to start the process toward realistic disclosure is the call for honesty, accountability, and responsibility. As an example, the SEC calls for openness and transparency in reporting; fair disclosure must go beyond formalities and timetables to the substance, the relevance at the core of basic reporting methods. Corporate governance apostles must take a deeper look than just board composition and procedures. Auditors must go beyond accepted processes and standards to a deeper level of questioning the validity of the reporting routines of companies they check.

What is at stake is the lack of symmetry between the real world and the fictions and conventions of accounting that Robert Olsten called to our attention. Traditional accounting is simply not reliable or relevant as a platform for management and strategy work.

Companies will find it increasingly urgent to deal with new challenges. Ultimately, it will be necessary to discuss and define what factors in reality are crucial indicators of company survival, growth, and earnings capability. Those factors are what stakeholders want to learn about. They are seldom or never reflected in a timely manner in accounting data.

In Chapters 3 and 4 we will discuss practical approaches to new, largely "accounting-free" reporting or accountability systems, models that can be applied individually and without delay, by any company that wants to get a better grip over its situation. These approaches have been implemented with great results and can open up an era of experimentation that gives companies freedom to take initiatives. We are convinced that out of such an experimental spirit will arise something better than what we have now.

What Damage Does the Present System Create?

A friend of the status quo might offer a last line of defense for it: Given the fact that all models by nature must offer a simplified view of reality, could we not accept accounting as such an incomplete but still useful model? After all, a map can never give the whole picture—if it did, it would be unwieldy and complicated. So, can't we keep accounting anyway, even as a basis for decision making, despite all its faults? Are present practices only irrelevant, or do they, in fact, create serious damage? That was exactly the question that U.S. Senator Joseph Liebermann asked in a discussion with New York University accounting professor Baruch Lev, one of the pioneers in academia for new thinking and practices in accounting.[18]

Is it a question of serious damage, or just damage, when companies themselves, analysts, and other stakeholders, including the investing public, are misled by unreliable or irrelevant accounting, for instance in mergers and acquisitions, bond issues, and other due diligence processes? Is it serious damage, or just damage, when banks grant or refuse loan applications based primarily on accounting data?

As we have seen above, and as many academics, business watchdogs, analysts, regulators, and practitioners have noted, accounting offers innumerable opportunities for creative, aggressive, or downright dishonest practices. Some frequent kinds of financial statement tricks may be technically legal, yet they create a picture of the company that has little to do with the underlying reality. They are only misleading. And borderlines between more or less trustworthy accounting are getting increasingly blurred.[19]

Creative accounting is not necessarily a new problem,[20] but the situation today seems to be worse than it has been. The "recurring charge" scheme is reported to be used today by 30 percent of large, publicly traded companies in the United States, against only two or three percent before 1970.

The wave of accounting scandals has created a storm of protests and calls for new rules and regulations, tighter controls, and a higher level of business ethics.

The overwhelming majority of the demands for change have been limited to changes within the system, a reformist view of the situation. The Sarbanes-Oxley legislation is a case in point.

Small steps of change, or stricter supervision of existing practices, may be a tempting and convenient fast track for regulatory bodies to be seen to be doing something immediate about the disappearing confidence in accounting, auditing, and business in general. However, if our ambitions are higher, if we want to obtain more significant results, major changes cannot be avoided. It becomes more and more obvious that, even in the best of circumstances, with the strictest possible rules, the toughest supervision, and the highest ethical standards, accounting and accounting-based models give too much leeway for arbitrary, incomplete, and misleading pictures of a company. The so-far unchallenged position of the accounting system as a tool for many different kinds of decisions in business and the economy is untenable in the long run. The problems have reached a level close to intellectual, ethical, and management disaster. One basic reason, as we will discuss in more detail in Chapter 2, is that accounting does not adequately relate to the fundamentals of a company in the twenty-first century. It is dangerous to use old maps in a fast shifting landscape, or, as the outstanding banker Walter B. Wriston expressed it: "Flying by faulty instruments is dangerous."[21] The sooner we make the change to more adequate instruments, the better it is for all parties involved.

The focus needs to change from *accounting*, as an academic discipline, to *accountability*, with emphasis on finding honest and relevant tools for practical business and management applications, strategic decision-making, stakeholder reporting, valuation, risk management, auditing, and financing.

"The Emperor's New Clothes"

The Danish storyteller H.C. Andersen wrote a charming story about deception and public opinion, "The Emperor's New Clothes." As we all recall, it is about two rogues, who fool a whole city, including the emperor, as they present a (nonexisting) set of fabric, of which they make a beautiful (nonexisting) dress for the emperor. The scheme is close to success, when a young boy reveals the truth and exclaims, "But the emperor has no clothes!"

Blind belief, without questioning, reflections, and reason has a less charming, more detrimental face, fundamentalism. It can be defined as a set of dogmas that survive beyond their "best before" dates, without being affected by a changing environment or new evidence. We see its harsh consequences, when it blindly supports religious beliefs, be they Jewish, Christian, Islamic, or other.

"The Rear View Mirror"

Accounting data, by definition, belong in the past tense, while business decision making, also by definition, aims to the future. This conflict between the time perspectives of accounting and business decision making is impossible to overcome, if one wants to retain a minimum of honesty. Reflecting past performance is the one and only legitimate focus of accounting data. It is not necessarily a clear and reliable rear view mirror, but any other focus is definitely unreal.

Under the slogan "business as usual," accounting fundamentalists have tried to make business practitioners believe that it is possible to use past accounting data as the starting point for valid prognoses, perhaps in the form of trend extrapolations. They have also tried to make us believe in budgets and such questionable techniques as "discounted cash flow," "net present value," and "real options." The reality is that the future is, and always has been, genuinely unpredictable. On the admittedly arguable assumption that the world and the economy are even more exposed to sudden, dramatic change today than ever before, we will discuss this in some detail in the next chapter.

The belief in forecasts based on past accounting data or other forms of guess-work turns extremely dangerous when it is allowed to influence or guide the company risk management process.

The Risks of Accounting-Based Risk Management

A prime responsibility for any management is to ensure, as much as possible, the company's survival. This priority calls for a high level of attention to the risks a company may be exposed to. Much of what goes under the term risk management is, however, much too deeply rooted in accounting-based financial aspects, rather than business aspects.

In traditional—and traditionalist—risk management, the process basically aims at guessing, perhaps through devising scenarios, future events that may have a negative or detrimental impact on the company, estimating the probability of these events, and then designing programs to protect the company against those events, giving priority to those that have been assigned the highest probability numbers. A clue to risk management in this school of thought is to use past data, mostly accounting-based, to predict future events. The reality of life does not support this process, simply because accounting data have no legitimate role, except listing past transactions.

Serious risk management must accept this reality. The uncertainty factors tend to be too many and too strong. Instead of trying to predict threats or other events, it must focus on reducing the sensitivity of the company to unpredictable forces. The only safe way to do this is to assess the dependencies the company is exposed to, areas or forces where outside influences can have a decisive damaging impact on the company.

One reason for the confusion may be unclear definitions of risk, as different from uncertainty. If risk is defined as possible outcomes among a range of known possibilities, such as for instance tossing a coin, or casting dice, probability calculation may have some meaning.

But that is not the situation that a company finds itself in. A company is, at any given time, in a situation of complete uncertainty. Influences that impact the company can come from any source, at any time, from competitors changing their technologies or marketing approach, from financial circumstances, such as currency changes, interest changes, or other, from key employees suddenly and unexpectedly getting hit by accidents or illness, or deciding to leave for other reasons, from government regulations, from opinion or trend shifts in the general public, from changing investor preferences, and any number of other influences. Never has this situation of complete uncertainty been as clear as it is in our time.

In situations of genuine uncertainty, there is only one way to act, and that is to attain the highest possible flexibility, or resilience, or, as we prefer to call it, "freedom to act." A more in-depth discussion is presented in the next chapter, and practical ways to handle it are discussed in Chapter 5. Past (as they are by definition) accounting data have very limited roles to play in this process.

THE VALUE MESS

The Search for "Real Value"

One of the serious problems in accounting is how it is used to show and calculate value. If the long history of bubbles has a lesson to convey to us, it must be that we should seriously question this use. The first question to ask regarding value is: Does any asset[22] have a "real" or "true" value? Let us take a good look at this issue, since it is basic to many applications of accounting.

The belief that there is a magic Grail in terms of objects having a "Real Value," which can be expressed in absolute and reliable numbers, is deeply rooted. That is why we can read such sentences as, "The company reserves the right not to sell any assets, if the bids do not reflect full value," or "The enterprise value is the starting point for bidding," or an analyst talking about raising or lowering "the target value" of a stock, or discussing what "the real value of the Euro" should be. Even frequently used terms as "true shareholder value," book titles such as *What Are Stocks Really Worth?*, or consultant formulas proclaiming "Economic Value Added" are as questionable as many companies' accounting proved to be in the early 2000s.

A Wilde View of Value—and Price

According to a quote from Oscar Wilde, "A cynic is a person who understands the price of everything, and the value of nothing." If that is true, many economists would classify as cynics. Well-respected "contrarian" David Dreman expressed the reality of this dilemma very well when he exposed the fluctuations of a stock price, previously in the trading range of $75 to $84: "Trouble was, the range of prices had nothing to do with the stock's real worth. People who purchased it at $60, or even $50, lost a bundle. Recent price: $5."[23]

The Bubbles Are Still Active

Share prices, whether shares of individual companies or industry groups, or whole stock markets, move up and down, sometimes slowly, sometimes in leaps and bounds. Do share prices ever represent something that could be called "true value"? If so, how come the share prices of tech companies as a group were cut in half over a few months in the early part of 2000, and some of the individual shares even more? Which day, hour, or minute did the share price represent the true value of the companies?

Currencies go up and down, just as share prices. In post–WW I Germany, stamps for normal letters were sold at nominations of billions of marks. A less dramatic, but still illustrative example is that since its introduction, the euro, the European Union currency, has been exposed to wide swings in relation to other currencies, among them the U.S. dollar. Desperate business writers and currency experts have asked what the real value of the euro is.

The huge swings in real estate prices in Japan, the United States, and Europe in later decades have clouded the views of real estate as a safe haven, where a mysterious "value" could be found and safeguarded. Anyone who has bought or sold a house recognizes the confusion about what the property is "really" worth. Realtors may establish a price range, aiming at something they could call a real or at least a fair value, but variations around that target are often substantial. In the end, success in making a deal invariably hinges on the right buyer showing up.

One of the strong buzzwords in the business community in the 1990s was shareholder value. Creating or increasing shareholder value has been widely trumpeted as the ultimate strategic objective for boards and managements. It has been used as a reason for innumerable mergers and acquisitions—although the goal has rarely been achieved. The basic challenge of defining what shareholder value actually is has been part of the problem.

So what about the "real stuff," commodities? And what about the most real of them all, gold, the metal that for a long time was used as the standard of world currencies? What is the real value of gold? Gold has a wide range of applications, from jewelry to teeth to currency reserves. It has outstanding physical qualities, corrosion-resistance as one of them, that gives it an aura of permanence that few other things can match. For thousands of years, gold as a metal has probably been more precisely defined in terms of quality and measurement methods than any other commodity. If value rests in the thing itself, one would think that gold should have a very stable value. What is the true story?

In the 1490s, the time of the origins of our accounting system, gold was priced at around $2,500/troy ounce in today's currency. It then went through dramatic swings up and down through the centuries. In the 1930s to the 1960s, gold was price-controlled to remain steady, at around $35. In the early 1980s gold was quoted and sold at $800 to $900. Twenty years later, after sometimes galloping, sometimes benign, inflation, one would think that gold, this example of lasting value, would have a price tag at least in the range of $1,000 or more. Instead, today it is sold worldwide at less than half of that, the mid-$400 range.

Shares, currencies, and even real estate seem to be fickle friends, if one is looking for real or objective value. Commodities, even gold, are no better.

Asset Valuation Has Always Been Difficult

Asset valuation has always been a difficult discipline in itself, under the best of circumstances. Thick volumes have been written about methods to calculate asset value, even dealing with the relatively simple physical assets of the agricultural and industrial economies. Very few of the writers of these volumes have dared to draw a bold conclusion from their difficulties, the conclusion that they may be on a wrong track in one of their basic assumptions: trying to assign an objective numerical value to a thing in itself. Since this is a core issue in business, accounting, and management, we will discuss it in some detail.

Case in Point—Assess the "Value" of a Machine

If you have a factory nearby, ask three colleagues, maybe three accountants, to assess the value of a machine, the same machine, on the floor, without comparing notes with each other. Chances are that the three independent assessments will result in at least four different price tags, and don't be surprised if there is a wide variation between them!

Then discuss with them how they arrived at the "value" or price label. Did they start with a purchase price? Did they estimate an "autopsy value"? Did any of them try to look at the value of the machine in terms of its contributions to the total manufacturing and marketing chain of the business it is used in?

The Value Enigma—or the Value Mess

Have you noticed the inevitable confusion when two parties in a discussion use the same word, but with different meanings? No matter how bright and well meaning they are, the result is usually a complete tangle. Imagine then, if the whole business world used one word, not for two but for several different meanings, without clear distinctions! And imagine, on top of that, that the word would be one of the core business concepts, the concept of value! No wonder we would have a mess—the Value Mess.

Most dictionaries[24] show eight or ten different definitions of the word value. Even if we limit ourselves to those frequently used in business contexts, several very different meanings of value are used interchangeably, without making it clear which meaning we refer to in each given case. Some definitions are different enough to put semantic confusion of the *value* word as one of the roots of the general confusion of accounting.

Let us look at four different but frequently mixed-up meanings of value:

1. Value as any number, for instance "What value did you enter into the table?" Let us call this Value^{amount}.

2. Value defined as the price we once paid for an item, adjusted or not by depreciation, for instance "What is the balance sheet value of that machine?" We can call this, if we like, Value^{historicprice} or Value$^{b.s.}$.

3. Value as a potential price or price range we may be able to obtain, if we were to sell an item, such as "What is the value of your house?" This could be called Value^{potentialprice}.

4. Value as the benefit, usefulness, contribution of an item, such as a machine, to the company production process, or the brand to the company marketing process. We could call this Value^{usefulness}.

The four meanings are very different, which is why confusion pops up practically every time the word *value* or *valuation* is used in a report or a statement. Imagine if we all were to be consistent, only one week of our lives, strictly defining the word *value* every time we used it! Imagine a financial analyst or a due diligence consultant who had to clarify his or her reports in these terms! Imagine a Wall Street journalist who had to do the same thing!

Value^{amount}

This can apply to any item. It must be expressed as a number, it is not necessarily linked to a currency, and, of course, has no relation to Value$^{b.s.}$, Value^{potentialprice}, or Value^{usefulness}.

Value$^{b.s.}$

Balance sheets were traditionally seen as indicators of company value. The asset side lists prices we once paid for some (but not all!) of the things the company owns, the liability side lists some (but not all!) of its obligations. In both cases they may or may not be adjusted by arbitrary or conventional amounts.

The price we paid for an item can be interesting, as a memory of an historic transaction, which is what value is, in this sense. This is fine; we all need memory support, and it may be good to have a record of the prices we once paid for an item. We can list the amounts in relatively precise terms, which accountants and legislators like. Then again, Value$^{b.s.}$, the amounts on the balance sheets, have nothing to do with what we may or may not get for those items if we want to sell them, Value^{potentialprice}, nor with their contribution to the company's business results, Value^{usefulness}. In fact, the price we paid must be lower than the Value^{usefulness} of the item to our business at the time of purchase. If not, we should not have bought it in the first place. And once the transaction has been made and registered, it is a historic fact without any further impact on the business. On top of this comes the fact that, today, many of the most significant resources for company survival or success have never been purchased the traditional way and have consequently not even come close to the balance sheet.

Value^{potentialprice}

This is an indication of what we might get if we were to sell an item, in the near or distant future. Value in this sense has always been a hard nut to crack for economists of the old schools, since we deal with uncertainty in many dimensions. One dimension is the fact that we do not know anything about the future, which makes it impossible to know what we may get for an item tomorrow, or next week, or next year. The listings in real estate advertising are examples of that category, along with analyst predictions of future stock prices.

A key dimension is the fact that the price ultimately comes out as a result of a negotiation between two or more interested, and often emotionally involved, parties. When we sell a house, or a car, or a share, or, in fact, anything, we know that the price we will finally get depends entirely on whether "the right buyer" shows up.

When Value^{potentialprice} is expressed as a number, in a currency, it gets a totally undeserved air of precision. In reality, it is never precise. It is always a guesstimate. Value^{potentialprice} rests in the mind of a buyer. Consequently, as commodity, real estate, and stock markets show, it can swing wildly from year to year, from day to day, or from hour to hour. It is not an intrinsic, objective measure, such as for instance length or weight. There is never a "correct" Value^{potentialprice} and it has no relation, or only an occasional relation, to either Value$^{b.s.}$ or Value^{usefulness}.

Fortunately, this fundamental truth is gradually, although slowly, getting recognized. Traditional economists are getting their old ideas challenged by members of the so-called behavioral economic schools of thought, for instance such outstanding academics as the winners of the 2002 economics prize in memory of Alfred Nobel, Dr. Daniel Kahneman and Dr. Vernon Smith.

Value^{usefulness}

In many ways, Value^{usefulness} is the most genuine form of Value. It can well be argued that the only "real" value of an item is the benefit someone derives from it.

One of the most significant, but sometimes neglected, aspects of Value^{usefulness} is that it can be expressed only in terms of usefulness:

- To a defined person or a defined company
- In a given context, a given set of circumstances
- At a specific time

Change one of these parameters and the Value^{usefulness} changes! Value^{usefulness} can never be used as a general or an absolute term. A share may be useful in my portfolio, given my investment priorities, at this time (!), but not in someone else's. Company A would be more useful, would produce or contribute more, if merged with company X than with company Z. There is no once-and-for-all valid value or even a "fair value" of Company A.

Any single item is useful only in a closely defined context. One step on a ladder has no value without the other steps. All links in a chain are required for the chain to be useful. One single machine on the factory floor is useless if isolated from the rest of the production process—and from the product and marketing context of the company.

The conclusion is that Value^{usefulness} is not an objective quality; ultimately it is only a perception or a feeling. Consequently, shocking to some, *it cannot be expressed in numbers*, only in words.

Total confusion arises when variations of Value^{amount}, Value$^{b.s.}$, or Value^{potentialprice} are interpreted as having the meaning of Value^{usefulness}, such as the benefit or contribution of these items to the business operations. Then we are going far beyond reality, into the Value Mess. The four value concepts must be kept apart and clearly defined.

The paradox, which may seem hard to recognize by traditionalists, is that:

- Value^{amount} and Value$^{b.s.}$ can be expressed in relatively precise numbers—not necessarily meaningful numbers, except as an historic record, but precise.
- Value^{potentialprice} is a meaningful number only if one believes that the future is predictable. This condition is more and more questionable, or in fact dead wrong, as for instance stock markets, real estate markets, commodity markets, and currency markets show increasingly clearly. Just look at the Value^{potentialprice} of a sample of stocks as predicted (or, rather, guessed) by Wall Street experts, the specialized analysts, in the year before and after 2001. Alternatively, this truth can lead to tolerating very broad price ranges, which again reduces the benefits of the guesswork. How helpful is it, if an analyst predicts a stock to be really "worth" anything between $100 and a dime?
- Value^{usefulness} is a very meaningful concept. However, it is never precise, nor is it generally applicable. It must always be defined in a specific context, for a defined kind of application, at a certain time, in a defined set of condi-

tions, very much including the emotional situation of the players. These conditions are rarely constant. Consequently, valuation methods looking at usefulness can, by definition, never result in a precise number, in fact, not really in a number at all!

In this light, balance sheets are confusing instruments, to say the least. The *British Journal of Accountancy,* as early as September 1994, reviewed a report, "Making Corporate Reports Valuable," and called the balance sheet "an inconsistent hodgepodge of costs and values."

Case in Point—Value Judgments

When the Bank of England auctions off tons of gold, it is an indication that the usefulness of gold, in this case to defend the value of the British pound, has diminished.

Affection value may lead someone to pay a higher price for something that totally lacks value for another person.

There is a sign outside an antiques shop, "Junk Bought—Antiques Sold," obviously indicating that the seller and the buyer assign very different value to the same thing.

Or think of the French expression: "The best way to make a woman beautiful is a bottle of good wine—consumed by her spouse."

In the investment community, the fight between those who believe in value investing and those who advocate growth investing is hard and sometimes bitter. As the market swings in one or the other direction, one or the other side feels the same kind of comfort and support that a sailor may get from a tailwind, until the weather changes. In reality, and especially in our time, value and growth are two fuzzy subjects. Whatever definition one tries to apply, the two aspects are mutually dependent on one another. Value, in most businesses, is a function of growth, but it is also a condition for growth.

Consider the value of a glass of water to someone who is stranded in the Sahara or the Mojave deserts, compared to the value of the same glass of water to a person standing near his kitchen tap in a regular home in New York or London. It is useless to look into the glass to find clues to the difference in value. The value criteria do not rest in the glass or in the water; they rest in external conditions outside the glass.

Toward a New Understanding of Value

Let us sum up a few factors to get a better understanding of how to deal with *value* from a management perspective, especially as it relates to company value or shareholder value.

Value Is a Subjective Parameter

Contrary to classical concepts, the Value^{usefulness} of any item is not a measurable, objective parameter. Value does not rest in the thing itself. The value, whether of gold, real estate, currencies, tulip bulbs, bandwidth, shares, or companies, is set in the minds of an interested party, a buyer, a seller, or in a dialogue or bidding process between two parties. Looking for an objective value is as futile as the search for the end of the rainbow. Swedish banker and industrialist Marcus Wallenberg, one of the international business leaders of the 1970s, expressed value as "a function of interest"—not bank interest but the interest someone has in an item.

The Market Cap of a Company Is Not Its Value

The market capitalization of a company, defined as share price times outstanding shares, does not adequately represent a value in any traditional sense. It is true that the price is a result of a bidding process between two parties, sellers and buyers. But since even in heavily traded stocks, only a fraction of all shares are traded in a given day, it must be assumed that the owners of most of the shares do not find it attractive to sell at the quoted price. Their implied perception of value is that the stock is worth more. This is also confirmed in takeover situations, when a buyer wants to get control of all shares or a big majority of them. As we all know, in such a situation the price is normally much higher than the previously quoted price. So, if market cap is not an intrinsic value of the company as such, then what is it? A suggestion is that it reflects, if anything, a range of perceptions held by a minority of shareholders wanting to sell and potential shareholders interested in buying, at a given moment. Those perceptions express a level of confidence that investors have in the company, its management and its business position—a combination of emotional indicators that are the primary basis for a share price.

Balance Sheet Numbers Relate to Price, Not to Value

The assets or the equity on a balance sheet are not related to Value (Value^{usefulness}). The value of a company as an ongoing concern cannot be assessed by adding numbers from a balance sheet, numbers that have their dark origins in old, later adjusted or manipulated purchase prices. This is equally true, even if the confusions and misconceptions of the balance sheet were to be further increased by including mind-based assets or items of "intellectual capital." Even money itself has different value to different people and in different situations.

New Ways to Create Wealth

Finally, as a distinctive feature of the present economy, there is a new view of how wealth is created today. This wealth creation process is very different from that in the second or third economies, and it is even less linked to physical assets on the balance sheet. We will come back to this issue in the next chapter.

DISTORTED METRICS

How to Correctly Measure the Wrong Things

Many of the ratios launched with great fanfare during the new economy mania were rather absurd. The same is true, however, of traditional ratios, based on accounting data. They turn equally absurd, when examined a little more closely. Here are some examples of absurd measures used with more or less straight faces by people who ought to know better:

Absurd "New Economy" Measures

Many of the measures used in the IT boom had very poor intellectual or economic underpinnings. Intellectually they failed, trying desperately to prove company-internal value factors, when the value factors, as always, were based in the minds of the market participants. Economically they failed, when the ratios showed no relations or very weak relations to company fundamentals, survival, earnings, and growth.

Most of the measures were top-line related, such as web site visits, eyeballs, engaged shoppers, mind-share, or other exposure-related measures. As a common denominator, they were only remotely linked to earnings. Yahoo, for a time, had wonderful eyeball data. The number of visitors showed dramatic increases and numbers. For a time, Yahoo had a share price of more than 1,700 times past earnings.

Some measures of this era were bottom-line related. One of the most persistent was "pro forma[25] earnings," an unsuccessful effort to introduce seemingly formal accounting-related views, inherited from the merger raiders of the 1980s, to a concept that was basically not agreeable to the business views of the new economy, as it was then perceived.

Absurd Traditional Measures

Many of the traditional measures are equally unrealistic, and equally unrelated to real indicators of company performance, although they hide their irrelevance in a veil of terminology drawing on the traditions of accounting respectability.

Price/Book Value

There are two problems with this ratio, which was traditionally used as a basic valuation formula. The first is that the price the stock market happens to be willing to pay at a given time has nothing to do with an objective or true value of the company. The price of a share, just like the price of any other product or service, is created in the minds of potential buyers and sellers. It reflects the attraction the potential buyers feel for the company at a given time. That attraction is based on several factors outside the company itself. Furthermore, the price is generated only by those who want to do business at a given moment.

Book value makes no sense at all, having no relationship whatsoever to the "value" of a company as a going concern. This has always been true. In the present economy, when the real value drivers of the company have never even come close to the balance sheet, it is more true than ever. "Substance" is by and large irrelevant, if not even an impediment to success.

Making price/book value a basis for decisions on whether to lend money, for selecting which companies to invest in, for consideration in a due diligence process, or for any other economic action, is just another dubious way to misuse accounting-based data.

Price/Equity

This ratio suffers from the vagaries of the price component and the lack of rationality of the equity component. On top of that, today, when physical assets are not the decisive factors for company success, this ratio makes about as much sense as it would be to define the value of a soccer team in relation to the size and weight of the ball the team plays with. And what happens when a company outsources part of its activities, that is, dumps some of its physical equity and replaces it with contracts with outside suppliers?

Return on Equity

The equity defined on a balance sheet is a meaningless number, the rest amount when some (not all!) of the company's (manipulated) liabilities have been deducted from some (not all!) of its (manipulated) assets. The "mega-charges" made in the early 2000s to accommodate accounting to the merger disasters of the late 1990s just underline how senseless these accounting manipulations are. Since the return is also a manipulated figure taken from a frequently unreliable income statement, this ratio, again, equals relating two meaningless numbers to each other.

Return on Capital Employed

In addition to the reliability problems it shares with other accounting-based indicators, this ratio is highly dangerous if used in a corporation as a directive or target for managers to work toward. It invariably tends to lead to a focus on trimming the Capital Employed factor by tempting managers to avoid long-term investments to obtain look-good short-term gains in the ratio.

Price/Earnings

This ratio may seem to make more sense, until, of course, one has considered the weaknesses around the price variable.

Case in Point—February 22, 2005

On this day, the Dow Jones Industrial Index fell by 174 points. The analyst community was mobilized in all media to come up with creative reasons why it was truly logical that it should go down. In the next three trading days it recovered the loss, by a generous margin. Lo and behold, the same analysts were out there to explain why it was quite obvious that it should go up! When was the price "right"? When did it reflect a "true value"?

The earnings component of P/E suffers from several weaknesses as well. Most important of them is the likelihood that the earnings reported on the income statement have very little to do with real earnings. Given the fact that the earnings of a company are, at best, a small net result of a subtraction of the total of various cost items from the overall sales figure, two big numbers, the earnings figure that comes out of the calculation is subject to severe risks of misrepresentation, willful or not, or just plain accounting errors in the process. *Fortune,* December 27, 2004, published an investment guide for 2005, "The 20 Best Bargains at a Glance." Among the companies listed, the spread of the P/E ratio was from a low of 10.3 to a high of 45.4! P/E ratios are and remain nothing but arbitrary numbers, especially since it seems that everyone has a different way to define the E.

What about consistency over time? While the average variations from year to year are much smaller, say from a low of 7 or 8 over the last few decades to a high of mid-40s, that variation in itself is too big to permit anyone to draw conclusions, especially as those averages hide great variations.

The conclusion remains that price/earnings is a ratio between two very dubious numbers. P/E ratios are as dangerous to use as guidelines for investment or other decisions, as, indeed, any other accounting-based ratios are.

Adding a time factor to the equation makes the fallacy of the P/E ratio even more obvious: If we use trailing earnings, which are at least recorded earnings, and draw conclusions of future performance from that, we fall into the unpredictability trap. And if we try to predict stock market prices and earnings and develop future P/E numbers, we do not merely fall in the trap: We jump right into it!

The Death of P/E—Or New Life?

Once upon a time, in old monarchies, the transfer of power from one king to another was dramatically expressed: "The king is dead! Long live the king!"

The P/E ratio is seen by many in the stock market as the king of all ratios. It is one of the most cherished formulas for assessing whether an individual share, an industry segment, or the stock market in general, is reasonably priced, even reasonably "valued." As we have seen above, neither one of the two numbers that make up the ratio are very reliable. As the stock market shows us every day, prices jump up and down, apparently without any logic. And we certainly cannot ask for more proof than we have gotten in later years that earnings numbers are unreliable, whether they refer to past earnings or guesses about future earnings. The fact is that P/E variations between companies, even in the same business, are so wide that they defy any logic explanations. The search for logic in these numbers is vain. In math, two negatives are said to make one positive. That does not mean that putting together two unreliable numbers transforms them into a reliable ratio!

As long as we try to find an explanation for P/E numbers in—numbers(!)— we are at a complete loss. What we need to do is recognize the fact that the stock market is largely controlled, not by numbers but by emotions! This is true about the stock market in general, but also about the individual investor and his or her relations to a portfolio.[26]

Time for a New P/E Ratio?

This leads us toward a dramatically different P/E, where the E does not stand for *earnings*, last year's, next year's or any other period's. Instead it stands for what really affects the stock market: *emotions*. Exhibit 1.1 is what a P/E chart of this kind could look like, over a period of time.

Does the chart in Exhibit 1.1 give us a magic way to make forecasts? Can it help us predict trend changes, help us see upturns or downturns before they happen? Unfortunately not! Not any more than the experts that Rich Karlgaard, publisher of *Forbes,* calls "The Priesthood: Pundits, Analysts and Economists."[27] In the same article Mr. Karlgaard also states: "Judged by any professional standard, the collected sayings of the priesthood are so bad as to be approaching quackery." The chart does not help us any more than so-called "technical analysis" or any other methods to predict the future. It can possibly help explain, afterwards,

EXHIBIT 1.1   PRICE EMOTIONS—A NEW AND MORE RELEVANT P/E RATIO

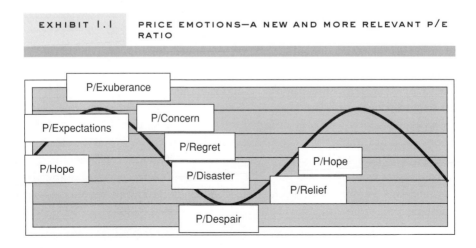

why things turned one way or the other. For a more in-depth discussion on predicting the future, please see Chapter 2.

When Is the Stock Market Reasonably Valued?

The traditional ratios discussed above have been used, and are still being used, by apparently serious financial analysts, not only for individual companies but also to try to assess whether the whole stock market is "reasonably valued."

In mid-September 2001, a week after the terrorist attacks on the World Trade Center and Pentagon, the Dow Jones Index, one of the trusted indices on the U.S. stock market, had fallen to around 8200. Financial analysts and media asked the question whether this was a reasonable level. Crystal balls were dug out from dusty cabinets to help answer the question. What appeared among the clouds in the crystal balls was tested against some of the ratios above, misguidedly called valuation models.

In its issue of October 8, 2001, *Business Week* correctly put the spotlight on the wide variation that four of these models produce. Conclusions ranged from an assessment that the market is undervalued by 15 percent to, at the other end, that it is overvalued by 40 percent! The "correct" stock market valuation, according to these models, should have been somewhere between a Dow of 5000 and a Dow of 9800!

Would any of us buy a thermometer that shows the temperature at a given point to be somewhere/anywhere between 30 and 60 degrees? Would we trust a scale at our fitness center showing our weight to be somewhere/anywhere between 50 and 100 kilos (or between 100 and 200 lbs)? (See Exhibit 1.2.)

Just as many of the absurd new economy measures were related to "top-line data," or "before the top-line data," so many of the equally absurd traditional ratios are related to "bottom-line data." Both, more often than not, are either guesswork or unreliable for other reasons.

Economic Laws or "Irrational" Human Factors?

It is increasingly accepted that economy and business are far from the numbers-based science it was once claimed to be. Behavioral economists and econo-psychologists have shown that assessment and valuation are controlled much more by irrational human factors than by economic laws. Value is in the eye of the beholder. This means a totally changed focus on what value factors to consider, define, and measure, and may provide a clue to why old economy fundamentalism is as far from reality as new economy enthusiasm. Financial factors are not what matters, essentially, and never have been. Nonfinancial forces control the development. Reality wins over accounting. Looking at and reporting on a company only from a financial perspective would be like looking at a car only

EXHIBIT 1.2   WOULD YOU ACCEPT A BATHROOM SCALE WITH THIS DEVIATION?

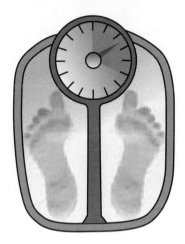

by checking the speedometer and the gasoline gauge, disregarding whether the engine is working, whether the tires are okay, and what it is supposed to be used for.

In a eulogy article in *Forbes*,[28] editor-in-chief Steve Forbes gives credit to Laury Minard, founding editor of *Forbes Global*. Steve Forbes's words reflect, not only on Laury Minard, but also on an important aspect of economics: *"He never allowed the numbers-laden discipline to... obscure the fact that economics is about real, breathing people. He knew the discipline's strengths and shortcomings."*

Get Real! An Emphasis on *Business*

While analyzing *financial statements* is largely irrelevant, analyzing *business performance* is highly relevant. In consequence, financial analysts should reassess their own profession. If they transform themselves into *business analysts* instead, they will have a chance to return to relevance and trust. Few experts have recognized this truth more clearly, and expressed it more succinctly, than Phil Dow, director of equity strategies at the Wall Street company Daine Rausher Wessel. He "predicts a renewed emphasis on a company's business—what its opportunities are, how those can be quantified, and how they compare with competition—to replace the previous obsession with price targets."[29]

Such an emphasis on the business is exactly what we have selected as a foundation for the alternative reporting system we suggest in Chapter 4, to replace one-eyed accounting-based reporting.

Case in Point—Lucent and Financial Analysts

Lucent is one of the companies that have suffered and seen a nearly free fall in share price. The reason we give it as an example is not to rub salt into the wounds of Lucent management. It is to illustrate the futility of financial analyst work. Here is what some financial analysts said during the process. We have omitted the names of the respective and respectable financial analyst firms who made the ratings. However, we have based the presentation on an article in *Forbes*, September 10, 2001, where more information is available:

Time:	Actual Price:	Rating:
July 2000	$49.50	BUY
Oct. 2000	$31.38	LONG-TERM BUY
Dec. 2000	$20.94	LONG-TERM ACCUMULATE
March 2001	$10.27	MARKET PERFORMER
June 2001	$ 8.32	BUY
July 2001	$ 6.67	STRONG BUY

Lucent, of course, is very much a postindustrial economy company. It is understandable that financial analysts, stuck with their 500-year-old arsenal of financial tools, have a hard time understanding and explaining what goes on in this economy. Against this background, this quote seems very appropriate: "We must be able to do better than that!"

As we will see in Chapter 4, it is possible to build a reporting system based on largely accounting-free, but measurable data, a reporting system that reflects what goes on in the companies and their environment, that defines better than accounting numbers the conditions for company survival, earnings, and growth. It is a system that takes reporting from guesswork top lines and unreliable bottom lines to meaningful baselines. It includes awareness that many of the forces that drive company performance (a) do not exist in the company, but outside it, and (b) are not reflected in any traditional accounting statements.

The Value of a Company Is Based on Perceptions

Most companies have strategic goals that ultimately relate to survival, earnings, and growth. If so, anything that is seen, for instance by a potential buyer, as a contribution to survival, earnings, and growth could be viewed as an asset, whether it is soft or hard or anywhere in between, or a combination. Anything that is seen to hamper survival, earnings, or growth is a liability, whether it is soft or hard or anywhere in between. Value is ultimately a factor based in somebody's mind, a (potential) buyer and/or seller. Value is a perception.

The chart above, showing the wide range of ratios, clearly indicates that the process of valuating a company is not a mathematical issue. It is not based on objective data. The same principle applies to the stock market as a whole. Valuation is entirely a matter of the eyes of the beholders, the perceptions of the stakeholders, not least their perceptions of the soundness of a business idea and its ability to reach its goals. Factors that support stakeholder perceptions of company goals are basic value drivers. This applies to any factors, no matter if they are hard, soft, liquid, or mixed. A truck, operated by a competent and motivated driver, can be seen as a value factor in a transportation company; it generates earnings and it is clearly related to the business idea. The same truck owned by another company may be perceived as a liability, restricting company flexibility, rather than as an asset.

What Is Shareholder Value?

An understanding of value is hard to reconcile with old beliefs in accounting. Neither does it match with accounting-based ratios used by financial analysts, then generously sprinkled over business and financial pages in our business media. It has serious implications for management priorities, given that creating shareholder value, in the full sense of it, is seen as an important priority.

Putting a Price Tag on a Company

If the value of a company is not in the thing itself, how does one arrive at a reasonable price?

The price of a share is ultimately a function of the willingness of present shareholders to stay as shareholders and the interest from new shareholders to join. It depends primarily on factors outside the company. Consequently, accounting data about the company are not the main source for decisions. Instead, decision making is initially the result of a four-stage process:

1. *The total savings volume in society.* This is a function of employment rates, cultural patterns, and a big mixed bag of sociological and psychological issues.

2. *The share of savings or investment funds that look to the stock market as an opportunity.* This, in turn, is a function of a complicated pattern of sentiments, most of them as far from "rational" number-crunching as can be.

3. *The perceived relative opportunities of various business groups.* These perceived relative opportunities swing fast, almost from hour to hour, and certainly from day to day. Just look at the changes in perceived opportunities of airlines, the hotel industry, health care, and the financial industry before or after September 11, 2001.

4. *The perceptions that shareholders and potential shareholders have of an individual company.* Most of these perceptions are based on impressions that go far beyond traditional calculations, P/E numbers, and other arbitrary data.

Hopefully, instead, they are based on an understanding of the company's business, its opportunities and risks, the people who run it, and other aspects of real business, not accounting.

Summing up, how do you put a price tag on a company? The answer is: The price of a company is the result of the same factors as the price of any other products or services—that is, the outcome of a three-step competition process among potential buyers:

1. *The competition for discretionary use of money:* choosing between saving or spending

2. *The substitute competition:* choosing between various investment opportunities

3. *The direct competition:* choosing an individual company

In the first stage, investing is an activity in the most fickle of all fields, that of discretionary spending. Potential investors can always freely decide to *invest or abstain,* that is, do something entirely different with their money. The decisions are entirely based on the priorities of potential buyers. Relevant indicators include broad consumer and investor confidence data. The sum of all these decisions affects the total amount of investments.

An individual company can realistically not do anything to affect these decisions. The figures it may publish in its reports does not influence decisions on that level.

In the next stage, decisions about *how* to save or invest are examples of substitute competition. The result of *perceptions of* macroeconomic conditions, tax rates, interest levels, inflation expectations, business trends, political choices, and so on, affect the choice between bank deposits, money market accounts, bonds, stocks, or other savings or investment alternatives.

An individual company cannot do much to influence these decisions but it can make itself more or less visible.

The final stage is one of direct competition, the decision on which company or share to buy. This decision is affected by the company's visibility and attraction level:

- The ability of the company to present itself to the market
- The brand position the company commands
- The strategic position of the company
- The confidence the investing public has in top management
- The perceptions on the size or growth rate of the market the company serves
- The liquidity or exit possibilities that the share offers
- A host of other factors

For shareholders to choose an individual company, several conditions have to be met:

- Prevailing conditions in key market segments must be attractive.
- Shareholders must understand and appreciate the business idea, what the company aims to achieve, and its ability to reach its goals.
- The company should be able to show its flexibility, "freedom to act," since this ability decides how much value added the company can expect to generate and how much of it the company can keep.
- Shareholders must have an idea of how the company is perceived in important stakeholder groups, since those perceptions define, among other things, such factors as market share and relative price level.
- The company must offer shareholder flexibility, that is, trading patterns that give shareholders exit possibilities.

These conditions can be measured and registered, *but not through accounting data.* Accounting-based ratios are also of very little help. The investing community needs and deserves more useful information systems.

NOTES

1. The two-liners appearing here and there under the chapter headlines are quoted from Hans V.A. Johnsson, *Analysts to Zhu Rong Ji: A New Economy ABC*, Sarasota, FL, 2000.
2. www.ACAUS.org_his.html.
3. For a broad and insightful discussion on the severe limitations of the reliability and relevance of accounting, see Robert E. Litan and Peter J. Wallison, "Beyond GAAP," in the Special Edition of *Regulation: The Cato Review of Business and Government*, Cato Institute, Washington DC, 2003. The two co-authors of the article enjoy a high level of credibility. Robert E. Litan is vice president for research and policy at the Kaufman Foundation and a senior fellow in the Economic Studies Program at the Brookings Institution. Peter J. Wallison is a resident scholar at the American Enterprise Institute and co-director of its Financial Institutions Project.
4. Arthur Levitt, former Chairman of the U.S. Securities and Exchange Commission, in *Directorship*, Greenwich, CT, July/August 1999.
5. Joanne Gordon, "Accounting: It's Not Just a Job, It's a Misdemeanor." *Forbes,* March 18, 2002.
6. For a detailed account of this case, look for instance in John A. Byrne, *Chainsaw: The Notorious Career of Al Dunlap in the Era of Profit-at-Any-Price*, Harper Business Books, New York, 1999. A short but still extensive summary of the book was published in *Business Week*, October 19, 1999.

7. For an in-depth presentation of this case, turn to *Forbes*, November 27, 2000.

8. According to a 2002 study directed by accounting professor Russell J. Lundholm of the University of Michigan, more than 150,000 earnings reports issued from 1988 to 1999 excluded certain expenditures from their pro forma earnings. The results of the study suggest that, with some well defined exceptions, "we should be skeptical of all expenses that companies exclude from their pro forma earnings." Mark Hulbert, "When Those One-Time Expenses Have a Refrain," *New York Times*, September 15, 2002.

9. See for instance David Henry, "Why Earnings Are Too Rosy," *Business Week*, August 13, 2001.

10. See for instance a study made by the accounting department of Florida Gulf Coast University, directed by accounting professor Deanna Oxender Burgess. The study was reported in *New York Times*, September 15, 2002.

11. In "When a Rosy Picture Should Raise a Red Flag," *New York Times*, July 18, 1999.

12. As in "Accounting Gets Radical," *Fortune*, April 16, 2001.

13. The U.S. Sarbanes-Oxley legislation is a case in point. Rather than trying to devise serious changes in existing reporting systems, the legislators just proposed—and enacted—"more of the same," stricter rules and tougher enforcement of existing regulation.

14. In his *The Structure of Scientific Revolutions*, University of Chicago Press, Chicago, 1996, 3rd edition.

15. James Gleick, *Chaos: The Amazing Science of the Unpredictable*, Vintage, London, and other publishers, 1998.

16. The concept of "the fourth economy" will be explained in some detail in Chapter 2.

17. The concept of a flat earth has, of course, got an unexpected revival and an entirely new meaning through the 2005 book by Thomas L. Friedman: *The World is Flat: A Brief History of the Twenty-First Century*. Farrar, Straus & Giroux. This book, incidentally, confirms many of the views on the present world and business situation that we present in Chapter 2, under the umbrella of "the fourth economy."

18. Reported by Professor Lev, in a conversation with HJ in December 1999.

19. See Howard M. Schilit, *Financial Shenanigans: How to Detect Accounting Gimmicks and Fraud in Financial Reports*, McGraw-Hill, New York and other places, 1993.

20. See "Are Those Revenues for Real?," *Forbes*, May 29, 2000.

21. Walter B. Wriston, *The Twilight of Sovereignty. How the Information Revolution Is Transforming Our World*, Charles Scribner's Sons, New York, et al., 1992.

22. See Justin Fox, "When Bubbles Burst," *Fortune*, June 11, 2001.

23. *Forbes*, Money & Investing, August 21, 2000.

24. As an example, *The American Heritage Dictionary (Second College Edition)* cites 10 different meanings of *value*, of which four or five are linked to business and accounting.

25. Pro forma earnings, as a concept, basically means that certain items, for instance such items that were deemed to be of a nonrecurring character, could be excluded from the income statement. The idea was that the earnings report would thus show more closely the earnings from the "normal" operations. The problem was that many companies excluded cost items that were, in fact, parts of normal operations, creating a more distorted or confused picture of the company's real earnings capacity, rather than the contrary.

26. For a thorough discussion of the role of psychology and emotions in investment decisions, see John Nofsinge, "Investor Madness: How Psychology Affects Your Investing and What to Do about It," *Financial Times*, Prentice Hall, NJ, 2002.

27. Richard Karlgaard, "Pity Pot Priesthood," *Forbes*, October 14, 2002. The article is well worth reading and is loaded with concise, excellent, and telling examples.

28. Steve Forbes, "Good Man, Too Early Gone," *Forbes*, Sept. 3, 2001.

29. Bethany McLean, "Investing: Finding Our Way," *Fortune*, Oct. 15, 2001.

CHAPTER 2

When Accounting Meets a New Reality

Fundamentalist accounting
feels the pressures on it mounting.

THE WORLD IN THE TWENTY-FIRST CENTURY

A mania has passed—an era has just begun.[1]

Many business practitioners, writers, and thinkers seem to agree that we live at the beginning of an era that is about to change much of what we have previously taken for granted in society and in the economy. Just as war and diplomacy will never be the same again, neither will business and the economy. Many ingrained patterns from earlier times will have to be reconsidered. In a wider context, this era could be called "the fourth world order." Since we focus primarily on the aspects for business and the economy, we will deal with it as "the fourth economy."

The dramatic changes are driven by a maelstrom of technological, economic, and social sources and forces. We invite you to review with us some of these changes and the far-reaching consequences they are likely to have for your business.

Some people may have an interest in lulling the business community into denial of the dramatic changes. They may try to make us see what happens as just another phase of "business as usual." We feel it is more appropriate to face reality: The sooner we recognize the fact that these changes will have consequences for all of us, the sooner we can start to take appropriate action. The changes will affect some of the holiest cows of the business and economic community. One of them is accounting.

The late twentieth century coined the term the "new economy." In many ways the "new economy" was a temporary phenomenon, a mania. It also quickly turned into a cliché. Those are two good reasons to avoid the term. Another reason is that it implies a *conflict* between a "new" and an "old" economy. This view is misguided. It is more fruitful to see the four economies as gradual layers of practices, technology levels, opportunities, and priorities.

While the fourth economy is distinctly different from previous economies, it does not necessarily replace them. Instead, the postindustrial fourth economy adds a new layer on top of the industrial, third economy, just as the industrial economy improved the earth-based second economy, in turn changing the first economy, the economy of hunters and gatherers:

- The hunter-gatherer economy lives on in some areas of the world, not to mention all who love hunting and fishing as serious spare-time activities.

- As long as we need food and clothing, metals, oil, wood, and paper, "earth-based" second economy businesses like farming, fishing, forestry, oil extraction, and mining will continue to be with us. Their productivity has been enhanced, first through advanced machinery provided by third economy mechanization, then through software, systems, and concepts supplied by fourth economy technologies.

- There is no sign that we will live without cars, trains, houses, or other hardware. The computers of the fourth economy need electric power, so power plants and utility systems are necessary. Even with telecom, e-mail, and e-trade, people and products need to move, so transportation systems and equipment, functions of an industrial economy, need to be built, maintained, and operated. The third economy is alive and well, reinforced by fourth economy methods and systems.

Each new economy has made significant contributions to society:

- The second economy was an improvement over the first economy: It provided a certain degree of stability and reliability in *basic supplies,* such as food and clothing.

- The third economy added machinery that gave us new physical strength and power, and added speed and efficiency to *physical processes,* including those in the second economy.

- The fourth economy supports *mind-based processes* and takes them to previously unimaginable levels of strength, power, and speed. For the first time in the history of the world, we are seeing changes brought about by an almost complete conquest of time and distance. This includes productivity enhancement processes in second and third economy businesses.

Overall, the new conditions raise earnings and returns. They create new wealth.

Case in Point—India

Few countries offer a more dramatic example of this coexistence between the four economies than India: Hunting and fishing still exists. Villages, with very basic second-economy agriculture as their dominating source of employment, coexist with textile and engineering manufacturing plants typical of the early third-economy industrial era. High-tech companies, software-based "Cyberabad" and fiber optic-based "Fiberabad," are at the leading edge of the fourth economy. The contribution of fourth-economy technologies is increasing fast, based, among other things, on an efficient education system, which turns out more than 100,000 engineers a year. India's high-tech exports are growing fast. As proof of international acceptance of India's capabilities, one in three of the global top 500 multinationals outsource software work to India's companies. And yet, farming by oxen goes on next door....

Cases in Point—Ford and General Electric

Are these third economy companies, or fourth?

Both of these companies can be seen as typical third economy companies, steeped in the heavy manufacturing tradition of the nineteenth century. Yet, these companies are rapidly transforming themselves, using e-trade, software, outsourcing, and other concepts and technologies generated by fourth economy pioneers like Cisco, Microsoft, Amazon.com, and E-Bay. Ford divested itself of much of its manufacturing resources and sent back $12 billion of earlier "fixed asset" capital to its shareholders in early 2000, while in the last few years it has invested about the same amount in intangibles, such as brand names, including Aston Martin, Jaguar, Land Rover, and Volvo. It has shed assets you can touch, traditional third economy balance sheet assets, and bought what exists in the minds of customers and other stakeholders, a major characteristic of the fourth economy.

General Electric, spurred by its forward-looking former CEO, Jack Welch Jr., and present CEO, Jeff Immelt, has made an all-out effort to switch to an e-business company. In Welch's words, "The E in GE now has an entirely new meaning." The expertise GE has gained in business-to-business e-trade has, in fact, become a "product" in itself, a multibillion-dollar product that GE now sells to outside companies. Time is a valuable resource in the fourth economy. GE has introduced systems that allow it to dispatch service engineers in 4 hours rather than the traditional 18 hours. Double gain is in increased productivity and higher customer satisfaction. For intangibles the GE concepts also emphasize fast exchange of experience between employees and divisions. GE has discovered, and put into practice, a fourth economy tenet that we will discuss in detail later, "minds in interaction," communications in the broadest sense, as one of the prime value drivers in today's economy.

The Twenty-First Century as a Burning Glass— A Convergence of Sources and Forces

The new trends affect the *economy* but they originate in *society*.[2] What is new in the change from the third to the fourth economy? Simply put, we are exposed to a barrage of forces that move us from an industrial to a postindustrial world.

As the pioneers of "behavioral economics" have made increasingly clear, the *driving forces* of economy and business are human attitudes, feelings, and preferences, influences outside the accounting-based, numbers-oriented classical economy.[3] A quick look at some of them will show how broad the range of these driving forces is.

Each of the trends we can distinguish is huge in itself. The impact is raised to the nth degree through their *convergence* at this time. The early twenty-first century is the focus spot for a burning glass of hot issues, together creating a fire of change.

New Sciences and Technologies

The fourth economy is a high-tech economy with a broad technology base, including but certainly not limited to infotech. Biotech, with DNA, cloning, stemcell research, and new openings in pharma; astronomy with "superstring" theory; physics with quantum physics, quantum mechanics, with other quantum technologies, and nanophysics; sensory networks, holography, new materials; chaos and complexity theory; new forms of energy; new perspectives on time; these are only a few examples of forces that impact the whole society, the economy, and individual companies.

A Crossnational Awareness

The fourth economy, with unlimited data storage, real-time communications, new telecom techniques, and the Internet as only a few components, builds on broad and strong crossnational awareness, working in a WWW environment, a World Without Walls.

An Unlimited Base for Wealth Creation

In the fourth economy, economic growth is generated by minds in interaction, not primarily by physical resources. Contrary to physical assets, the human mind is not a fixed, limited resource. For the first time in history, the fourth economy offers potential for unlimited growth. This affects many business conventions, practices, and metrics. The human DNA, the genome project, an entirely "mind-based" innovation, has already had more impact and created more value than any discovery of new gold mines would have done.

Multiculturalism

The fourth economy thrives on variety, diversity, multiculturalism, based on "minds in interaction" as the most distinctive source of wealth creation and productivity enhancement.

A Search for Common Protocols

The fourth economy calls for common protocols, along with a high tolerance for "trial-and-error" development.

Case in Point—The Mars Orbiter Disaster

A Mars probe was misguided because, in the final moments, mistakes were made between U.S. and metric measurement systems. The fact that the United States still maintains a nonmetric measurement system would perhaps be something to smile at, if it were not for the huge costs to the U.S. economy, in a time of global trade and communication. Of course, the United States has taken one step of change in the right direction: Since some years now, drinks are measured in liters and milliliters, rather than gallons. Seemingly, this bold step into a global system has not had any negative consequences for the U.S. consumption of soft and not-so-soft drinks.

New Concepts of Time

In the fourth economy, by and large, time is a critical resource and a more significant competitive tool for many companies than capital.

New Waves of Creativity

The fourth economy has the potential to develop into a global win-win economy of practically unlimited creativity. Consequently, innovation, and creativity turn into high-priority competitive tools.

New Forces of Conservatism

In the fourth economy, conservative forces on the "left" and on the "right" will oppose new ideas, exchange, transparency, and openness. In the long run, however, the World Without Walls is strongly positioned to show its value in winning over isolation.

New Priorities for Government

The role of governments will not disappear in the fourth economy, but it will be refocused toward investments in human development, education, health, and mind-based infrastructure.

Case in Point—The U.S. Cell Phone Disaster

One of the dramatic examples of the disasters that may happen when an important technology area goes off on a wrong track and fails to find a good, international technology platform is the U.S. experience of getting stuck with a suboptimal wireless communications protocol in a period of dramatic international development of wireless communications. While the systems used in the rest of the world are not necessarily perfect, anyone who has experienced the difference between U.S. and international wireless technology in the 1990s can testify to the superior quality, functionality, and user-friendliness of the latter. Staying too long in an analog system, rather than a digital, and in a technology standard not embraced by the rest of the world, the United States has seen the 1990s as largely a lost decade for wireless communications, while the rest of the world—especially Europe and Asia—has made extremely fast progress. This example of a wrong choice at an important technology crossroads has cost the United States enormous amounts in missed opportunities and lost investments, to the wireless industry, but even more to U.S. business and society at large.

The Fourth Economy and the Accounting Perspective

The fourth economy presents immediate and far-reaching challenges for governments, management, business, and the economy. It would be amazing, indeed, if a reporting system developed in the days of Columbus and Copernicus were still adequate in our times. In Chapter 1 we have presented abundant examples to show that the *reliability* of accounting is severely limited. The characteristics of the fourth economy cut deep into the *relevance* of accounting.

The Fourth Economy Has Consequences for Management

The forces of the fourth economy have strong impact on business and management. We need to be aware of the broad view for a full perspective, but then, for a sharper focus, we must boil down the broad range of confusing trends and influences to a short list of major factors.

An expression we have borrowed from somewhere is "Action without thinking is dangerous; thinking without action is useless." In practical business, we see the two as complementary: You can't have one without the other. We need new thinking to grasp what is going on in the dramatic paradigm shift to the fourth economy. We need well considered action to put thinking into practice. Appropriate action will call for new tools.

A fair amount of observation and thinking is beginning to emerge. Yet, by and large, the process has been remarkably slow in terms of developing appropriate management tools for the twenty-first century in accounting, business analysis, and other business procedures.

It is not easy to single out a limited number of the strongest movers in today's turmoil of influences. Some have tried the easy way out by just linking the "new economy" to information technology or "knowledge." Our review of sources and forces above shows a more ambitious approach. The fourth economy is more than IT.

In the distillation process from the broad view to a few major trends we have endeavored, as much as possible, to avoid arbitrary choices. To achieve that, we have tested our own ideas against many sources to select the most relevant factors from a big pool of possible alternatives. From our research and our management and consulting practice we have been bold enough to distill a short list of three distinct management consequences[4] of the fourth economy. While any selection of this kind can be argued, we have received enthusiastic endorsement of these three characteristics whenever we have presented them to academics and practitioners.

1. Our time is "The Age of Discontinuity."[5] An unprecedented pace of fast, unpredictable change is replacing step-by-step or "business as usual" patterns of previous economies. Change can have its origins in new technology, in political and religious turmoil, in natural events, or in shifting market trends.

   Fast, unpredictable change, and the impact it has on society, the economy, business, and human minds, was first called to the world's attention by Alvin Toffler, in his 1970 book *Future Shock*.[6] The future, in Toffler's reasoning, hits us with an impact similar to the "culture shock" that affects a traveler suddenly arriving in a country with a culture widely different from what he or she is used to. Peter Drucker, in the same vein, called our time "The Age of Discontinuity." This distinct feature of our age was confirmed from an entirely different corner, by General Colin Powell, when he accepted the nomination as U.S. Secretary of State. In his words, quoted in the *New York Times*, December 17, 2000: "Challenges and crises that we don't know anything about right now will come along."[7]

   The fact that life and business are genuinely unpredictable is valid everywhere. Once we accept this fact, the consequences are far-reaching. The challenges it generates for business leaders are clearly perceived (e.g., in business risk management).

   It has always been hard for society, and it is hard for some in the business community, to accept the law of nature that the future is genuinely unpredictable. It may be comforting to know that not even the witchcraft in Harry Potter's world can handle it: "It sounds like fortune-telling to me, and Professor McGonagall says that's a very imprecise branch of magic."[8]

2. Our time stands out as "The Age of Mind-Based Wealth Creation." In previous economies, natural resources, physical assets, and capital were driving

forces in wealth creation. Today, wealth is created primarily through the interaction of mind-based factors.

The changing emphasis from the *earth-based* second economy and the *capital-based* third economy to the *nonfinancial, mind-based value drivers* of the fourth economy was first signaled by management writers like Peter Drucker[9] (although the terms "fourth economy" and "mind-based" are our own). Robert J. Shiller and other "behavioral economists," such as Richard Thaler and his followers, have helped return economics to the domain of human, mind-based factors. In the early 1990s, many new initiatives were launched on the concept "intellectual capital." One writer who has helped add and assess, in hard economic terms, not only intellectual but emotional factors within and outside the company, especially loyalty, is Frederick F. Reichheld.[10]

3. A third major characteristic of our time is "The Network Economy." Strong and intricate networks of relationships, interdependence, connecting people, companies and countries, and their environment in real time are keys to survival, growth, and earnings.

The traditional "autistic" view of the company as an independent legal unit is increasingly being replaced by views of the company as a living organism.[11] The crucial aspect is the constant exchange, the symbiosis, between the company and its environment. Quite often, the most critical factors for a company's success or failure are not found within the company itself. They are found on the borderlines between the company and its environment. A consequence is that every company must be seen and evaluated in its context, not on its own.

The case for *the new interdependence*, the closely connected "network economy," globally, regionally, and for companies, crossing borders, industries, and business categories, was made by, among others, the outstanding banker Walter Wriston, in "The Twilight of Sovereignty,"[12] and by Kevin Kelly, in "New Rules for the New Economy."[13] In *Forbes* ASAP, Nov. 27, 2000, William H. Davidow and W. Brian Arthur presented an interesting discussion on interdependence and some of its consequences using the term "interconnectedness."

Of course, these fourth economy tenets interact in practical business. Like "The Three Tenors," each of "The Three Tenets" is powerful, one by one. Their full impact is felt, however, when they are coordinated into one performance.

Case in Point—Management Consequences in a Nutshell

Recent management trends such as just-in-time, daily deliveries, outsourcing, time-to-market, alliances, mergers and acquisitions, and others, are by and large a result of these three features, at the same time proving them and reinforcing them. They tend to reduce or eliminate traditional balance sheet assets as the carriers of company "value." Balance sheet assets are replaced with relationships with suppliers, customers, and business partners. Fast, unpredictable change, one of the three features, is in itself fed by "mind-based factors" accelerated by communications and relationships.

How Much Time Do We Have?

The previous big change, from earth-based to industrial economies, had a transition period of two to three hundred years. In some countries it has yet to come. The fourth economy is in its initial stages at this time, the early twenty-first century, perhaps to be compared with the third economy, when the first mechanical looms were introduced in Britain. Still, new conditions have erupted in such a short time that they have already undermined many traditional concepts. Many age-old solutions simply do not work in the new situation. Others will have to change, as we begin to perceive and understand the full impact of the new realities. In the words of Harry Emerson Fosdick: "The world moves so fast nowadays, that the person who says it can't be done, is frequently interrupted by somebody doing it."

Productivity—One of the Great Gains of the Fourth Economy

The dramatic difference brought out by the fourth economy is perhaps easiest to recognize in the productivity data: As new fourth economy processes, techniques, and methods are applied to second and third economy companies, output per work-hour goes up significantly. GE, cited earlier in this chapter, offers dramatic examples, as does the U.S. economy as a whole. While numbers can fluctuate, as in all statistics, the productivity trend has been the one consequence of fourth economy innovation that has backstaged all others. It has puzzled some economy bureaucrats, who have had to admit, sometimes reluctantly, that this economy may allow a higher "speed level," without raising the inflation specter.

New methods, concepts, and technologies will offer great opportunities to countries and companies who can benefit from them. An equally strong negative impact will hit people in areas or countries that either are left behind, for example, because of inadequate education systems, insufficient infrastructure, or tragic disasters, such as countries in sub-Saharan Africa, or that choose to stay behind, maybe for political or religious reasons, such as some Mid-Eastern countries. Staying out of ongoing global learning and exchange processes will have dire consequences, which cannot be compensated for by ever-so-abundant natural resources, such as copper and hydropower in African countries or oil in the Mid-East. The rift between those who choose to participate in the exchange, and those who do not, will not be an economic gap alone, although that is serious enough. It is bound to affect broad aspects of quality of life.[14]

ACCOUNTING AND ACCOUNTABILITY IN THE FOURTH ECONOMY

Without reliable and *relevant* metrics and tools adapted to today's fast-changing environment, business and management will be exposed to higher risks of failure than ever. Nothing should stand in the way of efforts to restore credibility, accountability, and relevance to the economic process, not even drastic changes in the role of accounting, should they be seen as necessary.

The focus needs to change from *accounting*, as an academic discipline, to *accountability*, with emphasis on finding honest and performance-based tools for practical business and management applications, strategic decision-making, stake-holder reporting, pricing, risk management, auditing, and financing.

Accountability is equally important to all companies, whether they see themselves mainly in the second, third, or fourth economies. Generally Accepted Accounting Principles were guidelines once supposed to help set up indications and warning signs. In the old economies they may have worked. In the fourth economy, their usefulness is severely limited. In the legendary phrase, the GAAP guidelines may now not be part of the solution; they may be part of the problem.[15]

The Dangers of Fundamentalism

Through history, and not least in later times, we have learned to see the dangers of fundamentalism, a nonintellectual attachment and loyalty to established dogmas and creeds. Some of the worst political and human disasters in history have been caused by people acting on blind beliefs without appropriate questioning, tempered reasoning, and efforts to adapt old doctrines to new circumstances. The strongholds of fundamentalism, often linked to authoritarian or dictatorial regimes, are characterized by isolation from dissenters, excessive trust in tradition, and by holding on to fixed sets of ideas long after the reality has changed,[16] like using century-old maps to drive through today's Los Angeles. In terms of economic and cultural development, authoritarian and fundamentalist regimes have seldom offered good opportunities for their people, compared to open societies. Given the characteristics of the fourth economy this difference is going to increase.

Fundamentalist accounting may turn out to play a dangerous role in this perspective. Accounting was originally created for a society and an economy in which, *compared to and contrary to our time, the pace of change was slow, the important assets were physical, and where the company could possibly be seen as a closed system.* The realities of twenty-first-century business have moved us far away from what once might have made fifteenth-century accounting relevant, even if accounting rules were applied with reasonable honesty and integrity.

The Conflict between a Traditional View and Today's Economy

Let us sum up the three tenets of the fourth economy and their consequences for management strategies and corporate accountability:

In a world...	Executives cannot...	Instead they must...
of fast, unpredictable change	rely on trend extrapolations, prognoses, or forecasts	prioritize flexibility and diagnoses
where wealth is created by minds in interaction	focus on material assets alone to explain success or failure	define and measure nonmaterial drivers of success or failure
where relationships are a condition for survival	limit their views and measurements to what happens within company walls	define and measure the impact of relationships

Accounting and the Three Tenets of the Fourth Economy

Over the centuries, accounting came to be used beyond its capacity as a broad support tool for management. Even in the twentieth century, accounting was never really helpful for such purposes. In the economy of the twenty-first century, accounting data are less useful than ever.

Modify or Abandon?

The conflicts raise the question of whether one should try to modify, complement, or completely replace existing systems. We feel that we need to develop better methods. The present system is beyond repair for all applications except registering transactions. It should be replaced as soon as we can agree that there are alternatives. Performance indicating success or failure can be tracked in systematic and manageable ways through experience-tested, non-accounting-based models.

Cost/Benefits of Accounting

Given the shrinking benefits of traditional accounting, we must also consider the huge resources it is allowed to consume. Companies and countries spend enormous amounts of money, staffpower, equipment, software, and other resources on their accounting systems.

To the extent that these priorities are dictated by tax legislation or other government directives, it may be hard to argue about them, at least short term, until better systems have been adopted even by governments. If, however, companies continue to trust accounting-based models to manage the company's real performance, they are basically wasting their resources. Accounting does not support today's most burning strategic management needs. New reliable and relevant reporting systems are required to help company management, boards, investors, and others who depend on transparent information for their decision making. The longer we keep accounting as a major support system for decision making, the more problems will be experienced.

A Parallel with Recent Global Politics

The same parameters affect the world at large and the business community.

- The terrorist attacks on September 11, 2001, were apparently unpredicted, even by the best-equipped intelligence organizations in the world.

- The war that they released is not fought for land, natural resources, or physical assets. It is fought—on both sides(!)—for "share of mind," for ideas, beliefs, and basic concepts.

- None of the parties, not even the United States, despite its position as the only remaining superpower, can succeed in this war alone. Both sides need support, alliances, networks, relationships.

- Looking back in history is not going to help us deal with the challenges. The world has never been through anything like this before. Neither will old prescriptions help the business community to deal with the unprecedented challenges of our times.

Case in Point—Nokia: A Success Story of Leadership through Dynamic Change

Nokia, today a global leader in wireless communications, did not start out as a fourth-economy company. It started in the second, or possibly third, economy, as a forestry products company. As late as the 1970s, Nokia was still primarily a third economy company, making chemical products, industrial parts, and rubber boots. Its financial situation was shaky and its outlook for the future dim. The management of Nokia courageously made dramatic change in response to new circumstances. In the 1970s Nokia had taken its first steps into cable and telephone switch technology. The accepted wisdom in most countries at the time was that telephone companies needed government protection to survive and develop. Finland, by contrast, had an open climate, and encouraged competition at an early stage, even in telecom. In the early 1990s, Nokia sold off a range of other product lines and focused on mobile phone technology. It took courage on the part of Nokia's management to make the company leave its old position and platform in heavy industry and turn it into a fireball of advanced telecom technology. Together with other European suppliers, it developed a cutting-edge standard for wireless communications. This standard, the GSM, has been accepted as the global standard in most countries in the world, with the United States as the major exception, although it is now gradually winning ground also in the United States.

The takeoff for Nokia's dramatic change is closely related to the three tenets: accepting and welcoming fast, unpredictable change; shedding old economy "assets" that would have limited the necessary flexibility; and focusing on technology, brand-building, and customer satisfaction. In one customer's words: "Nokia was the only manufacturer that listened to us and didn't tell us what to do."[17] It also means focusing on other mind-based resources, and building alliances and relationships with other Finnish and foreign companies and organizations (e.g., in developing the victorious GSM cell phone technology and the Ericsson-inspired Bluetooth technology).

The stage is set. So, what does it take for companies and business executives to successfully deal with the challenges of discontinuity, mind-based wealth creation, and relationships and dependencies? That is what we will examine now.

HOW TO SUCCEED IN "THE AGE OF DISCONTINUITY"

More than ever before, the economy in general and most businesses are exposed to and dependent on fast, often totally unexpected and unpredictable change. As a consequence, executives must learn to accept flexibility, agility, or "freedom to act" as the company's first strategic priority.

Case in Point—Grizzly River Run

It is easy to understand why the Grizzly River Run is the most popular ride in Disney's new California Adventure Park. Looking at how it exposes the rafters to a whirling, soaking spin ride, including two waterfalls, it should perhaps be made a compulsory experience for all executives in the fourth economy.

"The Crystal-Ball Wall"

Turbulence is nothing new in the business community. Companies have started up, lived for a time, and then died. Only rarely do we find really long-lived companies, such as Swedish-Finnish Stora-Enso with a recorded lifetime of well over 700 years.

Learning to handle the challenges of fast, unpredictable change is a necessity for any board or management team in the twenty-first century. Traditional practices, forecasting, scenario building, trend extrapolation, planning based on past performance and "business as usual" are no longer useful. Instead, flexibility, agility, resilience, and "freedom to act" will be more and more important conditions for success. *Diagnosis* of threats and opportunities in the present situation will be more important than *prognoses*. Some executives and managers understand the serious difference between focusing on flexibility and relying on crystal balls. As *CFO* magazine writes in its issue of January 2005 (p. 54): "Even managers at businesses with sophisticated forecasting systems have run up against the crystal-ball wall." *CFO* then quotes Mitch Myers, VP of an instrument-making company in Tulsa: "We want to be fast and flexible. We don't want to be dependent on predictions about what's going to happen, like some psychic on a 1-900 number."

Most managers agree instinctively that change is faster now than it has ever been. While the average life span of *people* in most countries has gone up over the last 10 to 15 years, the average life span of *companies* has gone down. New companies spring up at an amazing speed, some of them as consequences of other dramatic changes—downsizing, outsourcing, and restructuring of bigger companies—some based on new technologies, some on new market needs, some for other reasons. A few of these companies grow fast to global leadership. Cisco is one example. Other companies die young, perhaps too young, or they survive under a different name, sometimes as a result of another strong business trend of our time, mergers and acquisitions.

The fast pace of change is not the only dimension to consider. It adds to the drama that change comes in so many shapes and from so many corners: technological change, change in marketing methods, new actors coming in from new countries, new constellations of stakeholders and companies, government action, deregulation or reregulation, international politics, and changing public opinions, trends, and fashions.

Management as Whitewater Kayak-Rafting

Any executive today can provide dozens of examples from his or her own experience to confirm the totally mind-boggling pace of fast, unpredictable change today.

Percy Barnevik, former chairman of the Swiss-Swedish engineering company Asea Brown Boveri, ABB, goes beyond the tame expression of "the winds of change." Barnevik makes it more drastic:[18] "Earlier, we could use the metaphor of sailing, when we discussed management. Today, management is more like whitewater kayak-rafting in class E rivers." What Barnevik talks about, really, is management as a Grizzly River Run, but in real life, not in a theme park.

The Death of "Business as Usual"

A simple consequence of the unpredictability of today's life is that traditional methods of forecasting, based on trend extrapolation in various forms, must be seriously questioned, whatever purposes they are used for. In this economy they have lost whatever usefulness and credibility they may once have had.

Management has traditionally relied heavily on forecasting, often based on past performance. The best advice a CEO traditionally offered to calm his clients, employees, and other concerned stakeholders was to proclaim "business as usual." This expression came to serve as a lifeline and a tranquilizer. In crises or difficult times it gave a feeling of comfort. It was an equivalent, at management level, to the famous security blanket of Linus, George Schulz's unforgettable cartoon character. In our "Age of Discontinuity" it is questionable if there is something like business as usual at all. So much in every new situation is without precedent. Contrary to the old adage, history does not repeat itself.

Unexpected competitors come in from unexpected corners. It took some time before Vodafone realized that one of their wireless competitors was the third economy steel and heavy manufacturing giant Mannesman.

Starting from garages and basements, young managers and entrepreneurs with ideas and visions come in directly from school and build up, in a short period of time, global companies that outperform old-timers. Point One Tele-communications, starting as a three-person company, became an unexpected competitor to the big telecom companies, when Point One introduced new technology, fiberglass and Internet, and used unconventional financing, leasing equipment and capacity rather than owning them.

New technologies shoot up fast and change all the rules of the game, and gene technology changes the very rules of life itself. Fashions shape trends in totally unpredictable ways, for everything from watches and cell phones to reading and TV viewing. While we can recognize an existing trend, we can never anticipate when a new trend will come up, nor can we predict the end of an ongoing trend.

Nobody Can Predict the Future!

Cases in Point—The Future is Unknowable

Alan Greenspan has gained a reputation as one of the most respected leaders of the U.S. Federal Reserve Bank. According to a Reuters release, in January 2000, when he was renominated for a fourth period, he made perhaps one of his most concise comments: "The future is always ultimately unknowable." If anyone does, Alan Greenspan should know what he is talking about. After all, before his time as Fed Chairman, he started and ran an economic forecasting firm!

The Blizzard of the Century

In the late winter of 2001, all weather forecasters agreed that New York would be hit by one of the worst snow emergencies ever, one that would totally cripple the city. High-tech equipment, satellites, automatic sensors and advanced computers, every instrument supported what may well be the best-educated and -experienced weather professionals in the world. No word of doubt entered the forecasts. Planes and plans were canceled. The outcome was a light touch of snow, nothing that anyone should ever have worried about.

The Record Budget Surplus

In the fall of 2000, toward the end of the Clinton administration, forecasts of the most enormous surplus ever in the U.S. federal budget dominated the U.S. political scene. Over the next 5 or 10 years, a surplus amounting to trillions of dollars would swamp the U.S. coffers. The budget would go from its traditional big red numbers into an era of black or blue for many years, maybe forever. When the Bush administration took over, this was one of the few legacies of its predecessors that it initially adopted into its own policy base. Spending patterns on education and defense were developed, and on top of that, record-breaking tax cuts were administered. The rosy picture lasted through the spring of 2001. As summer came, so did the realism. Once again, forecasters, in this case the most prominent financial experts, with the most advanced resources and mathematical models at their disposal, had made fools of themselves, or rather proved what humankind has known for thousands of years: The future is genuinely unpredictable.

Mr. Greenspan's remarks are in no way sensational. The failed New York weather forecast is not unique. The vagaries of national financial trends are commonplace. Some commentators have accused the IMF for being clueless, because of their failure to predict the economic meltdowns in Russia and in Asia and other financial crises. Others have accused the CIA and the FBI for not predicting the terrorist attacks on New York and the Pentagon in September 2001. Both accusations are unfair. Every one of us knows, or should know, from history, theory, and our own experience, that the future is completely and genuinely unpredictable. We cannot predict the short-range future and certainly not the long-range future.

Yet, through the ages it has always been an intriguing pursuit to try to predict the future. The Aztecs read the future from the blood-dripping intestines of animals and young girls. The ancient Greeks asked the Oracle of Delphi. In the United States, groundhogs, otherwise little known animals, are used to predict six months' weather, depending on the shadow they cast or don't cast on a certain day. Hemlines have been seen as predictors of the ups and downs of business. The thickness of Alan Greenspan's briefcase has been used to predict interest rate changes.

Since it has always been known that it is impossible for normal humans to predict the future, all traditional cultures and most religions have cautiously limited the right to make predictions. Forecasting was a prerogative for the gods or spirits. If necessary, the gods used priests, oracles, shamans, soothsayers or other fortune-tellers as intermediaries, to act on behalf of the gods, equipped with supernatural or divine powers of attorney. It is not until our time that we have delegated such talents to mere mortals, consultants, analysts, and CNBC panelists.

Cases in Point—More Lessons from History

History tells us that even highly intelligent people fail dramatically when they try to make predictions. Here are a few examples from history that we can laugh at in the aftermath:

A president of the Michigan Savings Bank advised one of Henry Ford's lawyers, Horace Reckham, not to invest in the Ford Motor Company. His comments were: "The horse is here to stay, but the automobile is only a fad." Reckham did not heed the advice. He bought $5,000 worth of Ford shares, and sold them later for $12.5 million.

In 1949, the magazine *Popular Mechanics* made a forecast of the development of the future of computers: "Computers in the future may perhaps only weigh 1.5 tons."

Lord Kelvin, one of the world's leading mathematicians and physicists of his time, at the turn of the twentieth century, was very concise in his verdict: "Radio has no future."

Practically all political scientists had predicted a massive victory for Al Gore in the 2000 presidential election in the United States. As one of them, Thomas H. Holbrook of the University of Wisconsin, who predicted a 60 percent share of the vote, admitted that "the election outcome left a bit of egg on the faces of the academic forecasters."

People Are Not Stupid

Please do not read these quotes as examples of the stupidity of the people who make the forecasts. On the contrary, these predictions come from specialists in their fields, enjoying a high level of respect and credibility. The examples just illustrate how even the most qualified experts are subject to the laws of nature: "The future is genuinely unpredictable."

All of us can add other examples of predictions, forecasts, and assumptions that have gone wrong, examples from our reading or our own personal experience. Let us end this passage with a quote from another time that proves that intelligent people can certify to this even in earlier, perhaps less dramatic times: Edmund Burke (1729–1797), in a 1791 letter to a member of the National Assembly, said, "You can never plan the future by the past."

Case in Point—A Demand for Meaningless Predictions

One of Alan Greenspan's associates in the forecasting business, later working for Bear Stearns, was Steve Gibson. In an interview he gave to Virginia Postrel, quoted in Postrel's book, *The Future and its Enemies*,[19] he recounts how "a lot of people would rather have utterly meaningless predictions than no predictions at all."

Against our best judgment, many of us take a peek at the horoscopes in our daily newspapers. Other forecasting methods, reading coffee or tea leaves, shuffling Tarot cards, gazing into crystal balls, and palm reading have a large number of true believers and supporters.

Most of us do not admit to taking horoscopes seriously. We would not trust them as reliable guidelines to what will happen today, tomorrow, or next week. Most of us do not go to psychics or card-readers and other forms of fortune-tellers for help in making important decisions, for instance before making strategic decisions about our company's future. At least we would hardly confess that we did. Rational thinking and generations of hard-earned experience lead us to base decisions about life, work, love, and investing on other parameters. We accept, at least intellectually, that *the future is genuinely unpredictable*.

Butterflies and the Berlin Wall

If we need to reinforce what Alan Greenspan and the rest of us know by experience, we can go to science to learn more. In later years, chaos and complexity researchers[20] have convincingly shown the same thing. The best-publicized example from chaos and complexity theory, of course, is the case of the butterfly in the jungles of the Amazonas, whose wing movements may release a typhoon in the Pacific Ocean, on the other side of the globe. And nobody would be able to predict it.

Case in Point—Not Even the CIA!

The fact is that no forecasters or experts, not even the best-equipped or the best-informed experts, including the CIA and the big international media networks, predicted any of the great events of recent history, including the fall of the Berlin Wall, the fall of the Shah and the subsequent surge of the Islamic Revolution in Iran, the Asian economic crisis in the 1990s, the terrorist attacks on the New York World Trade Towers and the Pentagon in September 2001, or the Asian tsunami in December 2004.

The trendiest of all trend forecasters, Faith Popcorn, states, in her 1992 book, *The Popcorn Report*, "You have to see the future to deal with the present." Our view is exactly opposite: In our management work we have to carefully examine *the present*, especially the quality and strength of the company's business position, its relationships, to have any chance at all to deal with the future. (There is more about how to do this in Chapter 4.)

The Last Bastion of Fortune-Telling

Isn't it strange that the same people who laugh at fortune tellers take economists seriously? (*The Rotarian*, July 2000).

In our time, there is actually only one segment of society that we can think of where well-educated people practice fortune-telling as a serious pursuit. It is the privileged brahmin caste of "fortune-sellers," the group of financial analysts, who look into your face from the TV screen and predict, without a twinkle or a smile, how share prices are going to change over the next hours, days, or months, or how an individual company is going to develop over the next five or ten years, or how the economy, or inflation, or productivity, or interest rates, or currencies, or . . . and, consequently, how you should invest or disinvest today. If someone feels that we exaggerate, just check your favorite business and financial media! But this is not only a media issue. If it were, we could dismiss it as entertainment. It is worse than that.

Some companies, and many governments, even in highly developed countries, maintain big departments of fortune-tellers, in the form of well-educated bureaucrats, who do nothing but pursue *the impossible dream*, predicting the future. And at the top of the pay ladder, we find highly paid consultants accepting assignments aimed at predicting future developments and trends. Some of them even publish serious books about it.[21]

Case in Point—Nine of the Last Five Recessions

Famous MIT economist and 1970 Nobel laureate Paul A. Samuelson called this fact to our attention in an article in *Newsweek,* September 19, 1996: "Wall Street indexes predicted nine out of the last five recessions."

A specific problem is that the main instrument that executives have been taught to lean to in their business operations, fifteenth-century accounting and its derivatives, leaves us totally in the dark.

Cases in Point—Three Do-It-Yourself Experiments

Just for the fun of it, and to avoid the feeling that we exaggerate, here are three experiments that anyone can make:

1. Dig out some old copies of business or finance magazines or newspapers, read their forecasts for the period that has elapsed, and compare with what really happened. In some exceptional cases, you may find that the difference between prediction and reality was small. There is nothing to say that guesses about the future have to come out wrong. Guesses can go either way. Chances are, however, that you will have a good laugh at the comparison.

2. Go back to your own company files of a couple of years ago and review some of the planning or forecasting documents that the management team discussed and perhaps acted on. Check how much of the forecasts came close to the real outcome!

3. Find a newspaper page showing the development of stock prices over a day, a month, or a longer period. They register what really happened, so they are safe. Now take a marker or a pen and try to establish a point, or a few points, for each of the curves and decide when you would have felt comfortable to go in and make a forecast!

Truth and Some of its Consequences

Case in Point—Disclaimer, Please!

Technical skeptic Paul Kurtz, in Amherst, NY, has made it his mission to reveal all kinds of humbug or unscientific claims. As part of his mission, at one time he asked a large number of newspapers to disclaim their astrology columns as entertainment.[22] Only 80 of the 1,200 newspapers complied with Kurtz's request to put a disclaimer on astrology columns.

What would happen if Mr. Kurtz made the same request for a disclaimer to analysts or consultants who are in the business of forecasting? Chances are that very few of those who live a good life making forecasts would comply with such a request, perhaps at best the same proportion as the newspapers disclaiming their astrology columns. To top it off, these consultants charge big money for their services, far exceeding the fees charged by their colleagues, the legendary little old back-alley ladies in the old-fashioned crystal-ball reading business.

In *The Elements of Style*[23] by William Strunk Jr. and E.B. White, a book that has taught generations of Americans to be cautious about how they use language, the writers bring up the expression *the foreseeable future*. They comment that it is "a cliché, and a fuzzy one. How much of the future is foreseeable? Ten minutes? Ten years? Any of it? By whom is it foreseeable? Seers? Experts? Everybody?" As is often the case in the advice found in this book, it is not only the problems of grammar or form one should be aware of. It is the thinking that matters. The thinking failure behind the expression *the foreseeable future* is of course that *no one* can foresee the future. Claiming to be able to do that, and charging real money for it, is worse than a language gaffe. At best, it is fuzzy thinking; at worst it is unethical, or plain dishonest.

Why Spoil the Fun?

The sad truth is that a clear warning label should be made compulsory for financial analysts, advisers, writers, and consultants to display prominently in all their material and statements:

We accept that,
since we are not equipped with divine powers,
we cannot predict the future.

Unfortunately, such a dose of realism might spoil some of the fun for many people, just as a ride in Disneyland or going to a futuristic space movie would be less exciting for children and grownups, if one were reminded the whole time that all of it is only a game, a show that tricks and tickles our imagination rather than reflecting reality.

The warning label should not be seen as a reason for anyone to ban fun, fantasy, or imagination from our lives. If we wish, we can still read horoscopes as entertainment, *as long as we keep the line clear between imagination and reality*. It is when we mix imagination and reality that we are on a dangerous track. Psychiatrists can tell us horror stories about what happens to people who lose the ability to keep them apart.

Serious Diagnosis—More Reliable than Prognoses

So what do you do when you need a platform for decisions that are going to shape a company's future one way or the other? Peter Drucker expresses his view this way:[24] "I don't speculate about the future. It's not given to mortals to see the future. All one can do is analyze the present, *especially those parts that do not fit what everybody knows and takes for granted*" (emphasis added). If this is the advice given by one of the greatest management thinkers of our time, anyone who disagrees has a strong burden of proof on his or her shoulders.

Fortunately, experience-based methods exist, methods that examine many of those parts. In Chapter 4, we review one such method that diagnoses a company's business position systematically by the links the company has to stakeholders and influence factors.[25]

Case in Point—The Super Bowl Predictor

For non-American readers it may be necessary to mention what the Super Bowl is: It is the final championship game of the (American) Football Season. The Super Bowl game, followed by some 800 million TV viewers at millions of Super Bowl parties, takes place annually at the end of January. The Super Bowl Predictor tells the world how the stock market will end the year: If the winner is a team with its roots in one of the two earlier leagues, the AFL, the stock market will end the year lower. If, on the other hand, the winning team is firmly anchored in the other league, the NFL, the market will end the year up. Claims are that it has been correct more than 80 percent of the last third of a century, which beats most gurus, professional analysts, university professors, and econometric models.

But American football is not well known in Europe. Since European investors also feel the need for economic indicators, they have developed their own soccer-based equivalent. The well-heeled British business and financial magazine *The Economist* reports on a scientific study that clearly links success in the European soccer championships to accelerated economic growth. The study shows that the country that wins the European championship one year can look forward to three years of higher growth than other European countries.

In *A Random Walk Down Wall Street*,[26] Burton G. Malkiel expresses the difficulties in predicting future earnings, dividends, and other accounting-based data with utmost care and restraint, when he calls it "a most hazardous occupation" and warns: "It requires not only the knowledge and skill of an economist, but also the acumen of a psychologist." He could have added that predictions also require *the supernatural powers of a shaman*.

Accounting, Analysts, and Astrology

We live with a wall of time before our eyes. No matter how much humankind has tried through the ages to peer through that wall, it has never succeeded. On top of this, accounting is and has always been an instrument to register past transactions. Its only legitimate focus is on the past. When accounting is used to look to the future, it turns to trend extrapolation, assuming step-by-step development and business as usual. This clashes completely with the reality of fast, unpredictable change. Any efforts to use accounting-based data to guide future-related decisions are doomed.

We are not going to discuss the significance of forecasts based on the Super Bowl Predictor, the European Soccer Championships, crystal-ball gazing, palm reading, astrology, hemline measurements, or the Santa Claus Rally theory. We will limit ourselves to discussing the value and usefulness of prognosis models where the apparently precise art of accounting has been misused as a tool for forecasting, in the Harry Potter terminology: *a very imprecise branch of magic*.

"Business research" (read: *analysis*) has been in a crisis since the legal and regulatory system put pressure on Wall Street firms to separate the business of analysts from the investment business. Under the old system, the costs of "research departments," easily amounting to hundreds of millions of dollars for each one of the major companies, were hidden or lumped together in the commissions that banking, brokerage, and investment firms earned on their investment banking deals. Today, the research departments need to find customers willing to pay up front for "research." That has put them to the challenge that other companies in a market economy constantly face: having their customers and clients experience that they get value for money, when they buy a product or service. The new situation, where costs are exposed, has led to sharp cuts, in some cases 50 percent or more, in analyst salaries, as well as to drastic reductions in research staff. The harsh realities of the market economy confirm that when the costs are brought to the surface, the lack of usefulness in the work made by analysts leads to a commensurate lack of willingness to spend money on analyst reports. *Business Week*, in its issue of January 31, 2005, suggests that financial research is "looking more and more like an expensive luxury."

"Past Performance Is No Indication of Future Results"

That sentence in mutual funds ads reflects the tough reality. History does not repeat itself, certainly not the parts of company history reflected in accounting. The only thing history teaches us in this context, as historian David McCullough has repeatedly emphasized, is that, at any given moment in history, development could have gone in endless numbers of directions. The development that finally happened was only one of an unlimited number of possibilities. This, of course, is true of companies as well. At any given point, a company's development can go in an endless number of totally unexpected directions. A competitor can come up with an entirely new solution. An executive can be killed in an air crash. Sudden changes in currency exchange rates or interest rates can occur overnight. Staff members can be hijacked.

For anyone interested in a company's future, accounting-based historic data are close to meaningless. Yet, forecasting based on an extension of the past is exactly what we see and hear (e.g., in the form of P/E forecasts based on a company's performance in previous years).

Case in Point—When Business Predictions Meet Reality

Here are some scattered quotes collected at random from financial and business media. They show what happens when accounting-related predictions meet reality. Please note that the forecasts and estimates in these cases are not for many years in advance, they are for the running period, or even the past period(!):

Boeing Co., the world's largest aircraft maker, on Wednesday said profits rose 36 percent in the fourth quarter, beating Wall Street forecasts.

Bank One Corp., instead of earning an expected half million dollars in the fourth quarter, said on Wednesday it lost about that amount in the period.

Tyco International Ltd said on Wednesday its fiscal first-quarter net income increased 29 percent, beating Wall Street estimates.

US Airways said on Wednesday it lost a greater-than-expected $89 million in the fourth quarter before special items, blaming higher fuel costs and competition from both low-cost and major network airlines.

Union Carbide Corp. warned Thursday that it would post a larger-than-expected loss in the fourth quarter because of soaring energy and raw material costs.

Exxon reported a huge rise in fourth-quarter income, far surpassing analysts' forecasts.

American Greetings lost more than 40 percent of its market value, when it announced that earnings would be way below analysts' forecasts.

The popular Internet auction site eBay Inc. Thursday reported a fourth quarter profit that was larger than forecasts.

The fourth-quarter performance of the U.S. economy was weaker than predicted by Wall Street economists.

Reliant reported earnings of 25 cents a share, short of analyst estimates of 33 cents.

These examples were collected during a few days in January 2001, but one can find similar statements practically every business day, year round. Note the expressions that should trigger loud warning bells: *higher than expectations, beating estimates, lower than expectations, better than anticipated, not as good as anticipated, far surpassing* or *far short of analysts' forecasts*. The percentage deviations from forecasts varied from 5 or 10 percent to 30, 40, or 50 percent; accounting-based forecasts and trend extrapolations gone sour! Yes, of course there are also cases of *met expectations*—anyone would get it right sometimes, even tossing a coin, drawing blind cards, throwing darts, or trusting a horoscope. Note also that *higher than* indicates a failed prediction, just as much as *lower than*!

We are not criticizing companies or other executives, nor analysts or other experts. Most of the time they do as well as they can. The point is that forecasting is *always* and *unavoidably an imprecise branch of magic*, no matter how good the accounting data of past performance seem to be. In every given moment, the potential development trends go far beyond what we can imagine. Life is simply too complex for predictions.

This applies beyond companies. Forecasting is equally impossible, for the same reasons, in the realm of national economics. Candidates in the 2000 U.S. presidential elections tried to get into the field of economic forecasting, related to the expected huge future budget surpluses. In the words of one of the experts:[27] "Both campaigns are using the best forecasting techniques available. Having said that, those techniques have proven to be consistently and completely wrong."

Even the area where forecasting techniques are perhaps the most scientific, weather forecasting, is in the same precarious situation. After the unanimous, and completely failed, meteorologist prediction of a major blizzard in the northeastern U.S., March 2001, cited earlier, one of the professional weather forecasters coined the term *premature prediction*. He could have sold the term to his forecasting colleagues in the financial field, who can use it not only for unusual blizzard-like events on Wall Street but to excuse the misfits in their everyday job. Indeed, most if not *all* predictions seem to be premature.

Caught in the Forecasting Web

Additional warning signals come to us from the big lawsuits against WorldCom, Enron, HealthSouth, Cuc/Cendant, and others after their record-breaking accounting fraud. The common denominator is that these and other companies tried to give their investors and others the impression that they were unbeatable earnings machines that could deliver unbroken chains of profit increases. When the vagaries of real ups and downs in their business did not match the promises of constant growth that the companies had presented in their forecasts, the companies and their top management, instead of facing the reality, changed accounting data to meet the forecasts! The companies were caught in the forecasting webs they had laid out, themselves. The invariably tricky business of making forecasts, which no one should trust, turned into a trap where the hunters were caught, along with the innocent prey, investors and other interested parties. These are scary examples of how forecasts are turned into self-fulfilling prophecies, even if it takes crimes to fulfill them!

There Are Simple Ways to Goof...

Practically any guessing game about the future is as good as any other. Tossing coins or reading tea leaves may turn out to give equally good indications of future market or economic performance as other methods. The Super Bowl Predictor and the Soccer Championship Indicator both have better track records than most experts. Checking the order flow to cardboard box manufacturers may sound like an odd and oversimplified predictor of business up- and downturns, but may in fact be one of the best.

...and More Sophisticated Ways

The fact that any simple guessing game is about as good as any other method for forecasting the future never stopped Mayan priests, African shamans, Greek oracles, Chinese I Ching diviners, or our own financial analysts and consultants from launching more sophisticated methods. Today's analysts have launched complicated methods in this spirit, including drawing cross patterns in "technical analysis" and combining forecasting-backcasting with fancy names like net present value, discounted cash flow, and real options. There are even companies that sell management performance solutions based on "forecasting software."

Following the collapse of Long Term Capital Management, Greenwich, CT, in 1998, Sir Howard Davies, Chairman of the UK's FSA, was quoted as saying, "The LTCM risk model told them that the loss they incurred on one day at the end of August 1998 should have occurred once every 80 trillion years. It happened again the following week."

As will appear later, we have very few objections to cash flow. In fact, we believe it is one of the few reasonably reliable instruments from the realm of accounting. However, even this good tool can be misused, drawing the reputation of accounting further down the drain. A safe way to misuse it is to try to imagine *future*(!) cash flows.

This is how discounted cash flow processes, originated and advocated by quite reputable accounting and auditing firms, basically work:

1. A SWAT team of consultants go deeply into the history and the books of the client company.

2. After a thorough study, the team comes up with predictions based on a whole lot of accounting factors, including past performance data.

3. These predictions are recalculated into estimates (read: *guesses*) of future revenues, market trends, earnings, cash flow, and other accounting parameters, 2, 5, 10, or infinite(!) numbers of years ahead.

4. They are then back-calculated, with assumptions of future interest rates, market shares, currency exchange rates, and so on, ending up in a figure supposedly showing a present "value" of the company.

The Ethics of Forecasting

We see it as a serious issue that professional consultants, analysts, and financial institutions continue to use and sell corporate astrology, although they must know it is against all common sense. Discounted cash flow (DCF) processes are an obvious case in point. They pretend that the value of a company can be assessed by calculating future financial results, for instance cash flows.

VALUE^{usefulness} is a perception that cannot be calculated by mathematical methods.

Future cash flows cannot be assessed with any claim of credibility, since the future is genuinely unpredictable. The uncertainty is much too big, even for a short period. To presume that cash flows can be predicted for periods of 5 to 10 years is absurd.

Does More Information Give Better Prognoses?

Unfortunately not! The number of possible developments at any point in time is unlimited.

Does Expertise Make Better Prognoses Possible?

Unfortunately not! All experience shows that expert predictions are no more reliable than those of amateurs. Unpredictable chance plays too big a role.

more variables a probability factor, say ±20 percent, more for longer-prognosis periods, and then feeding all those variables through a calculation program, which is easy with existing software, will result in a total probability span. The end results of these operations, however, do not tend to make DCF sellers any happier. Results invariably come out with a "value" defined with a devastating probability span, say, $100 million to ±$500 million or more, up to infinity. And then we have not taken into account the fact that reality, more often than not, is much more complex than even the most imaginative forecasts or estimates can be.

Studies to Prove

Innumerable studies have proven that discounted cash flow methods, at best, are useless. An example is a study[29] from the Department of Business Administration of the University of Stockholm, Sweden. It is based on empirical facts, not, as most cases used in the selling process, on theoretical calculations. It is also unbiased in the sense that it was not sponsored by any consulting company. Its initial conclusion is as straightforward as it is sobering: "(Discounted) cash flow valuation does not generate correct expectations of future share price development." Another conclusion was phrased even more bluntly: "It is our opinion that investors and analysts should not base their investment decisions on (discounted) cash flow valuation." There is nothing surprising about one of the reasons the research project group gives for the warnings, which are as clear as they are academically restrained: "The prognoses made about the future and the discount interest rate chosen are the most significant variables. Both of them are fraught with substantial uncertainty."

And then, critics have not touched another issue that we have met several times in our experience of analyzing companies: Even if one were to accept the general flaws, there might be just one single fatal threat that had not been considered or expected, which could be enough to turn the whole forecast upside-down.

"Unhatched Chickens"

It is bad enough from an ethical point of view to use such forecasting methods as "valuation" models in a decision-making process. It is even worse, when data from such questionable processes are fed directly into company accounting, polluting income statements and balance sheets.

In *Forbes,* February 19, 2001, under the headline "Unhatched Chickens," Elizabeth Macdonald, a journalist who keeps a sharp eye on shoddy accounting practices, writes about a credit card issuing company that does just that: "To calculate profits that are still to come, the card issuer makes guesses about future losses from bad loans and about how long the average account will stay on the

Real options, just as net present value, are basically just other forms of D calculation. They base the whole process on assumptions of future accounti data, which, in our view, is enough to discredit the model from the outset. T calculation proceeds to show decision trees, cash flow trees, event trees, ai switching options. Another questionable thing about it is that various future alte natives are being assigned a probability number. This may first look like a cautio move. However, since what is going to happen in the future goes way beyon most of what we can even imagine today, and the real impact of such future even is likely to deviate very much from anything we can guess, it is as unreliable as an other forecasts. (Compare with the Long Term Capital Management example above!) It is hard to understand why the method has the word "real" in its name

It is not surprising that such methods can be launched. The consulting mar-ket, like any other business, has its share of charlatans and gold-diggers. What is surprising is that otherwise serious analysts, corporate officers, and other intelli-gent persons on the client side have let themselves be led into using them, not as a late-night party game or pastime but for use in serious and critical strategic sit-uations. Much to our surprise, we have seen them applied, without a smile or an excuse, in due diligence projects, in strategic company crossroads situations, in venture capital financing, and in risk management processes. The most benevo-lent explanation is that accounting has its loyal believers, who have retained such respect for it from their years in business school that anything related to account-ing gets an air of respectability.[28] This seems to be especially true if "results" are served with an array of decimals, graphs, charts, mathematical formulas, and com-puter hocus-pocus.

The weakness of the methods is not that they are poorly sold or executed. The mathematical formulas are impressive. The weakness is that the methods ar incompatible with a hard, undeniable fact of life: *The future is genuinely unpre dictable.* As indicated by the randomly chosen quotes above, this applies even t short time periods, one quarter or less, and even when several of the paramete seem to be well known. Chances are always, especially today, that unexpect factors or forces pop up from nowhere and destroy the planner's or forecaste sand castles.

Can DCF Be Made Meaningful?

Are there ways to make discounted cash flow projects more meaningful? there is one way: to apply a probability range to each of the underlying fact

It can be done; we have done it as a demo on several occasions. For each factor, say five years' projections of sales volumes, revenues, profit margins, ket trends, costs, earnings, currencies, interest rates, and cash flow, there are ai 10 to 20 underlying support factors or variables. That makes for 100 to 150 ables, each of them estimated over five years. Giving each one of these 1 books throwing off interest. The resulting hypothetical earnings are discounted back into today's dollars and called profit." Macdonald asks a poignant question: "How do you foretell the future, when you do not know when or if a recession will hit?" She also concludes that such income statements are more art than science.

We feel that even that conclusion is kinder than it could have been. We would use less friendly terms. When such methods are used to distort accounting to the extent that the income statement is an expression of wishful thinking rather than reality reporting, then accounting itself becomes discredited. And when companies in the banking and finance business do it, there is no way they should get away with a disclaimer.

What Does One Do When One Must Make Decisions about the Future?

Faced with genuine unpredictability and uncertainty about what the future has to offer, the board and management of a company need to find ways to deal with their main responsibility, the future of the company. Anyone making evaluations of companies in a due diligence process has the future of the company or companies in their focus. Much of the work of auditors and risk managers is equally focused on what happens next, not what happened in the past. Also, investors and lenders are certainly looking for future returns and payback ability, not for past performance.

This is why it is important to find better ways to support decision making than guesswork and crystal-ball gazing. In Chapters 3 and 4 we will show that the case is not hopeless; better methods than those traditionally applied can, indeed, be developed.

HOW TO SUCCEED IN AN AGE OF MIND-BASED WEALTH CREATION

The economy in general and most businesses today have moved into a new era of wealth-creation. Today, wealth is not created primarily by physical assets. Wealth-creation is driven mainly by mind-based performance factors, not reflected in accounting. Consequently, the successful executive must develop ways to identify, measure, and report on these value drivers.

In the fourth economy, every company will need to look outside the accounting box to find and develop the most important drivers of company survival, earnings and growth. Boards and management need to identify and measure them, report on them, use them in serious due diligence, include them in auditing and risk management, and assess them in lending, financing, and investment decisions.

From Physical to Mind-Based Value Drivers

In the second economy, when wealth was defined in terms of agricultural land, forests, mines, or fishing waters, being rich could be described in terms of acreage, harvest capacity, number of cattle heads (originally the same word as capital!), or ore content. The task of management was to use and expand these physical resources, usually through production and distribution to local markets.

In the third economy, when wealth was generated by manufacturing resources, factories, machinery, and equipment, being rich was owning physical resources used primarily for producing physical products. The task of management was the proper use and growth of hardware and capital. The production and distribution focus expanded to national and later to international markets.

In the fourth economy, a consistent feature is that wealth and growth are generated by *minds in interaction*. This has far-reaching consequences, not only on management and economy in a narrow sense, but on politics, education, maybe even religion and philosophy. The focus is on problem solving with a minimum of physical resources involved.

The interaction component is the important element. Nothing happens, in business or elsewhere, without interaction. *Minds in interaction* is more than celebrating the bright genius of a Curie, a Linnaeus, a Newton, or an Einstein. Intellectual capital is part of it, but only a beginning. The human mind, not least in a business context, is more than intellect. The real focus must be on the process of free and open exchange of ideas, thoughts, and opinions as a key to growth and wealth. Wealth-creation goes beyond the intellectual scope to the emotional fields, ultimately to rely on the total process of human interaction and relationships.

Mind-Based—More than Intellectual

A popular concept about the "new economy" of the 1990s was to define it as a knowledge- or information-driven economy. When discussing new wealth drivers, one often gets the Pavlovian reflex, "Oh, you mean 'intellectual capital'?" Unfortunately, or fortunately, it is not as simple as that.

Pioneers like Leif Edvinsson launched the *intellectual capital* concept in the early 1990s. It represented a big step forward. Before that, the only resources recognized by accountants were hard assets and liquid assets, tangibles, and cash and cash-equivalents. (Even today, there are stalwarts in the accounting community who are only barely prepared to accept anything else.[30])

Wealth creation in the fourth economy is driven by something else than physical assets. We can see it in the relative decline of the prices of traditional physical assets, commodities, such as metals, even gold(!), and industries based on metals, wood, and other raw material, with relatively small amounts of mind-based value added.

Many economists in the 1950s believed that developing countries with big mineral resources would move up to a better economy and better quality of life for their people if they exported those basic commodities. UN and other data show that this never happened. Positive economic development has more to do with diversified economies, especially if they are also at least partly democratic. Taiwan, with practically no natural resources, has done better than oil-rich Nigeria or climate-blessed Zimbabwe. Developing human talent is a more critical factor in the twenty-first century than mineral resources.

Mind-based wealth drivers in the fourth economy are more than knowledge, information, or "intellectual capital." They include such basic concepts and emotional factors as culture, perceptions, attitudes, and opinions. This is obvious even from using a poor indicator such as stock prices. Of the market capitalization of industrial companies in the early 1980s, tangible assets represented some 60 percent. Twenty years later, that figure was 10 to 15 percent. And a large part of the intangibles part, the 85 to 90 percent of the price, is represented by more than intellectual capital. When Coca-Cola, for example, had a market cap of 15 times its book value, who would say that it was based on intellectual assets? It is *mind-based* in the sense that its share price rests on perceptions in the minds of millions of soft-drink customers around the world who prefer to quench their thirst with Coke rather than with Pepsi or any other alternative. But it is not *intellectual*; to most Coke-lovers, their preference is much more *emotional*.

The same goes for many other examples of brand recognition, which is perceived as a very strong driver of company share price in our economy, a major part for companies such as LVMH. When GE has a high stock price, it is fair to assume that much of it is related to appreciation of its top management. Preference and loyalty are important mind-based factors, and clearly contribute to company earnings and revenue,[31] but they are not necessarily intellectual.

Some proponents of the term *intellectual capital* maintain that we can call all of the nonphysical factors *intellectual*, whether they are in fact *intellectual* or predominantly *emotional*, such as loyalties and relationships, or something else. We do not agree. Any dictionary can provide clear and accepted definitions[32] of the words *intellect* and *intellectual*, distinct from and, indeed, often opposed to *emotional*. Messing with the meaning of these words would add more confusion to an issue that many perceive to be difficult anyway. Using language carelessly is equal to debasing a currency.

In today's world even the concept *intellectual capital,* once a significant innovation, is only a station on a much longer journey. The range of value drivers is much broader and much deeper. Putting *intellectual capital* items on a balance sheet would hardly make it better; it would only add to the mess.

Assets Do Not Create Wealth—Action Does!

Creation of new or added wealth has never been a matter of *items*, whether hard, physical assets, liquid, financial assets, or soft, mind-based assets. New wealth has always been created through *interaction* between various kinds of resources. The process is similar to what happens when active ingredients in a chemical process or in a baking bowl are mixed and the interaction starts. Dynamic forces, not static assets, create wealth.

Proportions between the three kinds of assets may vary. There is no doubt that our economy benefits from a high share of mind-based resources in the wealth-creation process, while for instance in the third economy, capital was often a major and sometimes limiting factor. The amazing thing today is that mind-based processes, without much material underpinning, can build whole industries and thriving businesses, a form of wealth-creation that is more unique and more miraculous than ever the old alchemists could dream about in their wildest imagination. In fact, most of the top 100 U.S. companies at this time are based on creative minds in action, rather than on natural or other fixed assets.

The past is prologue. In the fourth economy, management must learn to identify, measure, and manage a broad array of relationships and mind-based performance factors—their action and interaction. When company growth and earnings are largely generated by *minds in interaction*, then the interaction process is what management should focus on. It is also what should be shown in reporting systems worth their salt.

The new, bigger role of mind-based nonfinancial factors, intellectual or emotional, means among other things a reshuffling of the traditional roles of capital and labor. In the twentieth century, mass-manufacturing Taylorist methods aimed at standardizing industrial work to a level where one person's contribution was impossible to distinguish from another's. Labor became a collective pool of anonymous, exchangeable individuals. Capital, on the other hand, was owned by individuals, who exercised their power as owners to run the companies or strongly influence the process. Today, the reverse is true in many fourth economy businesses: Work is performed by individuals with very specific skills and qualities, hard to replace, while capital has developed into anonymous, collective flows that move freely between industries and across borders. Capital ownership, through mutual funds, pension funds, and other financial intermediaries, has become several steps removed from the influence that traditionally accompanied it.

Mind Over Matter

Perhaps this is the most dramatic aspect of change in our time: the switch of the whole economy from physical, material resources to mind-based resources as drivers of the economy. Even a brief survey gives ample examples.

Employment

Two-thirds or more of the U.S. workforce today move and process ideas, not physical products. Companies and businesses in the second and third economies have increased their productivity, often by applying fourth economy systems and concepts, so they can maintain valuable production with less people. Employment growth is in mind-based fourth economy companies, often in small start-up companies.

Companies

According to a *Business Week* listing[33] of the 25 biggest companies in the United States in 1969, 1979, 1989, and 1999, only four companies had stayed on the list for the whole period: AT&T, Exxon, IBM, and General Electric. The 1979 list had a majority of companies in natural resources or companies directly serving the second economy–related natural resources industry, while there was only one natural resource company on the 1999 list: Exxon. The old quote about a typical third economy company, General Motors, "What is good for GM is good for America," does not seem to apply today. GM did not even make the 1999 list, although, by many standards, the U.S. economy had never been better. Two-thirds of the 1999 companies were in pharmaceuticals, high tech, services, and other businesses with relatively modest assets on traditional balance sheets. Instead, their share prices rest almost entirely on mind-based assets, including investor perceptions of their ability to manage and develop mind-based forces.

Stock Market

As we discussed in Chapter 1, it is too simplistic to equate price to the magic word *value*. Ups and downs in stock prices depend largely on investor perceptions. So which way do investor perceptions go? Let us compare various categories of mutual fund prices as an example.

For an investment of $10,000 in August 1991, over the decade through August 2001, the change in fund price was approximately:

- 0–2 times for funds holding second economy companies: agriculture, natural resources, and basic materials (including gold)

- 1–4 times for third economy funds: manufacturing, industrial equipment, chemical industry, etc.

- 5–12 times for funds with fourth economy holdings: media, information, entertainment, electronics, computers, software, financial services, etc. (*Source:* Fidelity Select Funds report, Boston, August 31, 2001.)

This means that even after the adjustment of stock prices in 2000–2001, fourth economy shares still had a comfortable lead, in terms of buyer appreciation, over third and second economy shares.

Personal Wealth

Of the 100 wealthiest persons in the world at the beginning of the twenty-first century, only a few, such as the sheik of Bahrein, had old, inherited wealth based on hard assets. Most of the richest persons were new on the list, having created their wealth in a very short time span. Many of them had gained their position on the list through fourth-economy enterprises, related to software, computers, finance, or communications, with their net worth based on other than traditional hard assets.

Product Pricing

Over the 1990s the U.S. export value in dollars quadrupled, while the physical weight stayed the same! In other words, price per ton went up four times! What happened was that exports of products and services switched from base materials to electronics, pharmaceuticals, software, entertainment, and services (i.e., to products and services with a high share of mind-based content). Brand recognition, a mind-based factor, is in the same range as an indicator of perceived value added in the sense of what buyers are prepared to pay for. Well known branded products can serve as an example, from consumer products, such as Coke and Ester Lauder cosmetics, to Ford's acquisitions of Jaguar and Volvo, or to companies that specialize entirely in owning brands, such as the LVMH.

Basic Insight

In the age of mind-based nonfinancial performance factors, management and reporting must give up their fixation on tangible assets and find ways to assess all kinds of value drivers, ultimately the factors that make companies survive, prosper, and grow.

Traditional valuation methods, including accounting and accounting-based models, that assign a value to a product or a thing in itself, should be reconsidered.

End of Zero Sum

The new base for wealth-creation has given rise to one of the most spectacular phenomena of our economy, the potential for unlimited growth, a perspective that is hard to squeeze into the straitjackets of accounting.

In the second economy, when land was the base for wealth creation, we had a simple zero-sum situation: Since land is basically finite (the earth has obvious limits), one person's getting more land means someone else getting less. In the third economy, factories and machinery could expand one company's wealth without visibly hurting another company's. In the fourth economy, growth can even be generated by freely *sharing* mind-based resources. Linux, one of the typical fourth economy products, has built its success on that principle. This, of course, is not easy to accept for people steeped in second or even third economy thinking. It is certainly not easy to reconcile with accounting. As he showed in

Romeo and Juliet, Shakespeare would understand better than many accountants the fact that mind-based resources do not shrink when you share them—they grow:"The more I give to thee, the more I have, for both are infinite."

The Issue of Goodwill

In accounting, goodwill is by and large defined as the pocket-calculator difference, in a merger or acquisition, between the price paid for a company and the book value of the company's "equity." Very seldom are efforts made to examine more seriously the true content of the goodwill item, even less trying to itemize its components. This is indeed surprising, since in most mergers and acquisitions in later years this item has easily represented a major part of the purchasing price. The issue of goodwill write-offs puts one of the anomalies of traditional accounting under the microscope. For a start, it is an interesting case of misguided terminology, based on concepts that are no longer valid. But worse than that, it reveals the shaky grounds of how we treat the concept of value.

A brand name, a knowledge base, a corporate culture, a customer satisfaction record, a market position, a high level of employee motivation, a sound management structure, investor confidence, or other soft value drivers can survive and grow for ever, if they are properly maintained. But they do not exist in the company as such, and certainly not in their accounting records. They are generated in the minds of stakeholders or potential stakeholders, who weigh them against other things they know and feel about the company, especially in terms of what the ownership of that company can do for them, and how it fits into other priorities they have, as owner-operators, in a merger or an acquisition, or as owner-investors.

Case in Point—The Pseudoscience of Goodwill

The efforts to put goodwill on the balance sheets have led to another misconception. Without too much thinking, accounting experts decided to apply similar write-off rules to them as to traditional hard assets, despite their entirely different qualities. The result is that a whole pseudoscience has grown up around the treatment of goodwill. Thousands of lawyers, accountants, businesspeople, administrators, academics, consultants, politicians, and bureaucrats have been forced to spend a lot of time (some of them have built a comfortable livelihood on it) on an issue that is 99 percent imaginary, an issue that should not have been an issue at all.

Goodwill is an obvious aspect of goofy accounting. The fact that well educated and well paid experts have to spend time on it is an example of the damage created by our blind belief in an outdated system. The pseudo discussion on goodwill forces business leaders to divert their attention from serious, real business issues to a nonsense issue. Goodwill becomes an added cost item, a tax on business, much of the same kind, and perhaps magnitude, as the issue of exaggerated litigation costs.

Here is a word of truth and a wake-up call:

> The time has come for a radically new way to gauge corporate perform-
> ance. Every company today struggles to grow and manage its value. More
> and more of that value is derived from intangible assets such as human
> intelligence, brand recognition, customer service, and quality. But as of
> yet, we have no systematic way to measure these intangibles. That's why
> the gap between the numbers on a company's accounting statements and
> its market valuation continues to widen.[34]

HOW TO SUCCEED IN AN AGE OF INTERDEPENDENCE

More than ever before, the economy in general and most businesses
today are closely connected, interrelated, and interdependent. Consequently, the successful executive must find ways to identify, measure, evaluate, and benefit from networks, relationships, and dependencies.

Case in Point—Redefining the Company in a Network Economy

Dramatized by pictures of mobile phone users in different environments—the Tutsi
warrior, the Chinese farmer, the Scandinavian teenager, or the Arizona cowboy—
communications is shown as a lifestyle, a cultural and political phenomenon.

Telecom is just one factor that makes interdependence a stronger force than ever,
between individuals, companies, and countries. *Homo connectus* becomes a characteristic of modern man, for good or bad, not just an outflow of new technology.

Basically, in this situation we need to redefine the company from "a collection of
(physical) assets" to "a node in a network of relationships." The need to understand
and manage the company in its living environment, in a connected economy, will lead
management to a new focus on what is good for a company: moving from a balance
sheet focus to a relationship focus, and learning to define, measure, and manage good
and bad relationships.

The Sound of One Hand Clapping, or the Value of One Link in the Chain

In classic Zen philosophy, students are encouraged to think (in isolation, on top
of it!) for hours or days, maybe weeks, over seemingly contradictory or meaningless statements, such as "What is the sound of one hand clapping?" Another
apparently meaningless statement to consider would be "What is the value of one
link in a chain?" Obviously, a chain has a value only as long as all the links in it

do their job, together. If one link fails, the value of the whole chain is zero. Calculating the value of one link in a chain appears as futile as some of the classic Zen exercises.

Obviously, it is debatable whether one isolated unit in a production chain has a value at all. In a living business, earnings and growth are always generated in a process of interaction.

The traditional company-centered view reflects the prevalent worldview from the origins of accounting, the fifteenth century, placing the earth (later the sun) as a fixed and finite body at the center of the universe. Astronomers today help us see the universe rather as an infinite and interactive network of balancing dynamic tensions and relationships.

By the same token, the business universe, and every company that lives in it, is best described as a network of relationships. This is most obvious in "virtual" companies, e-businesses and dot-coms, but the trend is wider than that.

What Is a Company?

To grasp the scope of the change process we are in, we need to consider some very basic issues. One of them is the question of how to define a company. Fundamentalists in the business community have tended to define a company either in strictly legal terms, or as a range of assets, perhaps even relating these assets to the balance sheet. This inward-looking focus leads them to believe that the company itself has control over its survival, growth, and earnings. Their planning tends to start from the products and services the company offers, an inside-out perspective.

The reality is that a company, at least in our time, is best defined as a network of relationships. The success or failure of the company is largely based on the relationships between the company and its stakeholders. This does not reduce the need for strict and transparent reporting! An important foundation for the new reporting methods we propose is that, contrary to what many believe, the significant relationships between a company and its environment can be defined and measured in relation to the company's business strength.

This emphasis on the relationships and the links between a company and its environment also explains a critical issue: No matter how big a company is, be it a Microsoft, a General Electric, or a Citibank, the environment is always bigger. It is the environment that makes the rules and defines the parameters for company survival, growth, and earnings, an outside-in perspective.

Accounting data and financial key ratios play no, or a very small, part in this process. Contrary to fundamentalists, who believe that the balance sheet gives valid indications on the company's position, and that the earnings statement helps define its result, support for such evaluations must be found in other areas, which we discuss in more detail in Chapter 3.

A Declaration of Interdependence

Companies, like other living organisms, depend on links with the world around them, with external stakeholders, competitors, and other parties. The golden opportunities as well as major threats are frequently located at the edge of the company, its link to the outside world. As a consequence, all instruments we use to support management, reporting, valuation, auditing, and credit management must include or even focus on the process of interaction.

The birth of the United States, one of the truly dramatic events in world history, was launched with the Declaration of Independence. It defined, among other things, the freedom that the colonists perceived as essential to their well-being. For companies in the fourth economy, freedom of choice, or freedom to act, is a significant strategic goal, perhaps the ultimate strategic goal. The role played by company relationships is a key to company freedom to act. Perhaps it would be appropriate to launch a Declaration of Interdependence to emphasize the importance of relationships, more critical for company survival, earnings, and growth than capital and fixed assets.

From Vertical to Virtual

Yet, accounting-based balance sheet analysis is still used (e.g., in banking), against all common sense, as if nothing had happened in 500 years. Old manufacturing companies were highly vertical, with General Motors into the 1980s as a prime example. They had all functions, from foundries and glassworks to employee cafeterias, inside the company. That gave them a very massive balance sheet, which, in the third economy, was a thing to be proud of. It proved that the company had valuable resources.

Today, companies split up into fragments, with subsidiary companies, independent contractors, and external subsuppliers creating more and more of the total value added. Very few analysts today would maintain that a heavy balance sheet in itself is an indication of success or a sign of good payback ability. Yet, even today it can be hard for a company to get a loan from a bank without offering collateral in the form of "substance" on a balance sheet.

From Balance Sheets to Relationships

Outsourcing is one of the strong trends in business today. When companies outsource manufacturing, they move some of their "assets," such as factories and machinery, off their balance sheets. At the same time they move out the people that go with these operations. They replace those assets by building up a relationship with one or several suppliers. The telecom equipment company Ericsson did it in 2001 by physically turning over six factories and more than 4,000 workers to a contract manufacturer, Flextronics International, Ltd.

From an accounting perspective, the issue is that traditional "hard assets" booked on the balance sheets are replaced with relationships. Since relationships are not seen or recorded in accounting, as we know it, the result is a disappearance act, worthy of a rabbit-juggling magician.

Manufacturing is not the only resource that is made to disappear this way. Companies hand over the selling function to independent resellers or franchisees, make R&D contracts with universities or research companies, scrap their truck fleets for distribution suppliers, hire outside consultants for executive search, corporate communications, and strategic advice, and leave much of their back office work to companies like Kinko's. If they do not go all the way by outsourcing whole chunks of work, they go half way through leasing contracts and similar arrangements. Contracts and relationships replace ownership.

The company is no longer contained within the walls that are built up by accounting and legal definitions. The company becomes a network, where the borderlines are hard or impossible to define with old terminology.

The same goes for other management trends today. Japanese car manufacturers were among the first to invite suppliers to be part of the total value chain. They make contracts for parts suppliers to deliver their goods directly to the assembly line, and even to keep track of the need to refill supplies automatically. Even more, suppliers are invited to be part of design and creative processes.

Traditional autistic accounting does not show the whole picture, only a small fraction of it, if even that. Today, in the connected economy, it is obvious that any reporting system, if it wants to claim to be fair and useful, has to reach outside the box and include relationships in the reporting system!

Case in Point—The Virtual Salmon Company

A simple example shows how this applies to a living company. And it is not even a company in the high-tech field. It is, seen from the outside, a company in a fairly mundane business, selling fish. The company is called Truefresh. What is remarkable about it? Check the story, and draw your own conclusions:

Truefresh is based in New England. It has delivery contracts, but not employment contracts, with salmon fishermen along the coasts of Maine and Massachusetts. The fishermen deliver their catch to a freezing facility. Truefresh does not own this facility, but it has a contract with it, including a license for a flash-freeze process that creates high-quality frozen salmon. Each fish is individually packaged at the freezing facility, wrapped in Truefresh-marked plastic wrapping. The fish are then delivered across the United States through a network of freezer trucks, none of them owned by Truefresh but working for Truefresh on a contract basis. At the outer end of the network are resellers. Again, these resellers are not owned or employed by Truefresh but working for Truefresh on a commission basis.

Truefresh has a very limited number of employees. What about its balance sheet? Well, maybe a couple of desks and computers. Not much to show a traditional banker. The whole "value" of Truefresh is in its network, its relationships.

The story of the virtual, almost totally "dematerialized" company Truefresh tells us a lot. One thing is the true value of relationships. That is really the only asset Truefresh has: relationships with suppliers, partners, resellers, and customers. Through this buildup, it also has a very high level of flexibility. Unfortunately, for friends of the *status quo*, this asset does not show up in accounting.

"If I Have a Dollar..."

There is no need to be too sophisticated or philosophical about these matters. Demonstrating the value of relationships, interaction, exchange, can be as simple as the following example. It also shows one of the distinct differences between physical and mind-based factors:

> If I have a dollar and you have a dollar, and you give me your dollar and I give you my dollar, what do we have? Still one dollar each. But if I have an idea and you have an idea, and I give you my idea, and you give me your idea, what do we have? Well, two ideas each, of course. And those ideas, again, may generate totally new thoughts...

You can expand the process, if you like. Add motivation or "zest" to the process, by instilling not only ideas but emotions, ambitions, drive! What do you get? Chances are you get action, ending up in tangible results.

Expand it in another direction: If the exchange goes on between persons of the same background, you may not get too many breakthrough results. But if people with very different backgrounds and views of life get together and start swapping, then real things can happen!

Ever Heard of Metcalfe's Law?

We have all heard about the dismal Murphy's Law, telling us that everything that can go wrong, will, and the revealing Parkinson's Law that says that any job will take the time we have to perform it.

In today's economy, new "laws" have seen the light. Without comparing them head on, they are, in some regards, as essential to this economy as Newton's Law of Gravity has been to many of the basic concepts of the old, industrial, mechanistic economy. Three of the new laws are "Moore's Law," "Metcalfe's Law," and "Brown's Law:"

- *Moore's Law*, briefly, states that the capacity of integrated circuits tends to double every 12 or 18 months.
- *Metcalfe's Law* says that the value, in terms of usefulness, of individual nodes in a network is generated through the interaction process between the nodes and that it grows by the square of the number of the nodes. One cell phone is useless, two cell phones are better, but it is really when millions of

cell phones interact with each other that the usefulness of the cell phone sky rockets.

- *Brown's Law*, after John Sealy Brown, adds a further dimension to interaction. It maintains that connecting individual nodes is not enough but that groups, communities, play a major role and need to be connected. The usefulness of any system actually grows by the square of the number of communities connected.

While Moore's law shows how the volume of interaction can and will grow with new technology, both Metcalfe's and Brown's laws make these growing possibilities for *interaction the real source of value, and also define value in the sense of usefulness.*

In all its simplicity, the example of how an interchange of ideas creates growth, rather than an interchange of dollars or physical resources, points to an entirely different foundation for wealth-creation today than in the land- or capital-based periods. On top of that, Moore's law shows that technology supports this process. Metcalfe's and Brown's laws show how the process can be accelerated to the nth degree. Together, the laws demonstrate the unlimited opportunities for exponential growth that lie ahead of us, a win–win situation for the world if ever there has been one.

The Expanding Economic Universe

Not only astronomers talk about a fast expanding universe. We live in an expanding economic universe, largely explained by the fact that wealth-generation today rests on *basically infinite* nonmaterial performance factors and relationships, unrestricted by the traditional limitations inherent and unavoidable in a universe based on physical assets.

Alert corporations, whether consciously recognizing these laws or not, have made it a strategic priority to speed up interaction, idea exchange, to benefit from its value creation power. One of them is General Electric, making a priority of idea exchange to increase profits and turn technology investments from costs to profit. Says Noel Tichy[35] of the School of Business of the University of Michigan: "No one, but no one, is as good as (the former GE CEO) Welch at taking a concept to its extreme and logical conclusion." He then recounts examples of how GE systematically works to take ideas developed in one division of the giant company to benefit operations and economies in widely different divisions, and, even further, actively share such new ideas with other companies for mutual profit.

This is a conceptually different approach from what was normal corporate behavior in the old economy. By their very nature, geo-based and other physical assets are limited by number, dimensions, weight, or other measures. As a consequence, companies were protective of their physical assets. Sharing them generously was an absurd idea. Perpetuating that tradition, probably out of force of habit, many companies used hierarchic structures and strict departmentalization to limit interaction, rather than promote it, long into the 1980s.

An economy based on ideas and other mind-based factors is different. In principle, these production factors are unlimited. They do not shrink or disappear when they are given away. Instead, in most cases they grow (e.g., as suggested by Metcalfe's and Brown's Laws). When AOL and other companies in high-tech or IT-based industries give away software, it is not because they are stupid. The best way to increase their real wealth is a paradox: by giving some of it away.

Mind-based resources do not grow if they are put in a bank vault. They increase when they are part of an interactive process. The process, the interaction, is the catalyst of growth. The benefits may accrue to several or all parties involved. This is true of a lot of companies, not only in the IT or high-tech industries. In service industries, such as insurance, restaurants, car service, and retail business, much of the value-added in each transaction is created in the hot spot of interaction between the customer and the company representative, the instant that Jan Carlzon, then CEO of Scandinavian Airlines, called *the moment of truth*. A good service engineer, waitress, hotel receptionist, or sales representative creates value, ideally both for the company and for the client, in each transaction. Instead of zero-sum, we have a win–win situation. A consequence is that it is a totally meaningless exercise to report on a company, or to try to assess or audit a company without diagnosing carefully the context, the relationships that it works in.

Accounting-Based Models in Times of Networks and Relationships

Case in Point—At the Center of the Age of Connectedness

The mobile phone industry is a quintessential industry in the age of networks and relationships. The changes it has brought about to the connectedness of today's world are second to no other industry, perhaps with the silicon chip business as a close contender. Companies like Ericsson, Motorola, and Nokia have changed the world, and not only the world of business. Their technologies have spread truly worldwide. Pictures of reindeer-herding Samis in the Arctic and Masai warriors in Kenya using their mobile phones do not surprise us any more than those of Japanese teenagers or Hong Kong bankers using theirs. The technologies now in the pipeline from these companies and others in the business, including the Bluetooth technology, are likely to continue to have great impact on us. They are certainly in the vanguard of creating tools for the connection or relationship industry.

Perhaps surprisingly, these companies have been late in adopting one of the networking techniques that entered classical third-economy companies, like the machinery industry and the automotive industry decades ago, outsourcing. The mobile phone makers, by and large, kept their manufacturing in-house. Not until the early years of the twenty-first century did Motorola and Ericsson start farming out some of their mobile phone manufacturing to outside companies. Nokia, at this writing, still retains most or all of its handset manufacturing in-house.

Case in Point—The Virtual Car Manufacturer

The Cunningham Motor Company is one of the few new American automotive companies. Its product is a top-of-the-line sports car, to be sold at a price in the $250,000 range. Where will it be made? It depends on how you define "made." It will actually be made by a virtual company. The design is made by Cunningham, although using outside design expertise as well. Engines will be supplied from another manufacturer. All other parts will be made and assembled in segments, finally to be put together by an outside assembly specialist. The batteries? It is a fair guess that they will come from Exide, the battery company that shares its driving force with Cunningham: Detroit's leading car enthusiast, Robert A. Lutz, the man behind the idea of the virtual car company. The company is still only an idea, but a realistic concept, a virtual car company. The strong element in the company is not going to be a heavy balance sheet, but rather an unusual dependence on relationships, Mr. Lutz's relationships within the automotive industry.

Measuring Dependencies: Flexibility

Flexibility is a crucial indicator of company success. A company with a heavy balance sheet, including big investments in fixed assets, real estate, factories, machinery, and so on, loses its freedom to act. It tends to be locked into the business it has chosen.

In a world of no change, that position can have its benefits, from cost and other perspectives. But few companies, if any, today live in a world without change. The demands of change, flexibility, are at the top of the list for most companies. Only companies that prioritize relationships over fixed assets have a chance to adapt to new situations.

But even relationships can put flexibility to a test. In a traditional situation, the balance sheets, no matter how misleading they are, can give some indication as to how "locked in" a company is. Where balance sheets make no sense at all, as is the case in a growing share of companies, how do we measure the dependencies the company has in its relations with other stakeholders and parties?

A new reporting system will have to provide us with methods and metrics to report and measure dependencies. Fortunately, such measures exist, although not in our traditional accounting system. They are an essential part of the new reporting system outlined in Chapter 4.

The Ultimate Strategic Asset: Freedom to Act

So what do you do, when the future is genuinely unpredictable, when you have to make decisions that involve the future, and when accounting-based models are the only kind you feel familiar with?

As early as the nineteenth century, a famous German general, Count Moltke, who was considered an outstanding strategist of his time, defined any leader's ultimate strategic goal as "freedom to act." If that was an important—no, *the* most important—definition of strategic goals to a nineteenth-century general, is it not likely to be even more important for a business leader in surviving today's fast changing, unpredictable business environment?

"Freedom to act" can be a strategic goal in other contexts as well. In *The Paradox of American Power,*[36] Dr. Joseph S. Nye, Jr., defines *power* as "the ability to obtain the outcome you want," which is another way of expressing "freedom to act." As the subtitle of Dr. Nye's book indicates, "Why the world's only super-power can't go it alone," Nye emphasizes strongly that even a country as strong as the United States must work through partnerships, alliances to networks to keep and develop its position, its power, or, in our terminology, its "freedom to act." In relations between nations, a strong country can always resort to war as the ultimate way to get their will. However, as Nye underlines, even for strong countries it is often advantageous to influence the world through relationships. Companies, even very big ones, do not have the option of going to war against their competitors. Consequently, it is even more in their interests to maintain, monitor, and manage their relationships. As we will see in Part II, the Baseline Reporting system provides practical tools to do just that, under the assumption that every company, like every other living organism, lives through its relationships with the environment, and that no company, not even GE or Microsoft, is bigger than its environment. Dr. Nye's thinking, at the national level, is totally compatible with Baseline Reporting on the company level.

Companies today realize that flexibility, the ability and freedom to act, is the most critical of any company strategic assets. It is, in fact, the first and indispensable step to competitive advantage. Every strategic move a company takes must support its agility, resilience, flexibility, and ability to cope with the unexpected, because the unexpected is what we all must expect and be prepared for. In any transaction, the party that has the highest degree of freedom to act also has the strongest negotiating position.

Anything in the company itself, in its resource allocation or in its environment, that limits a company's flexibility, its freedom to act, should be seen as a potential risk factor, a liability if you wish to use a balance sheet term. Any way to increase a company's flexibility is in principle a strategic plus factor, an asset. A new road to accountability must include a search for such factors. In this situation, "liabilities" are anything that limits flexibility, and "assets" are anything that enhances flexibility.

The Strategic Road to "Freedom to Act"

The road to a higher "freedom to act" is not a mystery. In fact, it follows a step-by-step process, which starts with the focus of this chapter, with relationships:

1. A company that has good relations with its stakeholders tends to get in return at the very least acceptance, very often more than that, active support, from forces in its environment.

2. A company that gets acceptance and support from its environment meets few restrictions or hurdles.

3. Reduced restrictions and hurdles leads to a strong position in any negotiations.

4. A strong negotiating position leads to higher value added and a bigger share of retained value added.

5. Increased value added and a bigger retained share of the value added means better earnings, better chances of survival, and opportunities for growth.

How Do You Get Freedom to Act?

Accounting does not show it. You get it by reaching a business position where no party or factor in the company's environment can or wants to interfere with the company's plans or to hurt the company in any significant way. The company with the least interference from stakeholders has the best chances to survive, grow, and deliver shareholder value.

Can You Measure Freedom to Act?

The answer is yes! Here are some items to consider:

- The environment creates the platform for all living organisms, including companies.

- All life, in business or otherwise, calls for an exchange with the world around the organism, in this case the company.

- The environment is always bigger than even the biggest company, and thus sets the conditions for company survival, growth, and earnings.

- The exchange between the company and its environment flows through relationships.

- Relationships are established when at least one of the parties set a value, positive or negative, on the relationship, that is, when the relationship has some kind of significance for one or both parties.

- Relationships can be defined and measured. The RealBiz® system has been developed to do just that. It even includes a measurement unit for freedom to act, the BIZ index.

In the next chapter we will see how this strategic priority, flexibility, nimbleness, freedom to act, can be monitored, measured, and made part of a new reporting system.

The Basic Issue: Why Companies Succeed or Fail

As always, the worst alternative, once a problem has been diagnosed, is to do nothing about it, to stick our heads in the sand and hope the problem will disappear. Many seem to advocate such an approach when it comes to accounting. A better way to come to grips with the shortcomings of accounting, however difficult it may seem, is to try to apply new thinking and *action* in order to create a new reporting system, one that works in the fourth economy.

Can it be done? We examine that question in Chapters 3 and 4.

NOTES

1. The expression should be duly credited to an important article by Bill Powell, "The New New World Order," *Fortune*, May 14, 2001. In the same article, the author confirms our view that the fourth economy is based on more than IT: "The Internet is indeed a hugely important technology (though not necessarily the most important technology)."

2. Peter Drucker, *Post-Capitalist Society*, Harper Collins, New York, 1993.

3. Robert J. Schiller, professor at Yale and one of the proponents of behavioral economy, expresses it well in an article headlined, "How Wall Street Learns to Look the Other Way," *New York Times*, Feb. 8, 2005: "Perhaps these (accounting) scandals would be a little less likely..., if more of us professors integrated business education into a broader historical and psychological context."

4. We have tried to identify sources and support we have found for our selection. It has always been difficult to attribute ownership to ideas. In our society of fast, free, and abundant information flows, it is harder than ever to identify how and where ideas are generated, modified, combined, and finally reach a presentation stage. If we have omitted sources we should have quoted, it is not on purpose.

5. The title of a landmark book by Peter F. Drucker.

6. Alvin Toffler, *Future Shock*, Random House, New York, 1970.

7. Colin Powell's words were, of course, confirmed in a drastic and tragic way through the unexpected terrorist attacks of September 11, 2001.

8. From J.K. Rowling, *Harry Potter and the Sorcerer's Stone*, U.S. paperback edition, Scholastic Inc., New York and other locations, 1999.

9. For instance in his *Post-Capitalist Society,* HarperCollins, New York, 1993.

10. For instance in his *The Loyalty Effect*, Harvard Business School Press, Boston, 1996.

11. See for instance Arie De Geus, Dutch executive and author, *The Company as a Living Organism*, Harper Business Books, New York, 1998.

12. Macmillan Publishing, New York, 1992.

13. Penguin Group, New York and other places, 1998.

14. For an enlightening review of this perspective, see Jared Diamond, *COLLAPSE. How Societies Choose to Fail or Succeed,* Viking, New York, 2004.

15. For more background this issue, see an article in the *Journal of Accountancy,* October 2000.)

16. For a parallel to this from a field outside accounting, see a book by Episcopalian bishop John Shelby Spong, *A New Christianity for a New World,* HarperCollins, New York, 2001. Bishop Spong argues that even in religions there are doctrines that were created for a different time, and that need to be revised to be relevant in new situations.

17. Paul Craig, General Manager, Orange, Bristol, as reported in *Business Week's* Special Issue on twenty-first-century capitalism.

18. In *Directorship*, Greenwich, CT, March 1998.

19. Virginia Postrel, *The Future and its Enemies*, Touchstone/Simon and Schuster, New York, 1999.

20. James Gleick, *Chaos. The Amazing Science of the Unpredictable,* William Heinemann Ltd, Great Britain, 1988.

21. See e.g. Tom Copeland, Tim Koller, Jack Murrin, *Valuation. Measuring and Managing the Value of Companies,* Wiley, New York and other cities, 1994, with the support of McKinsey.

22. See an article appropriately called "Bah, Humbug!," *Forbes*, March 6, 2000.

23. William Strunk Jr. and E.B. White, *The Elements of Style*, 3rd edition, Allyn & Bacon, Needham Heights, MA, 1979.

24. In an interview in *Wired,* August 1996, quoted by Virginia Postrel in *The Future and its Enemies* (op.cit.)

25. Since this is one of very few diagnosis methods that have gained general recognition, a more detailed description of it will be made in Chapter 4.

26. 1999 revised edition.

27. Stanley Collender, managing director of the federal budget consulting group of Fleischman Hillard. Mr. Collender was proven dead right, and the predictors dead wrong, less than one year later, when the predicted surplus flood had dwindled to a mere brook, later to turn into huge deficits.

28. A surprising example of this attitude is a sentence in an article by Geoffrey Colvin, *Fortune*, Oct. 15, 2001, in his column, Value Driven, "In the real world, unlike in the dream, stocks are worth the sum of future cash flows, discounted

to the present at some (sic!) appropriate rate." Our position on this is explained in Chapter 1, "The Value Mess".

29. Jonas Harrysson, Ola Matthisson: "Kassaflödesvärdering" ("Cash Flow Valuation"), Department of Business Administration, Stockholm University, Stockholm, Sweden, 2000.

30. See for instance Accounting Standard # 38, issued 1999 by the International Accounting Standards Board.

31. See (op. cit.) Frederick Reichheld, *The Loyalty Effect*, Harvard Business Press, 1998.

32. See for instance *American Heritage Dictionary*.

33. "From GM to Cisco in Just Four Decades," *Business Week*, Feb. 7, 2000.

34. Jon Low, Tony Siesfeld, and David Larcker, "Capital Thinking," *Forbes*, August 23, 1999.

35. For a detailed report, please turn to *Forbes*, January 24, 2000.

36. Joseph S. Nye, Jr., *The Paradox of American Power: Why the World's Only Superpower Can't Go it Alone*, Oxford University Press, Oxford and other places, 2002.

CHAPTER 3

The Search for Adequate Reporting

SEC will move to glory,
When it learns the real story.

THE NEED FOR ALTERNATIVES

The summary of the failures of traditional accounting that we have presented in Chapters 1 and 2, although far from complete, makes it obvious that the world business community has an obligation to its stakeholders to search for other, better ways to base decisions on companies than those offered by accounting. Tentative efforts have been made over the last 5 or 10 years to create such complementary or alternative methods to provide nonaccounting-based support for management decision making and to create adequate reporting on company performance, ultimately on company success and failure.

This search process has necessarily involved efforts to get down to very basic levels of business thinking. Some of the efforts have focused on specific areas of company performance, such as customer relations, employee productivity or investor satisfaction. Such focused approaches may be very useful in providing in-depth discussions on crucial company performance factors, although they lack in concepts of overall performance. Other work, such as scorecard methods, have encouraged boards and management to select their own priorities and make measurements and take action in areas perceived as critical to a certain company at a certain time. While very useful in finding specific approaches for temporary problems, they lack the scope and ambition to solve general company assessment needs.

All in all, this multifaceted work has shown that alternative, nonaccounting-based assessments of company performance are both desirable and, indeed, feasible. In their most ambitious forms, new assessment methods have focused on new ways to identify rock-bottom company fundamentals. However, few serious initiatives have been taken to offer overall, all-inclusive assessment methods unhampered by the accounting framework and mindset.

Essential criteria for business success or failure have traditionally been called the fundamentals of business. In the second economy, success was defined either as increasing the acreage or generating higher returns from existing areas. In the third economy, fundamentals were mainly related to ownership and use of physical production resources and other forms of fixed assets, capital. Since these assets were typically purchased from outside suppliers, they were registered on the balance sheet. A "strong" balance sheet, with plenty of hard assets, buildings, real estate, factories, machinery, inventory, and capital assets, was seen as a fundamental indicator of company success. Hard assets gave a feeling of comfort and were seen as both support for survival and conditions for future growth.

The fourth economy presents new challenges in defining company fundamentals. The more companies advance into the fourth economy, the less significant is the information provided by the balance sheets. A trend to watch is the increasing degree of outsourcing, even by traditional manufacturing companies, a trend that, of course, takes resources away from the balance sheet. An indicator, although not very precise, of this change is the relationship between equity and share prices. In the 1970s this relationship was often 1:1, in the early 1990s it had typically shifted to 1:3, and today, in the early twenty-first century, it is often 1:10 or even 1:20. What this process shows, in very broad terms, is that much of what the stock market appreciates in a company is now nowhere near the balance sheet.

Several of the basic conditions for success or failure are different in the fourth economy, such as the three characteristics we discussed in Chapter 2: fast, unpredictable change, mind-based wealth creation; and relationships or interdependence. Consequently, before creating a new reporting system, adapted to the twenty-first century, we need to define new, relevant fundamentals for companies at this time.

An essential difference is that criteria for success or failure need not or should not be looked for only within the company. An assessment system for today must include metrics on the relationships between the company and its business and political environment. Companies fail for reasons that could have been avoided or managed, if they had been aware of their sensitivity to problems in the business environment and taken appropriate steps in time. Such external conditions include macroeconomic factors and politically decided changes: trade regulation, tax changes, interest rates, customs regulations, currency exchange rates, building codes, energy prices, environmental rules, and so forth. While they may be difficult or impossible for an individual company to influence, it is a priority management task to systematically diagnose its links to external factors, keep track of them, assess them, and make sure that the company monitors and reacts to them in a sensible and sensitive way.

One way to look at this is to ask, "What makes a company great?" Fortunately, we are being helped by others who have considered this key question. Among them are two research associates at the Stanford Graduate School of Business, James C. Collins and William C. Lazier. They examined more than 300 companies, a mix of successful and disastrous companies, looking for long-term greatness, not only temporary success.[1] In the end they felt that the following four criteria, more than anything else, defined great companies:

1. Performance—a track record of meeting company objectives, with cash flow as one of the key indicators
2. Impact—influence and leadership in its business
3. Reputation—admired and respected by people outside the company
4. Longevity—staying power

Traditional accounting does not offer much help in this ambitious process, nor was it ever intended for such tasks. Accounting, with its focus on the past in terms of business transactions performed, gives no support for broader views and strategic decision making. Most of the information on the balance sheet, for an increasing number of companies today, is largely irrelevant, or even misguiding. The income statement can be relevant, in today's economy, as in the past, provided that it reports real earnings. However, to really get under the surface and assess critical strengths and weaknesses in companies today, we must search for more relevant fundamentals, criteria for success or failure that go beyond accounting.

EARLY EFFORTS: THE "SCORECARDS" APPROACH

Several attempts have been made in the pursuit of such critical clues, both those focusing primarily on the bright side, opportunities, and those focusing mainly on the risks or threats, potential problems. In real life, of course, both need to be assessed, since one is fairly often a mirror image of the other. In the accounting and auditing world, several of the big consulting organizations have initiated evaluation projects. In recent management literature, also look for terms like *key performance measures* or *performance indicators*, *business process management*, or *enterprise performance management*, or, in focusing on the negative side, look for terms like *enterprise risk management*.

One of the first successful efforts at going beyond accounting data to assess and manage companies was *The Balanced Scorecard*.[2] Broader performance measures were included in this model, boiling them down to a 5- to 10-item "balanced scorecard" for assessment and management monitoring. Both accounting-based data and other factors can be included.

The authors of this system, in addition to practical advice and a broad array of case stories, present an interesting discussion on the role and relevance of financial measurements in what they call the "Information Age." While they generously allow a role even in their system for financial data and a financial perspective of a company, one of their significant contributions to the development of new assessment models is their introduction of measurements as good as or better than financial measures. Those measures may include for instance employee retention, satisfaction, and productivity measurements, measures for research and product development, measures for customer relations, image, and reputation, and customer satisfaction and retention. They also comment on areas where measurements seem to be more difficult to make, such as employee accomplishment and development. The creators of the Balanced Scorecard and its followers made a remarkable contribution in demonstrating clearly that alternative measures to traditional accounting were, in fact, useful, necessary, and feasible.

Intellectual and Emotional Capital

Various measures of *intellectual capital* were introduced in the 1990s by Leif Edvinsson, Karl Erik Sveiby, Thomas Stewart, and others. Their input represented an important step forward, in that they created attention to and understanding of the fact that other than physical assets were significant in building company performance.

In the 1990s, the Scandinavian insurance group Skandia gave Leif Edvinsson the opportunity to make a full-scale experiment with the "intellectual capital" concept. Results included annual reports that listed categories of intellectual assets and attributed numbers to them. A whole battery of new terms saw the light of day, in addition to "intellectual capital," also a range of its components, "human capital," "structural capital," "customer capital," "organizational capital," "innovation capital," and "process capital." "The Skandia Navigator" was created as an instrument to manage these assets.

The contribution generated by the whole discussion about intellectual capital was significant. It raised the awareness level of the risks and problems created by the limited perspective of accounting and its focus on physical assets. The trap that some of the proponents of intellectual capital fell into was that, while they pretended to oppose accounting, they in fact adopted much of the premises and terminology of the accounting mindset. By using the terms *capital* or *assets* for many concepts that did not have the characteristics of capital, they even suggested an expansion of the rule of accounting and displayed their basic attachment to balance sheets.

If the first problem was in expanding the interpretation of the terms *capital* or *assets*, their other core problem was in the term *intellectual*. As every business-person knows, the issue of success or failure in business is not only, perhaps not even primarily, a matter of intellectual factors. Many of the most successful business leaders in the world have stated, and shown by their examples, that emotional and relationship issues are at least as significant. Research corroborates this view, such as Daniel Goleman's models for measuring very significant emotional factors, combined in his measures of "EQ," and Frederick Reichheld's models for measuring loyalty.[3] Reichheld's calculations of the value of customer loyalty in the insurance business and the automotive business for instance are specific, to the point, and convincing. Some of the work of the school of behavioral economists has added to the understanding that business and the economy are much more than financial calculations and much more than intellectual.

Rankings and Ratings

Rankings made by the big business media offer interesting approaches to crucial success indicators. Accounting firms and analysts have also introduced rating systems that offer food for thought. Some academics in the accounting field have added input to the debate. In our work we have considered many of these proposals and recommendations. However, what we see as a problem with many of them is that they have not been able or willing to shake off the limitations that are part and parcel of the accounting heritage.

Business Week

In its annual quest for the best performers among the S&P 500, *Business Week* uses eight criteria: sales growth, earnings growth, and total shareholder returns, all in a three-year and a one-year perspective. Added to those data are margins and return on equity, in both cases for one year.

We feel that these criteria rely too much on the data presented by the companies in their accounting-based reports to be really useful. They suffer from many of the fallacies of accounting, especially in their time perspective, reflecting, as all accounting data do, lagging, rather than leading, indicators.

Fortune

In its annual survey of "Most Admired Companies," *Fortune* goes several steps further. Its ranking parameters include a limited set of qualitative data, along with accounting-based data. *Fortune* states "eight attributes of reputation":

1. Innovativeness
2. Quality of Management
3. People Management
4. Financial Soundness
5. Use of Corporate Assets
6. Long-Term Investment
7. Social Responsibility
8. Quality of Products/Services

This program, with its mix of qualitative and accounting-based parameters, has been well received in the business community. Reaching or defending a high position on the "Most Admired" list has become a goal in itself for many companies. Any company that gains a top position in its industry is sure to gain in shareholder value and other benefits. By the same token, being pushed off the list can be fatal. The fact that the *Fortune* listing is based on views from outside the company itself is, in our view, a big step forward from traditional introspective accounting.[4]

Many other ranking or "valuation" methods exist in this search process, both traditional, using accounting data, and more innovative, using broader performance measures.

The Big Accounting Companies

Some of the big accounting companies have made substantial contributions to the development of new thinking.

Ernst & Young research, summed up in "Measures that Matter,"[5] represents a breakthrough in that it made a big hole in previously all-important accounting-based financial assessment systems. "Measures that Matter" includes some items from "Most Admired" and adds a few others. It measures eight nonfinancial factors:

1. Quality of Management
2. Effectiveness of New Product Development
3. Strength of Market Position
4. Strength of Corporate Culture
5. Effectiveness of Corporate Compensation Policies
6. Quality of Investor Communications
7. Quality of Products and Services
8. Level of Customer Satisfaction

The most ground-breaking conclusion in "Measures that Matter" is the confirmation that investors and other stakeholders *do* care about nonfinancial value drivers. No companies can afford to neglect this concern. Especially companies that have remained strongly focused on accounting-based data need to learn to identify and get comfortable working with nonfinancial measures.

Cap Gemini Ernst & Young, together with *Forbes* magazine, has initiated a valuable and insightful discussion about a "Value Creation Index."[6]

Initiatives resting mainly on accounting data include Stewart & Stern's Market Value Added (MVA) and Economic Value Added (EVA). MVA can be described as an improved "goodwill" accounting method. EVA is basically a variety of old accounting but includes some additional (although also accounting-based) perspectives.

The CEO of PricewaterhouseCoopers, Samuel A. DiPiazza, Jr., and Robert G. Eccles, president of Advisory Capital Partners, have joined forces in writing *Building Public Trust: The Future of Corporate Reporting*.[7] The authors, from a top-level professional background, emphasize the need for companies to accept their responsibility for providing complete, accurate, and trustworthy information. The information required in the present phase of our economy goes far beyond regulated and manipulated accounting data to include information on nonfinancial "value drivers." The authors present a "Three-Tier Model of Corporate Transparency" to move company reporting beyond traditional accounting.

Jonathan Low and Pam Cohen Kalafut, with their roots in the Cap Gemini Ernst & Young Center for Business Innovation, have co-authored *Invisible Advantage: How Intangibles are Driving Business Performance*,[8] aimed at decoding many aspects of "the intangibles economy." Their work excels in listing and explaining many of the value drivers that explain how and why companies succeed and fail in today's economy. They are fairly unique in including networks and alliances in the driving forces, an aspect that they explain in an excellent way.

One of the more radical members of accounting academia, professor Baruch Lev of New York University, has published a well-structured study of the impact of intangibles under the title *Intangibles: Management, Measurement, and Reporting*.[9] As could be expected, this book is well documented, but also fairly orthodox to many traditional accounting views.

The mentions we have made here of recent books that touch on various efforts to move into nonfinancial reporting are far from complete. What they show is that many great minds have put their efforts in action to show that conventional accounting is, at best, inadequate, and that the world today requires new initiatives to satisfy the call for relevant and timely transparency in a world that has changed substantially, not only from the time when accounting was developed, the fifteenth century, but also from the very recent twentieth century.

THE CHALLENGE IN PRACTICE: COMBINING A BROAD, ALL-INCLUSIVE PERSPECTIVE WITH A MANAGEABLE NUMBER OF FACTORS

In creating these listings, indexes, and performance measures, much thought has obviously gone into the selection of nonfinancial criteria. Theoretically, any number of factors or performance drivers can be listed. Some factors may be more significant to certain companies, in specific situations, than other factors. As a practical approach, we have found that it is possible to define a few distinctive main categories that appear to apply to all or most companies. These main categories can then be broken down in components adapted to company needs.

Some of the methods that have been launched in the last 5 or 10 years are lopsided, in that they approach some aspects, often important aspects, but fail to take a total, overall view. Some of them tend to focus exclusively on customer-related issues, others on employee-related factors, others again on management methods. While these segments are certainly important, the basic requirements for a new reporting system must include a total, not a partial, perspective of the company in its context.

The three characteristics of the economy of the twenty-first century we discussed in detail in the previous chapter—the three tenets of the beginning fourth economy—appear to be a natural framework for a realistic adaptation of company reporting to the demands of our time. They could support a set of basic, realistic, and broadly acceptable fundamentals for companies in our time.

These three factors have served as important guidelines when we have worked toward designing meaningful, all-inclusive reporting systems for management and governance in our time. They show the way to leading indicators of company success or failure, and clues to survival, earnings, and growth.

A reporting system for our time should be able to identify how individual companies manage these characteristics and to provide appropriate metrics for it.

BACK TO THE CRUCIAL QUESTION: WHAT MAKES COMPANIES FAIL OR PROSPER IN THE TWENTY-FIRST CENTURY?

In the fourth economy, as in previous economies, there are any number of reasons why companies fail or prosper. Frequent reasons for failure include sudden changes in customer tastes, technology shifts in customer or supplier areas, new competition factors, new marketing and sales approaches, poor quality control, excessive costs, low levels of new product development, unexpected political decisions, misguided strategies, or management mistakes.

Company failures, of course, are not necessarily bad under all circumstances. In a dynamic economy, some failures can be healthy, a kind of cleansing or, in Schumpeter's well-known term: "creative destruction." Strangely, it is often more difficult to explain reasons for success, but easier to find those who claim credit for it. "Victory finds a hundred fathers; defeat is an orphan." We all know that "pure luck" is a factor, although it seldom gets the credit it deserves, neither in management literature nor in real life. Everybody is happy to take his or her share of responsibility in times of success. When failure hits, it is more difficult to find the persons who accept the role they played.

An adequate analysis and reporting system, whether for management and corporate governance or for external stakeholder information, should provide valid twenty-first-century indicators of real company success or failures, providing reasonable answers to the question why some companies fail while others prosper. Answers to that question should help us redefine the basics of twenty-first-century strategic management. It could help create new management and support tools for a wide range of important applications. The stakes are high in these and other cases:

- For boards and management, who have the main responsibility and who may have to pay the penalty for a failure in one form or another, just as they get the credit for success, sometimes with little to go for one or the other

- For owners, investors, and lenders, whose money may go down the drain or give extraordinary returns

- For consultants in mergers and acquisitions, with at least a partial responsibility for the success or failure of major undertakings

- For auditors, internal and external, who may be accused for not having seen the signs on the wall, in case of unexpected problems

- For other stakeholders, including employees, who may find their futures shattered or at least dramatically altered—or get rewards in terms of salary increases, promotions, or bonus rainfall

In Search of New Fundamentals

A new reporting system must be better than accounting in demonstrating critical clues to company success and failure. Which success factors are critical or fundamental for companies in the fourth economy? Obviously, they are not only, not even primarily, the physical assets measured in traditional accounting.

We need a system that identifies, measures, and evaluates those factors in a company's life, including its business and political environment, that are likely to significantly affect company survival, earnings, or growth, as well as factors in the company or its environment that may put its survival, earnings, and growth at risk. A surprising result of such a process to some traditionalists is that old-time "assets" will sometimes show up on the liability side, while old-time "liabilities" may turn out to be very valuable.

Change Is on Its Way. . .

The reporting and ranking initiatives we have listed above indicate that a search for new data is a recognized need. New input from management thinkers and practitioners, among them Walter B. Wriston, Peter Drucker, Kevin Kelly, Marc Goyder, and many others, has also alerted many in the business community to the fact that a new era is on its way, or, indeed, is already here.

However, in our view some of this input suffers from severe weaknesses. Some are still closely linked to accounting-based mindsets. Others have launched ideas that are strong in theory but weak in terms of realistic, experience-based performance. Theory is fine. Conferences are excellent. Articles are valuable. And, as the late Danish-American entertainer Victor Borge once remarked: "You have to start somewhere."[10]

. . . But Where Is the Action?

Business leaders are not known to stay in the theory corner too long. Many in the business community feel an urge to go from theory to practice. Testing new concepts and ideas in real life is a more businesslike way than infinite series of academic research. This is why we have chosen a practical approach, consistently submitting our thoughts to the hard tests of reality. *Thinking without action is useless.*

Many warnings and challenges from accounting academics, the SEC, and similar bodies have emphasized the need for fair, reliable, and relevant reporting standards. They have questioned some aspects of accounting, but hesitated to go as far as we do, relegating accounting to a backstage role.

Such hesitation is understandable, given the centuries of accounting traditions and legislation. There are substantial forces that resist change. Some of the reasons for the resistance are real and well worth considering, especially since, until now, few realistic all-inclusive alternatives to accounting have been presented. Other reasons fall in one or the other of the well-known obstacles to all change: "We have never done it before" and "It may be difficult."

The platform for our work on these issues includes these considerations:

- Decisions are made for the future. Yet we recognize that the future is genuinely unpredictable. This apparent conflict must be solved.

- We also recognize that the past is not a clue to the future. Hence a need for leading, not lagging, indicators.

- We are used to accounting, which takes all data back to currencies. Nonfinancial indicators, by definition, cannot be measured in financial terms. Consequently we need to develop nonfinancial measurements that are at least as reliable as accounting data.

- It must be possible to collect relevant data at reasonable costs and effort.

- As we develop new measurements that provide more relevant information than accounting data, we must be able to deal with the potential conflict between a company's need to protect its business secrets and stakeholder interest in transparency.

- In a situation where the general public is used to accounting-based presentations, the new measurements must be presented in understandable terms.

These considerations have guided our development work toward a new reporting and management system, fit for our time.

It Can Be Done!

New accountability-oriented practices that deal with these concerns do not need to be a utopian dream. Much of the work in the 1990s proved that it is possible to develop down-to-earth, commonsense-based, and feasible approaches that meet these requirements. We can say this with confidence because we have done it in practice, in real life, with real companies, in a wide variety of contexts, and for a long enough time for participant companies to have experienced the beneficial results.

Our recommendations are not derived from accounting or consultant theory. They build on real-life experience of companies of widely varied sizes, from small, closely held companies to multidivisional corporations, from companies in hundreds of various industries and businesses, and from companies in established market economies, emerging economy countries, and post-communist countries.

In our work we have benefited from some of the thinking that other pioneers have brought to the process. To that we have added our own experience, from more than 1,500 business reviews, and the conclusions we have drawn from this work.

Action on the Macro Level: A Lengthy Process

Will changes require new legislation or endless committee work in national or international organizations? Not necessarily.

Action along new lines will be required on two levels, the macroeconomy level and the specific company level. In our view, they also represent two different time perspectives.

Change on the macro level will probably be a lengthy process. The fields of economy, finance, and business are surrounded by more than five centuries of traditions, regulation, and legislation. Even when the need for change is as broadly recognized as it is today, lifting the existing cobweb of establishment-supported codes will be a daunting task. It is hard to imagine a modern equivalent to di Pacioli, a single person going back to a monk cell and exiting some months later with a "heureka," a new system, fit for all.

Organizations like the SEC, FASB, the IASC, the IIA, and similar bodies on national and international levels, will have to initiate committees, run meetings, hold hearings, and publish papers. Given the need to listen to many parties with entrenched interests, and to reach consensus or at least diplomatic compromises, rather than bold solutions, these committees will require plenty of time to arrive at generally accepted recommendations for change. Changes in legislation, again both nationally and internationally, may take even longer. The quote from Horace about the mountains that gave birth to a mouse will no doubt be relevant many times in this process.

Our comments are not intended to ridicule the process. The slow pace is understandable, if the objective is to reach global consensus, and create new all-encompassing standards and broadly based legislation. However, in the search for new methods, other approaches may offer faster results.

Action on the Company Level, Now!

If the lengthy academic and bureaucratic process were the only way, it would mean that the already severe disparities between the old maps and the new terrain would continue to grow. Accounting would continue to distance itself more and more from reality and accountability.

In the established industrial economy it was a natural approach to wait for centrally dictated solutions to many problems. In the fourth economy, characteristically, there is more room for the entrepreneurial spirit. This is why we advocate a more aggressive alternative, making use of private initiatives. Individual companies, consultancies, and grass-roots business organizations may take a part in finding new ways to get out of the accounting hassles. Some of these will be based on solid thinking, others may be more of a trial-and-error nature.

Companies could start developing such systems for internal use, creating inside reporting that reflects parameters that are relevant to them in the fourth economy. Later, when they feel comfortable with them, they could use the same models in their reporting to external stakeholders.

Why should companies, and finally business organizations and regulators, want to get into this minefield of pioneering work? And will it not create total chaos, if disparate initiatives pop up from any number of creative minds? Will there still be a chance to make intelligent comparisons between companies, businesses, and other organizations, if a hundred flowers are allowed to blossom?

Some Basic Requirements

We believe common sense can win over theories and bureaucracy, so we think it is worth the effort to get the heavy stone to start rolling.

A new accounting and accountability system will have to be based on *business realities*, rather than on accounting theory. What is more, it has to be based on *today's* business realities, not on 500-year-old traditions. Can it be done?

A reasonable and creative approach may be to ask the classic "zero-base" question from management meetings and seminars: If we had *not* had the 500 years of accounting tradition since Luca di Pacioli, how would we devise systems to show the important coordinates of successful companies? How would we define indicators that support good governance and operational and strategic guidelines for management? How would we create reporting that provides honesty and fairness to investors, that facilitates reasonable pricing of companies, that helps auditing and risk management, and that supports healthy risk-balanced financing? Whatever such systems would look like, they are likely to be as different from existing accounting as the navigation systems of the spaceship *Columbia* are from those of the *Niña, Pinta,* and *Santa Maria* of the 1490s.

A new reporting system must help reveal or indicate why companies fail or prosper in the fourth economy. It would aim to be:

- *Relevant* as a platform for strategic management and board decisions
- *Informative* in providing meaningful information about the company for investors, analysts, and other stakeholders
- *Objective*, meaning that the norms and priorities of the person who makes the report should not influence the outcome
- *Measurable*, to allow for comparisons over time and for comparisons with other businesses, irrespective of company size, type of business, or geographic location
- *Consistent*, to minimize any possibilities of manipulating the results

In the next chapter we outline a coherent model that meets these requirements, a reporting system that defines and monitors important determinants or indicators of company success and failure, to help management and other stakeholders make intelligent strategic choices.

Our aim is to show traditionalists that an out-of-the box model can work also in this traditions-laden field, to create awareness that viable alternatives to accounting-based reporting can be devised. That may help ease the uncertainty and fear that many will experience, when it becomes more and more obvious that old models are inevitably breaking down.

NOTES

1. *Details in Beyond Entrepreneurship: Turning Your Business into an Enduring Great Company*, Prentice Hall, New York, 1992.

2. For more details on this approach, see Robert S. Kaplan and David P. Norton, *The Balanced Scorecard*, Harvard Business School Press, Boston, Massachusetts, © 1996, printed in many editions. Much additional material on this method has been published in business media.

3. See Daniel Goleman, *Emotional Intelligence: Why it Can Matter More Than IQ*, Bantam Books, New York and other places, 1995, and (op. cit.) Frederick F. Reichheld, *The Loyalty Effect: The Hidden Force Behind Growth, Profits and Lasting Value*, Harvard Business School Press, Boston, 1996.

4. For the 2005 update, see *Fortune*, March 7, 2005.

5. Ernst & Young LLP, Cambridge, MA, 1999.

6. This project, initiated by Ernst & Young in cooperation with *Forbes* magazine and Wharton School of Economics, is described in *Measuring the Future* and other literature that can be obtained from The Cap Gemini Ernst & Young Center for Business Innovation, www.businessinnovation.ey.com.

7. Samuel A. DiPiazza, Jr., and Robert G. Eccles, *Building Public Trust: The Future of Corporate Reporting*, Wiley, New York, 2002.

8. Perseus Publishing, NY, 2002.

9. Brookings Institution Press, Washington, DC, 2003.

10. For those who may have missed the context of Mr. Borge's remark, here is how it goes: Victor Borge is reported to have been asked by a TV reporter, at the end of a long interview, the question how he, being of European descent, felt about the old European tradition of kissing a lady's hand. Mr. Borge's answer: "Oh, I think it is a lovely tradition. And, besides, you have to start somewhere."

CHAPTER 4

Transparent Reporting Based on Today's Fundamentals

*Links with stakeholders are key
to business growth, not equity.*

There is an obvious need for better company reporting systems than those based on accounting, but is an alternative system feasible? We are looking for non-accounting ways to show indicators of company success or failure. Can they be found? This chapter verifies that it is, indeed, possible to develop new and better reporting methods, where lagging traditional accounting data give way to leading indicators and relevant metrics.

A system of this kind can be used by any company, any time, without waiting for national or international decisions or approval processes. Many of the data already exist in the company. The system has the potential to support and improve corporate governance and management, internal and external reporting, due diligence, auditing, risk management, investment/financing, lending decisions, and other aspects of strategic management decision making.

While we have been inspired by other efforts and by progressive experts in the business and academic community, no one else, as far as we know, seems to have dared to propose an all-inclusive reporting model that is meaningful, flexible enough to cover the needs of most companies, and meets the reasonable requirements of our time.

We are brave enough to stick our neck out and suggest specific action, methods, and systems. As we have emphasized, our proposals are based on business experience, not on accounting theory. Indeed, we have consciously tried to distance ourselves as much as possible from the mindset of conventional accounting.

The suggested system, Baseline Reporting, is comprehensive, reliable and well-tested. The system defines and measures easily understandable conditions for company performance and risk from four broadly recognizable perspectives. Each of the four perspectives presents well-defined indicators of company success or failure, indicators that most practitioners in the business community will acknowledge as relevant in today's economy.

Expect to find a framework based on logic, intuition, and experience, the three strong pillars of wisdom that management usually relies on in difficult situations. The framework applies recognizable indicators of company success or failure. The only legitimate role of accounting, that of registering business transactions, is incorporated in the system through an advanced cash performance statement.

What about metrics and measurements? We will get into this crucial subject later. Let it be said at this time that adequate metrics are available. The metrics are well tested, sufficiently precise, and with a level of relevance well above accounting in their role as platforms for strategic decisions.

This way, anyone with an interest in these issues can see that there are, indeed, practical, workable alternative solutions to the problems caused by malfunctioning accounting in a world of changing conditions. These solutions are available today. There is no need to wait. Any company that wants to improve its reporting performance can make the decision, on its own, to go from sounds to things, from thinking to action. This does not mean that the solutions we propose would be the only ones. On the contrary, continued contributions from many great minds will be expected. Our ambition is no more and no less than to try to help get a process started and to show that the task is, if not easy, at least manageable.

REPORTING TO SUPPORT PERFORMANCE, DISCLOSURE, AND STRATEGIC DECISION MAKING

As we will come back to in some detail later, we work from the premise that all strategic work should ultimately aim to help the company reach and maintain a maximum level of "freedom to act," a concept that is both well defined and measurable.

Freedom to act is nothing less than *the single most prominent condition for company survival, earnings, and growth.* A new system must offer ways for board and management to monitor company progress toward this goal. At the same time, it should help investors, analysts, auditors, and others concerned to follow the continued work of board and management in their pursuit of that goal.

A proposed control instrument incorporated in the system is a new way not only to check cash flow, but to measure *cash performance.* This new measure shows both the sources of company cash flow and *to what extent it is used for strategic pur-*

poses. At the same time it offers a link to traditional accounting, useful as long as legislation and traditions protect the conventional accounting system.

Baseline Reporting: Four Groups of Fundamentals

As shown in Exhibit 4.1, the four groups of fundamentals include one cash-based and three mind-based success parameters. To be successful, every company needs to:

1. Keep a clear focus—the Business Definition.

2. Keep company *networks* with significant stakeholders strong and supportive—the Business Position.

3. Identify and monitor significant stakeholder attitudes that work for or against the company—Stakeholder Management and Reputation.

4. Closely monitor its cash flow, whence, where, and why, and relate the cash use to company strategies—Cash Performance.

These four groups of fundamentals together provide a set of leading, not lagging, indicators of company success or failure. They offer a performance-based framework that any company management can apply in a consistent and systematic way, with adequate metrics. They give the board, management, and stakeholders inside and outside the company significant clues for setting priorities and for making decisions. All together, they help management prioritize the ultimate strategic goal: flexibility, *freedom to act*, as an indispensable condition for company survival, earnings, and growth.

EXHIBIT 4.1   THE FOUR GROUPS OF BASELINE FUNDAMENTALS

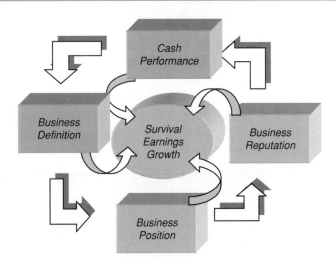

How Does Baseline Reporting Meet These Requirements?

The Business Definition

This answers the classical Peter Drucker question: "Which business are you in?" Baseline Reporting includes a carefully structured way to identify and present a clear Business Definition (Business idea, mission, vision) of the company. It goes beyond traditional "fluffy" statements to create a concise platform for explaining and assessing a company's direction.

The choice of Business Definition as a priority fundamental for business success is supported by, among others, Peter Drucker.[1]

The Business Position

This answers the crucial question: "Who controls the company?" Surprisingly often, the answer is that unexpected outside factors exercise a high degree of influence, even control, over a company. Baseline Reporting includes a computer-supported scan of the Business Position. It shows and measures the crucial dependencies and threats that limit or affect the company's most important strategic asset, its freedom to act.

The view of company relationships and connectivity as fundamental forces for company survival, growth, and earnings in a network economy is supported by, among others, Dutch executive and management writer Arie de Geus, and management writer Kevin Kelly,[2] and by thousands of users of the RealBiz® system.

Business Reputation

This is your competitive position in five fields. It deals with the significant question: "Who is on your side?" Stakeholder perceptions, largely an emotional factor, play a major role in expanding or limiting a company's competitive situation. Baseline Reporting measures a selection of leading indicators that help or hamper company success.

Making reputation a priority fundamental is supported by, among others, Ronald J. Alsop and Ron Alsop, who make a strong case for this perspective in their recent book[3] on the matter, and by Charles J. Fombrun.[4]

Cash Performance

Free cash flow is selected over other financial tools, partly since it is less subject to manipulation and thus more reliable than income statements and balance sheets. Baseline Reporting launches a Cash Performance metric, an advanced cash flow statement, with two added indicators, *linking cash flow to the company's defined strategies*.

For confirmation of this choice of fundamental over income statements and balance sheets, see for instance the editorial of *CFO* magazine, December 2002: "Although operating cash flow is not immune to manipulation, investors have increasingly turned to this measure as a more-reliable indicator of corporate performance than earnings."[5]

These four carefully selected parameters give a fairly complete picture of what drives a business in the fourth economy, which means they meet the all-inclusiveness test. They are all relevant to a company's chances of success in terms of survival, earnings, and growth. The data can be defined and measured to the desired precision level. They have been tested in companies of many sizes, in many businesses, and in many countries.[6] The system comes with clear suggestions for reporting and metrics. Some parts of it are computer supported, for speed, convenience, quality, and consistency.

A Permanent and Perfect System?

Do we propose a perfect and permanent system? If that were the goal, we could give up all efforts immediately. We will never find such a system to suit the fourth economy. The essence of this economy with its features of fast change, dynamics, creativity, interaction, and other characteristics goes against a search for something absolute and permanent. It is more natural to encourage experimentation, which is why we dare to propose something new.

Accountability Reborn

A performance-based reporting system of this kind has the potential to revive and reinforce the accountability once considered to be linked to present accounting. It helps board and management keep their focus on essential criteria for company success or failure and, when used for internal/external reporting, helps interested parties to follow the development of some of the most significant indicators of company progress.

Contrary to traditional accounting, with its built-in rear-view focus, this reporting system gives clear indications of the present situation, the starting pad from which the future takes off (Exhibit 4.2). It gives board and management, investors, and analysts sharp tools to assess business threats and opportunities, and makes it easier to visualize ways to strengthen the company's position. *No other reporting system that we know of can do this.*

WHY THE FOUR FUNDAMENTALS?

Starting Point for Success or Failure: The Business Definition

Companies with a clearly identified Business Definition find it easier to rally support from all concerned and to energize and focus all its resources toward a com-

EXHIBIT 4.2   BASELINE FUNDAMENTALS COMPARED TO PRESENT ACCOUNTING

Baseline Fundamentals	Compared to present accounting	How Baseline Reporting improves			
		Internal/external Reporting	Valuation and "Due Diligence"	Auditing/Risk Management	Banking/ Financing
Business Definition Shows the *needs* in the market that you try to fulfill and how it is done.	Not required in today's accounting.	Shows investors and other stakeholders where your company is going.	Benchmark for realistic valuation and "due diligence."	A testing stone for assessing the risk situation.	Shows company ambitions related to market needs.
Business Position Shows comp. *strategic* position, where it is in relation to outside forces.	Does not exist in accounting. Serious diagnosis instead of unreliable prognoses.	Measures and shows "freedom to act" and relates it to the strategy of the company.	Diagnoses the relations of the company, which reflect its business position.	Identifies threats and opportunities that are crucial to success or failure.	Platform to assess the company in its context. ("Payback ability")
Business Reputation "SMART" Dashboard shows Stakeholder perceptions that affect *operational* Position.	Does not exist in traditional accounting, which only recognizes "hard" and "liquid" assets.	Adds essential info on company situation, "tail wind" or "head wind."	Identifies critical value builders that may be at risk in M&A.	Shows strengths and weaknesses that may put the company at risk.	Gives leading indicators to company situation and performance.
Cash Performance Shows *real* earnings and relates cash use to strategies.	More reliable than income statements and less subject to deceptive accounting.	If provided with sensitivity comments, gives good view of strategy performance.	Shows earnings capacity and potential better than income statement.	More satisfactory from a control or risk management perspective.	Indicates "payback ability" better than income statement and balance sheet.

mon goal. The Business Definition is also the one and only company resource that can never be outsourced!

No company can be all things to all people. The Business Definition (business idea, vision, mission statement) expresses the choices of the board and management, but from an outside-in perspective. The answer to Peter Drucker's soul-searching question shows where the company or business unit wants to go, in market-oriented terms. This is why the starting point in Baseline Reporting is a thorough penetration of the Business Definition(s) of the company. The Business Definition is created in an outside-in process, which links the company situation to market and customer needs. It is the benchmark and the most important checkpoint for all subsequent decisions and evaluations. The result serves as a consistent guideline for employees, management, and the board, as well as for outside analysts and investors. It is the key statement against which all company strategies and other success or failure factors are measured.

When we talk about "Business Definition" in this context, we are not talking about a fluffy general statement that is more hype or spin. We are talking about a truly well worked out and clearly defined platform for the consolidated company and for individual business units.

In analyzing more than 1,500 businesses, we have found that defining a business idea is often the most difficult part of an analysis. The difficulties emphasize the importance of the process. Quite often the management team finds in this process that the company holds more separate businesses than it was aware of, or that the formal organization of the company is not in line with the structure of the business definitions.

The process starts by identifying a perceived need in a defined group of customers, a group that is big enough to provide a satisfactory base for the company's business. The company survives and prospers if it can satisfy this need, usually in competition with others.

The other side is the fact that the Business Definition expresses the willpower of the original entrepreneur in a new company, and of the owners and chief executives in more established companies. The official story is that businesses exist to satisfy customer needs. However, in reality it is equally true that they exist to provide an outlet for the ambitions, priorities, and drive of those in charge, the owners, the board members, or the top executives. The two sides, customer needs and owner ambitions, come together in the Business Definition.

The value that any assets, hard, soft, or liquid, create in an ongoing business, is based on how they are perceived by potential buyers to support the company's expressed and adopted mission. This is why the company's business definition, or that of each separate division, segment, business unit, or subsidiary, provides such essential benchmarks against which to check every resource the company uses and every step the company takes.

This is also why the business definition must be well communicated to all-important stakeholders, understood by them, and endorsed by them. The time when the business idea was a document that only appeared on the front page of the Annual Report is long gone, or should be.

The business definition expresses the essence of the business, and sums up the what, how, and why of the business. It defines briefly, and in operational terms, the strengths and strategies of the company. It gives every employee a clear background to his or her role in the company. It holds the business together and defines it, much more so than the legal definition of the company.

To be useful in practice, the business definition must be clear, concise, specific, and operational. The process of hammering out the business definition is crucial. Involvement from as many as possible of those concerned is a critical element.

All measurements in the proposed Baseline Reporting system are related to a sound and sharp business definition. The definition, however, is not cast in stone. It has to be reassessed with regular or irregular intervals, as market conditions and other parameters change.

A Sample Business Definition

You will want to reach a definition of this kind:

> The business of the company is to satisfy the need of the *(defined)* target audience by supplying, manufacturing, or marketing the product or service *(write the name or a brief description of the product or service; include the specific qualities of the product or service that match the product to the market or a market segment),* which is an immediate need /a planned need /a recurring/frequent need to *(indicate the market segment or the customer category with their basic qualities)* who need to *(specify briefly the customer need to be satisfied)* by *(summarize the main features of the product or service strategies).*

A 25-Question Process

For an even more formalized approach to a company's Business Definition, additional support can be obtained by answering a number of questions and checkpoints. Based on those answers, a management group can develop a specific and detailed description of what constitutes the heart of a business and what criteria should be sifted out as the essentials to monitor and prioritize.

We have found that a process that considers the following 25 questions—although it may seem cumbersome—is well worth the time it takes. It will help in phrasing and structuring your company's business idea, and in making it relevant to all stakeholders involved:

1. List all significant products/services the company sells, regardless of whom they are sold to.

2. List all important types of customers/clients to whom the company sells, by business group, size, or other relevant characteristics.

3. Make appropriate combinations between products/services and types of customers/clients.

4. Check, for each combination, the crucial question: Why does this customer/client buy this product/service? Give the answer preferably in the format: In order to be able to . . .

5. Proceed by asking: Why does this customer group want to be able to . . . ? If the answer is still specific to the products/services sold, repeat the question until the answer is no longer specific to the products/services sold.

6. Take the second-to-last answer (the last answer specific to the products/services sold) and use it as a definition of "customer need."

7. Verify that the definition does not contain comparatives, such as "better, stronger, wider" or similar. If it does, change to plain positives, "good, strong, wide" etc.

8. What circumstance generates the customer group's need as defined under Q6?

9. Who makes the final decision to buy or not to buy, and to choose one supplier over another?

10. What is the customer's typical situation when making the purchasing decision (Acute need, Planned need, Routine need, Unplanned need/spontaneous buying, Need based on feelings)?

11. Does the target audience include both end users and those who are not end users? They should be in only one of the two situations.

12. If the target audience is all resellers, who is then the end user?

13. Is there a geographical limitation for which customers we focus on?

14. Can the target audience refrain from satisfying their need for the next 12 months (Generic competition)?

15. What is your answer if the target audience asks you why they should use their money to satisfy this need?

16. Are the products/services exposed to *direct* competition (the customer can buy the same or a very similar product/service from someone else)?

17. In case of direct competition: What are the most important factors that the customer assesses when he or she decides from whom to buy? (Leave out price!) Name the leading direct competitor!

18. Can the need be satisfied by *substitute* competition (the customer can satisfy the need by a different method/product/service)?

19. In case of *substitute* competition: What method constitutes the most severe competition (most frequently chosen by the target group) in satisfying the need of the customers, as defined under Q6?

20. List the factors that influence the target group to choose between the alternative method and the one that your company offers! Select the two most important factors! (Leave out price!) Name the leading substitute competitor!

21. What are the most important competencies and resources we need to develop to respond to what is important to customers?

22. Which resources that can be destroyed or stolen are important for our competitive position?

23. What is the guesstimated growth rate of the market for your products/services in the geographic market you are focusing on? A simple number is quite satisfactory, say from a 0 for no growth (above inflation) to a +3 for very high growth. A shrinking market is listed as −3 (severely shrinking) to −1.

24. Summarize the answers to Q4 through Q23 by phrasing the Unique Buying Reason (UBR), the reason why the customers with the specified need should satisfy it in the way you recommend and buy from your company![7]

25. Repeat Q4 through Q24 until you have covered at least 80 percent of the gross profit of the company.

Working from the answers to the 25 questions, it is fairly easy to arrive at a concise and clear definition of business ideas. In the process, it is likely that several issues come up that call for difficult decisions and choices. Making these choices now helps avoid confusion later and supports intelligent decisions on organization, structure, and other policy issues.

The Company in Its Context: The Business Position

The purpose is to define and measure a company's interdependence with its environment, including strategically significant limitations to the company's freedom to act. In the network economy, a systematic review of the relationships is a powerful way for any company to gain control over its strategic situation. Listing and measuring the company's relationships gives more information about success and failure drivers, strengths and threats, than any financial statement.

Relationships: Crucial to Success or Failure

Relationships can support or restrict the company's freedom to act. The more we get into the fourth economy, the more we realize that the old concept of fixed boundaries between a company as a legal unit and its environment is getting outdated. Companies, like all living organisms, exist and thrive in a constant exchange with their environment.

The borderline between the company and its environment is elastic, and should be. Many important management trends now—outsourcing, contract manufacturing, R&D contracts, supplier contracts, various forms of dealer and reseller relationships, and partnerships and other alliances—tend to make the company's borderline less and less distinct. The links between the company and its environment are relationships. The variety and multitude of relationships, and the impact they can have on company survival, growth, and earnings, make it increasingly important to identify, monitor, and measure them.

Some companies choose to strip down their business structure to the basics. Instead of conventional complete vertical do-it-all organizations, with everything from ideas and concepts to manufacturing and marketing, they become "clusters of distributed capabilities."[8] Only the most essential business functions that add real, specific, and unique value are sure to stay within the legal framework of the company. By the same token, the borderline becomes the very "hot spot" in a company's sphere, the area where much of the strategic action takes place. Strategies are formed and expressed at the frontier, through relationships.

Relationships can be liberating forces and limiting straitjackets. To successfully manage a company, to evaluate its strategic potential and the threats it faces, no instrument is more important than a diagnosis of its relationships, alliances, competitors, and network counterparts. The board and management need convenient instruments to monitor this strategic resource. Since the whole concept of relationships goes against the grain of the traditional "autistic" accounting concept of setting up hard-to-penetrate walls between the company and its environment, we will discuss it in detail (and not only discuss it).

Baseline Reporting provides a practical, experience-based, and computer-supported system ready to help companies make this a regular part of their monitoring and reporting job.

Strategic Relationships Can Be Defined and Measured!

A company's strategic priority, its freedom to act, is largely dependent on conditions in the company's environment. A Business Position diagnosis shows the strategic links between the company and its environment, and how these links can create strengths and weaknesses in the company. Positive links between the company and its stakeholders are strong indicators of business success. Negative links indicate potential threats, each of which must be dealt with.

A software-supported process to do this in a systematic, controllable way is called RealBiz®, an important part of Baseline Reporting. Chapters 5 through 10 will show specific examples of the RealBiz® process in practice, applied to selected strategic decision-making areas: business planning, corporate governance and strategic management, due diligence, internal and external reporting, auditing and risk management, and investing, financing, and bank lending. This broad overall presentation will serve as a starter.

The system is not a theoretical, consultant-generated model. It is made up of what management writer Eric von Hippel calls "sticky knowledge," that is, practical knowledge that he labels as "costly to acquire, transfer and use in a new locus." The built-in knowledge in this system is derived from thousands of performed diagnoses of businesses of all sizes, from all industries, from different countries and legal environments. The problems Eric von Hippel brings out have been overcome by turning business diagnostics into an Internet service. Integrating the long experience of business diagnosis and analysis into a knowledge database makes the system the opposite of what von Hippel suggests: It becomes inexpensive, easy to transfer, and easy to use anywhere in the world.

It recognizes that we live in a world of *fast change*, a world in which the future is genuinely unpredictable. Unlike most existing systems for company assessment, it does not make predictions based on trend extrapolation or other guesses about future revenues or cash flows. It makes a thorough diagnosis of the present state of the company and the relationships it depends on. Actually, of the thousands of analyses made, no one has so far been seen as giving an incorrect picture of a company when checked against later development. This does not mean that this system claims to be able to predict the future. What it can do is help find and emphasize the really critical factors that prove to have a decisive influence on the company.

Unlike balance sheet–based systems, the system recognizes that traditional hard or fixed assets *may be a threat, a liability*, rather than a support factor. It uses only a minimum of items from the company's balance sheet to establish a few ratios defining its financial position. The reason for this link is that we live in a world that still assigns meaning to accounting-based data. When, some time in the future, general agreement has been reached on the futility of balance sheet measures, the system can be modified to eliminate this link. The Business Position is defined through a *systematic review of the relationships* that the company depends on for its survival, earnings, and growth.

The method uses the best available source of knowledge about the company: its top management. The computer-supported interview is frequently completed in 5 or 6 hours for a company with one business area, plus another 1 to 2 hours for each additional business area. The process generates a clear and easy-to-read report, and it cannot be manipulated. The result of the process is a specific and unique diagnosis of the company, complete with graphs, charts, tables, and text, with logic and conclusions explained in detail.

The report becomes the platform of the Position Statement. Linked to the Business Definition, the suggested Position Statement shows how each one of a company's significant relationships can affect its success or failure. The clue to the process is a clear *structure of all important relationships*. To achieve this, all such relationships are classified by category and strength level. Can it be done? Are not relationships something very "fuzzy" and imprecise? Not really; here is how RealBiz® works its way through the apparent jungle of relationships.

Relationships Can Be Defined and Classified

Any relationship or dependency, in business or human relations (or in relations between countries!), can be classified in one of *four categories*:

1. Dominating (where we decide the conditions for the exchange with the other party)
2. "Underdog" (where the other party decides the conditions for the exchange)
3. Alliance (win–win)
4. Competitive (zero sum)

Relationships Can Be Measured

The *strength* or potential impact of each relationship is the next step. The system measures the strength on a scale from 1 to 3, where 1 is a "normal" relationship, 2 is a very strong relationship, and 3 is a relationship that, if broken, can be fatal to one or both parties. This broad classification in three strength groups is quite satisfactory: Strategies are never about decimals; strategies are about making choices between major avenues.

Combining Categories and Strength Levels

The system ends up positioning all significant relationships in one of 12 classes:

- Dominating *(D1, D2, D3)*
- "Underdog" *(U1, U2, U3)*
- Alliance *(A1, A2, A3)*
- Competitive *(C1, C2, C3)*

This clear structure of relationships may seem like an oversimplification to some. However, it reflects important success/failure factors in a better way than any accounting-based system, without the fuzziness that accounting-oriented executives sometimes associate with the word *relationships.*

The system assesses each important relationship in terms of its impact, positive or negative, on the position of the company. The diagnosis of strengths and

EXHIBIT 4.3   BASELINE POSITION GRAPH SHOWS COMPANY
DEPENDENCIES

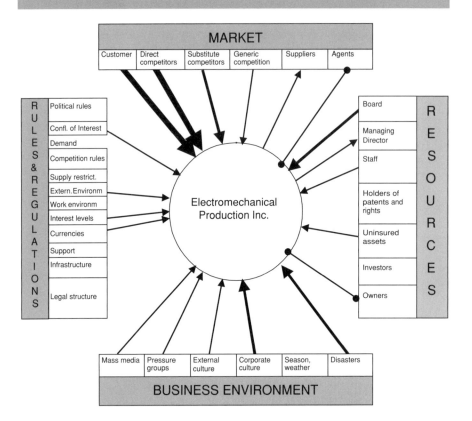

weaknesses of vital relationships for a real company ultimately ends up displayed in a graph. See Exhibit 4.3.

The Business Position graph in Exhibit 4.3 and its backup in the complete report offer a more concise review of the company's competitive position than any other method we have encountered. Details to explain the Position graph are part of the complete report. The common sense behind the system is that very strong relationships have a higher level of impact on the company than weak relationships. The specific benefit of the system is that competitive strengths and weaknesses are defined, measured, and presented in an easily communicated way that makes it easy for a board or management team to take coordinated action.

Here is a brief key to reading Exhibit 4.3 and its classification of relationships:

← Arrows pointing outward from the company are D relations, which means the company is the Dominating party in the relation.

→ Arrows pointing inward are U relations; thus the company is the "Underdog" in the relation.

•• Links combining the company with another party are A relations. They signify an Alliance relation where both parties tend to win, a win-win relationship.

↔ Arrows pointing both ways are C relations. They signify a Competitive relation, where one party's gain is the other party's loss.

— Thin lines signify weak relations, level 1: no major benefit or danger.

— Thicker lines signify strong relations, level 2: a warning signal.

■ Very thick lines signify fatal relations, level 3: a serious threat that must be dealt with.

Details of a Relationship Diagram

All level 1 relationships, whether *A1*, *D1*, *C1*, or *U1*, show relations that allow a satisfactory level of leeway or freedom to act. The relationship does not limit either party to any threatening degree. These relationships are desirable in the short and long run. Much strategic work in the company aims at changing other relationships to this strength category, which takes the company toward its strategic goal of freedom to act. Exhibit 4.3 shows several examples of U1, D1, and A1.

Level 2 relationships call for more attention. In an *A2* relation, both parties are quite dependent of one another. It may seem like a desirable relation, since it motivates both parties to continue to maintain their cooperation. If, however, one of the parties were to be eliminated for some reason, the loss could create a serious, although probably manageable situation.

A *D2* relation may also seem good for a time. However, the other party will probably act to get out of this relationship, or modify it, so in the long run it requires action to reduce one's dependence.

A *C2* relation points to competing relationships where the other party has the potential to damage the business. Action is required.

A *U2* relation means that the other party has the power to inflict serious damage to the business. Strategic action is strongly called for!

Exhibit 4.3 shows four examples of U2s. The first one is a strong dependency of the strongest substitute competitor. The reason why the system reached this conclusion was: "Y Inc. is outperforming our company in terms of geographical coverage according to the needs of the client, and functionality using new technology, and far better than our company regarding flexibility to solve crises."

The second is a board that is not quite up to its task. The reason why the system reached this conclusion was: "The Board has no external members and does not give management any significant input."

The third was the potential influence on the company in case of disaster: "High liability in case of a crime against the company."

The fourth is caused by unsatisfactory corporate culture: "Unclear strategy, reporting systems not quite adapted to company needs, problems with staffing, training, and environment responsibilities. Management style needs some improvements."

Level 3 relationships are crucial. They deserve the utmost attention:

- An *A3* relation indicates an alliance that is so strong that the other party would be eliminated, if one party disappears. Repositioning is urgently required!

- A *D3* relation may seem wonderful. You are in total control! However, experience shows that, since the environment around the company is always bigger, even such a position is untenable in the long run. It is strongly suggested that strategic action to get out of that position is taken before others do it to you! Well-known D3 examples are Microsoft (which contributed to their famous lawsuit) and the United States as the only superpower, a situation that is not as enviable as it may seem!

- A *C3* relation, where competing businesses or other factors can take such action that your company is eliminated, calls for strong strategic action, either by redefining the business idea, by reviewing the means of competition, or by strengthening your company's financial power *vis-a-vis* the competitor.

- A *U3* relation is a potential bankruptcy risk. Strong, immediate strategic action to get out of this position is urgent! Various ways to do this can be envisaged. A company with several U3 relations is in serious danger of getting eliminated.

The company in Exhibit 4.3 suffers from two U3s! One is the fatal dependency on the biggest client: "The biggest client gives a gross profit of U.S. $180,000. The company has an inventory of $75,000 and equipment of $100,000 exclusively for that client." The other is the extreme situation of direct competition, where the system indicates: "X Inc. has a dominating market share, superior financial resources, and is superior to the company in terms of geographical coverage according to the needs of the client, much better than the company regarding competence for design support, and somewhat better than the company regarding flexibility to solve crises. X Inc. gives better value for money that the company does."

A "Kite" Graph

The kite graph in Exhibit 4.4 shows the competitiveness of the company in a slightly different, visually easily accessible form.

EXHIBIT 4.4   BASELINE KITE SHOWS COMPANY COMPETITIVENESS
ELECTROMECHANICAL PRODUCTION, INC.

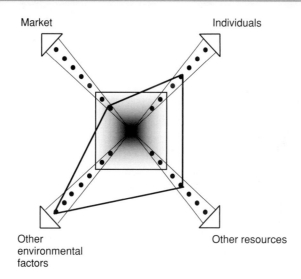

The kite shows the freedom to act of the same company as the previous exhibit. The bigger and more even are the wings of the kite, the better it flies, the stronger and more competitive is the company. Lines inside the central square indicate areas of weakness where forces acting against the company may be fatal.

In this case the kite outline is pushed into the central square by fatal dependencies on the biggest customer and the biggest direct competitor.

A BIZ Chart

A BIZ chart delivers a graphic measurement of the company's unique competitive advantage, its freedom to act, and shows where it stands compared with other companies that have been reviewed. See Exhibit 4.5.

The BIZ index can vary from −6, which is a very difficult situation, to +6, where no single factor can seriously hurt the company. The white bars show the results of more than 700 businesses. Each bar forms a risk class of 70 businesses.

The company Electromechanical Production, Inc., with a BIZ just above .2, belongs to risk class 2. It means that 80 percent of all reviewed businesses have a better freedom to act situation. The system equalizes between companies of various type, industry, size, or country.

A "Hot List" Shows the Threats

As an additional instrument, the system provides a "Hot List" that clearly shows potential threats that the company is exposed to. The threats are crucial in assess-

EXHIBIT 4.5   BIZ (**B**USINESS **I**NDEPENDENCE **Z**ONE) CHART

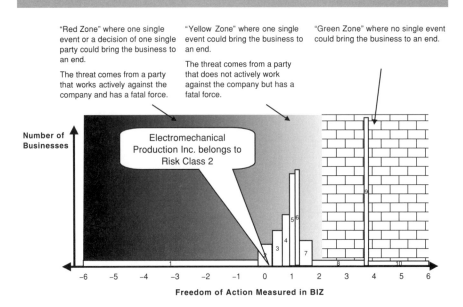

"Red Zone" where one single event or a decision of one single party could bring the business to an end.

The threat comes from a party that works actively against the company and has a fatal force.

"Yellow Zone" where one single event could bring the business to an end.

The threat comes from a party that does not actively work against the company but has a fatal force.

"Green Zone" where no single event could bring the business to an end.

Number of Businesses

Electromechanical Production Inc. belongs to Risk Class 2

Freedom of Action Measured in BIZ

ing the strengths and weaknesses of the company, and are consequently highly relevant:

- To the board and management of the company in choosing strategies and in evaluating various alternative courses that the company can take
- To a consultant or company representative considering a merger or acquisition, in a due diligence process
- To an auditor or risk manager, in a risk assessment process
- To any stakeholder, of whatever category, in assessing his or her ongoing relationship with the company
- To an investor or venture capitalist, before investing in the company
- To a banker or other lender, considering a loan

Corporate Sex Appeal: Who Is on Your Side?

Case in Point—Corporate Sex Appeal

Italian actress Sophia Loren, who should know what sex appeal is, quotes a viewpoint that applies to companies as well. In her words, "Sex appeal is 50 percent what you have and 50 percent what others think you have."

> ### Case in Point—A Word from Welch
>
> Jack Welch, the former CEO of General Electric, who is not known to be a "softie," summed it up a few years ago in an interview in *Management*: "When customers love you, they tend to buy from you, when employees like the company they work for, they do a good job, when investors trust you, they stay with you."

A Consensus Is Growing

As shown in Chapter 1, value is generated in the eyes of the beholder, such as a potential buyer. It is based on perceptions. A company's competitive position is defined, by and large, by stakeholder perceptions. Perceptions are affected by what viewers see as company performance. So, if you go back to Sophia Loren's guideline, a big share of what makes a company valuable in the minds of potential buyers and other stakeholders can be identified and measured through perception and performance indicators.

An international consensus is growing: Nonfinancial indicators are relevant, often more so than accounting data, and new concepts and platforms for defining them are on their way. As *CFO* magazine expressed it as early as 1995: "Like it or not, non-financial indicators are on their way," or in Virginia I. Postrel's words: "It is now the *intangible* economy, stupid."[9]

Most important decisions affecting a company's future are not made in the board room or the corner office. They are made by thousands of individuals "out there," customers, employees, investors, or other stakeholders. Keeping track of stakeholder perceptions is more than a marginal effort; it is one of the company fundamentals.[10] That is why the reputation of a company among defined stakeholders can be a strong support factor or, if negative, a bad hurdle. A good reputation is a tailwind that indicates success; a bad reputation makes the company work against a headwind.

The SMART (Stakeholder Management And Reputation Test) sheet we recommend is a flexible model to measure and show how strong support a company enjoys through these important indicators of success or failure.

Good or bad scores on these nonfinancial performance and perception factors are not cast in stone. A company can act to reinforce strengths and correct weaknesses before they get fatal. Companies that realize their significance have been known to move them to the top of the agenda at board meetings, before the traditional financial statements.

The SMART Approach

Baseline Reporting suggests a practical way of addressing the issue. Just as in the Business Definition and the Business Position segments, Baseline Reporting aims to support clarity and transparency in the Business Reputation segment. It shows how well your company competes for such important resources as market share, employee talent, financial resources, public support, and leadership performance.

The SMART approach identifies stakeholder perception factors that affect company success or failure. They can be measured at least as reliably as other assets. A few basic truths need to be considered:

- Do not pour new wine in old bottles; old bottles will sour the new wine.

- Call a spade a spade. A misguided terminology makes it difficult to take a realistic approach to realities.

- Apply appropriate measurements to measure what is really there, not what we would *like* to see there.

- In developing metrics for strategic choices, shoot for relevance over precision.

New Wine in Old Bottles?

The issue of intangible assets or similar terms seems to be the one aspect that has gained the most attention from those who seek to improve present accounting. They include the "Intellectual Capital" school, the Cap Gemini Ernst & Young project on a Value Creation Index, an SEC task force, even the IASC (# 38), and a Brookings Institute study.[11] This development work has been and is very important in breaking down some old taboos of accounting. The world is moving gradually toward a general agreement that the crucial value drivers are increasingly nonphysical.

However, some of these initiatives try to force the new situation to adjust to old accounting rules. Some proponents aim to treat "intangible assets" and "intellectual capital" like their physical counterparts, for instance by listing them on the balance sheets. They try to force new wine (intangibles) into old bottles (the old accounting system). This would only make the balance sheets even more unwieldy and confusing than they already are.

Call a Spade a Spade: Go Beyond Intellectual Capital

A basic requirement for an intelligent discussion is to adopt a clear, appropriate terminology. We have seen in Chapter 1 how a confusing terminology around the value concept makes a difficult situation worse.

The factors we have selected go far beyond "intellectual capital." In fact many of them are not intellectual—they are emotional—and they are not "capital" in any accepted sense of the word. Like other "assets," whatever impact they have is created in an interaction process. Ultimately, what counts is what they generate on the company's cash flow statement, when they interact to support company goals.

This does not mean that we do not recognize the importance of these factors. On the contrary, they are too important to be mistreated. They deserve to be taken seriously, for what they truly are, not for what one would like them to be. Certainly, motivated and knowledgeable employees play an important role in improving a company's value added. Customer perceptions, such as brand positioning and customer loyalty, affect a company's market share, price level, and repurchase frequency. Investor satisfaction creates loyal shareholders and reduces financing costs. They are value drivers, but not "assets" in any accepted meaning, neither do they have the characteristics of "capital."

What we need to recognize is that *nonfinancial* phenomena strongly affect a company's survival, earnings, and growth. Stakeholder perceptions influence stakeholder action, which affects company *performance*. So, let us call them what they are: *stakeholder-based performance drivers*. The SMART Dashboard makes them visible.

Measure What Is Really There, *Not* What One Would Like to See

Traditional accounting forces us to measure everything in dollars (or other currencies), since that is what accounting was developed for in the first place. Performance drivers reflected on the Reputation Dashboard are by definition nonfinancial. While they ultimately influence the cash flow and the value of the company, it would be inappropriate and confusing to measure each individual factor by any other metrics than one that reflects its inherent quality. Awareness, attitudes, opinions, and other perceptions should be measured in such terms. The intelligent business leader can make the required links between performance and perception data and company survival, earnings, and growth.

Metrics: Relevance Over (Apparent) Precision

The metrics issue is important. Trade organizations, research institutes, and consulting organizations have developed highly sophisticated attitude and opinion measurement processes. Companies that decide to adopt the recommendations of the SMART Dashboard will benefit from well-tested and recognized methods.

Even so, a few caveats can be justified:

1. If your company is not used to these kinds of measurements, dip your toes in the water. Do not jump in head first! Begin in a limited way and expand step by step.

2. Do not fall in the trap inherited from accounting, choosing apparent precision above relevance! Use simple scales, such as those suggested below.

3. There are reasons why *absolute* measures should not always be seen as the best kind. *Relative* measures, which provide a platform for comparisons, may do a better job.

Relative measures relate the metrics applied for each factor to the management's choice between three alternatives:

1. The Benchmark option—better than/worse than competition
2. The Progress option—better than/worse than last year, last quarter, or last month
3. The Target option—better than/worse than management objectives

An additional comment on precision: Any desired precision level usually can be achieved. However, a very high precision ambition may carry too high a price tag, in time and money. At least for a start, until management feels comfortable with the process, we recommend a reasonable precision level. In most cases, relevance is more important than precision to the nth degree. Original measurements may come in percentages or other formats, 7-level, 9-level, or other. For easy reading and comparability, we recommend that measurements are coordinated in a simple format as outlined below.

Perceptions and Performance

The contribution of specific stakeholder performance drivers can vary from company to company, from one business area to another within the same company, and even from one period to another in the same company. This parallels the variation of physical resources in individual companies. Priorities, definitions, and measurements of performance and perception factors exist or can be developed by the individual company.

Theoretically, a company can make up its own dashboard to include any number of performance drivers. In practice, a selection has to be made. Each company can narrow down its selection, if it feels that the 25 or so factors that we suggest are too much for a start. This, of course, is often done by companies using the "balanced scorecard" and similar approaches.

A Workable Part of Reporting

Based on these realities, Baseline Reporting establishes an instrument that is practical, intellectually sound, consistent, and accountable. It suggests a range of stakeholder-related performance drivers, which all have a potential to support or destroy company survival, earnings, and growth. However, it does not call these factors "assets" or "capital" and it does not simplistically aim to assign a currency "value" to them.

How to select the performance drivers? A viable approach is to assume that some *groups* of performance drivers apply to most companies (Exhibit 4.6). This can create a broadly agreeable structure, covering a range of important performance drivers.

EXHIBIT 4.6   **FIVE STAKEHOLDER GROUPS DRIVE COMPANY REPUTATION**

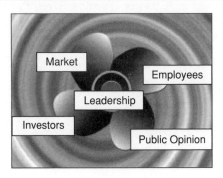

The following statements seem to enjoy a general acceptance level:

- All companies that sell in a market need to gain and retain a competitive position in the minds of customers and potential customers.
- All companies need to compete successfully in the market for talent and do a good job in keeping and developing good employees.
- All companies dependent on external financing need to compete for recognition among lenders and investors.
- Most companies also are better off if they can muster support from relevant public opinion makers.
- Most companies benefit from general appreciation and support for their leadership and the values they represent.

These statements are so obvious to many people that they can be listed as axioms as shown in Exhibit 4.7.

EXHIBIT 4.7   **FIVE VALUE-ADDED AXIOMS**

1. A company that is known, liked and preferred by its customers and potential customers gets more business at better price levels than a company that is not.
2. A company that attracts, motivates and keeps good people tends to increase productivity and reduce staff turnover costs.
3. A company that maintains good and open relations with the investment community gains confidence, a basic condition for investor support.
4. A company that is known and respected by those who create and influence its public framework finds more support and meets less obstacles than a company that is not.
5. A company whose management has defined and communicated clear and understandable visions and strategies finds it easier to gain cooperation and support from employees and other stakeholders.

From Generalities to Specifics:
The SMART Dashboard

The SMART Dashboard includes performance drivers that the company *does not own and cannot control, but may be able to influence.* The criterion is that these factors influence the progress of the company. Each of the five segments lists examples of four or five selected drivers of company success or failure, survival, earnings, and growth. The list we suggest is not necessarily complete, but can serve as a starting point for a company that wants to design its own dashboard to include nonfinancials in its reporting process. This may not be as difficult as it seems at first sight.

The five categories enjoy wide and unanimous appeal. General agreement is also beginning to evolve about a number of factors within the five categories (e.g., brand position, customer satisfaction and loyalty, employee expertise and motivation, productivity, innovation capacity, investor confidence, public opinion endorsement, board commitment, leadership, visions and strategies). That is a first step toward including them in improved company reporting.

The SMART Dashboard turns them into specific, measurable indicators of success or failure. Through breakdowns and applied metrics it goes all the way down to operational management and meaningful stakeholder reporting.

The selection of indicators may well be a matter of discussion. This also applies to the relative contribution that each category represents to a specific company's survival, earnings, and growth. In fact, some flexibility in selecting and prioritizing between dashboard items is not necessarily bad. The selection process itself offers an opportunity for strategic and operational discussions on priorities and success criteria within the board and the management team.

Some executives may feel uneasy about publicly reporting on these items. The data may be seen as too sensitive for sharing outside a small circle of board members and management. Such an attitude is understandable. It just proves that the data are significant. It is quite okay for a company to start the work toward building its dashboard only for internal decision making. However, after a time, when management feels comfortable with the process, it may move to use them also in external reporting. In the long run, external stakeholders have a justified interest in following the development of these forward-looking, wealth-creating leading indicators. To the extent a company chooses to report publicly on its development and progress in these regards, it provides valuable help to analysts (especially if analysts move to upgrade their work definition from financial to business analysis), to investors, and others who are interested in the company.

The Market

It is an axiom that a company that is known, liked, and preferred by customers and potential customers gets more business at better price levels than a company that is not.

The market is "where the buck starts," the major source of revenue. The Market segment measures crucial factors that affect the company's success or failure, ultimately in terms of market share and price level.

The market is specified in the Business Definition process. Customers' awareness of the company, their perceptions, the brand position in their minds, their satisfaction with the company and its products/services, their loyalty (e.g., expressed as repurchase and other factors), are crucial to the market share, price tolerance, and other company growth and earnings factors. Building and measuring such factors are an integrated part of any sensible company reporting system.

Case in Point—Whirlpool

Whirlpool has realized the importance of customer loyalty. It has made a point of keeping track of customer satisfaction and other perception and performance factors in the market segment. Not only does it follow these data as a marketing gimmick, but it has gone the whole way and integrated a responsibility for these performance and perception data all the way into its design and production systems.

When a brand-new washing machine model was discovered to leak after just a few washloads, warning bells started to ring all over. Production was stopped and a design change was made. But not only that; hundreds of customers who had bought the machine were immediately notified of the problem, and service staff were sent out to fix the faulty part. Whirlpool avoided potential liability lawsuits, and gained even more in customer loyalty and satisfaction.

The process leading to Market Share and Price Level follows a few logical steps, each of them measurable with generally available methods. They include measurements that many companies perform anyway, in developing their market strategies and tactics:

- *Awareness.* Obviously, a high percentage of customers and potential customers should at least be aware of the company's existence and the products/services it offers.

- *Brand Position.* Customers should have a clear, correct. and positive opinion about your company and its products and services. Your company should be recognized as one of the leaders in its business. Your company name and the brand names it represents should be strong and perform their role of attracting new customers and retaining old customers. Innumerable research projects that confirm the significance of strong brands have been made and the management literature includes heaps of books that report on the contributions that strong brand names make to company success.

- *Customer Satisfaction.* Present customer satisfaction levels are probably one of the most significant success criteria, in all categories. If they are happy with the way you serve them, the quality of your products/services, and the people they meet, your company is well on the way to market leadership. All available research confirms that just plain "good" is not nearly enough. The support that comes through a high level of customer satisfaction, and one of its results, customer loyalty, are universally recognized and accepted as a strong value driver. A Customer Satisfaction measure, by any of the several processes available in the market, is an indicator of value creation through its impact on market share, price sensitivity, and other earnings aspects.

- *Customer Loyalty.* In most companies, the frequency of repurchase by existing customers is an essential earnings factor. The work by Frederick Reichheld, *The Loyalty Effect*, provides a number of excellent examples.
- *"Zero Neglect"* (or *"First Choice"*). This measures "the moment of truth." Whenever a potential client or customer is in the market for your kind of product/service, he or she should have your alternative on the short list, preferably at the top. This measure, easy to assess in most circumstances, is a key success indicator closely linked to such data as Market Share and Price Level (Margin).

Employees

Another axiom states that a company that attracts, motivates, and keeps good people tends to increase productivity and reduce staff turnover costs.

Employees are a major cost and value-building factor in most companies. As companies move toward service, rather than products, employees are an increasingly immediate source of sales, revenue, and earnings. The Employee segment measures nonfinancial factors that contribute to productivity or innovation or other measures of Value Added per Employee.

The employee segment includes managers, workers, associates, and partners, and the potential employees the company may be looking for.

Their competence and professional skills, their enthusiasm, motivation and loyalty, the spirit with which they interact between themselves and with clients and customers, their willingness to endorse and work by the corporate mission and standards, the empowerment they get from management, the corporate culture, are crucial to productivity, innovation, and other company growth and earnings factors.

Case in Point—Southwest Airlines

In the turmoil of the airline industry at the beginning of the twenty-first century, one airline stands out above most others: Southwest Airlines. Its track record of survival, where several airlines have folded or merged; growth, where its competitors have stumbled and sometimes fallen and;uninterrupted earnings—unique in the industry—may have several good reasons. One of the distinctive features of Southwest Airlines is its stone-hard policy of never firing any of its employees.

Even when other airlines have cut tens of thousands of their employees, to a sum of close to 100,000 in the fall of 2001, Southwest kept its employees, as it has done throughout its history.

The Pavlov reflex of firing employees when times get tough has significant consequences, as has the other approach, that of keeping them. Basic to the decision making in favor of one or the other of these policies is the concept of whether employees are a cost factor or a value creation factor. Southwest Airlines seems to agree with Peter Drucker, when he maintains that managers need to understand that people are a resource and not a cost.

Factors in the employee segment help the company keep a focus on how it attracts, motivates, keeps, and develops the right employees.

Companies such as Southwest Airlines, that do everything in their power to avoid downsizing, in terms of firing employees, don't necessarily do it for their blue eyes. They claim significant and lasting benefits from the policy, both in the performance and the perception fields. Some of the benefits they cite include a high level of employee loyalty, gains zin productivity, savings in turnaround time, recruitment, and training costs, and when times change for the better again, a spillover into high customer satisfaction levels, and a spirit of innovation among employees, who know that it pays off to stay tuned to the company's needs and progress.

By contrast, companies who use their body of employees as an elastic tape measure have to take into account high severance and rehiring costs, potential lawsuits, lack of trust in management, losses of company expertise and customer relations, and risk-averse employees at low levels of enthusiasm.

It would be easy to make the case for the Southwest Airlines approach, even in business terms. Its earnings record and staying power in turbulent times seem to speak for themselves.

In the Employee segment, look at a logical sequence of steps toward Value Added per Employee, such as:

- *Awareness.* Potential employees must be aware that your company exists and is an attractive employer. To get the numbers, define your target groups for essential recruitments and measure awareness with easily available models and processes. Once you have them on board, there are two ways you need to go to develop your employees: the skills/brains way, through ongoing training, and the heart way, through sharing visions and providing motivation.

- *Training Investment/Employee.* In the fast-changing business climate of our time, the basic training an employee has when joining the company seldom lasts a lifetime. In most businesses, therefore, companies that invest actively in employee training programs have an edge over those who do not. While the amounts, in money and in time, that your company invests per employee, are not necessarily the only way to measure the accomplishment levels of your employees, they are an easy way to use measures that are easily available.

- *Expertise.* The performance of your employees should not only be half good—it should be the best in the business. Individual performance, team performance, and systems excellence all work in this direction and should be tracked and encouraged. Work from internal data or include customer reactions and satisfaction measures in your database.

- *Support for Visions.* Your employees must know and endorse your company's visions, goals, and objectives. Measure through attitude surveys (anonymous, of course!) or focus groups.

- *Motivation.* Employees must continuously be encouraged and motivated to do their best, to stretch beyond minimum requirements. Measure through attitude surveys (anonymous, of course!), focus groups, and/or customer reactions.

- *Empowerment.* If the company has the best people in the business and if they are motivated and committed, they must have freedom to do their job. The result is quality, innovation, and ultimately high Value Added per Employee. Make sure that your policies and, not least, your management practices maximize employee empowerment.

Investor/Finance Segment

Another axiom states that a company that maintains good and open relations with the investment community gains confidence—a basic condition for investor support.

The Investor/Finance segment measures critical factors that affect the cost and availability of capital and ultimately influences the share price of the company. It is a crucial aspect of the performance of the company.

The Investor/Finance segment includes shareholders, investors, lenders, analysts, financial journalists, and other financial influences. Their satisfaction with the company—obviously its overall return, but also such nonfinancial performance factors as reputation; market position; the quality and reliability of information it provides; and company leadership are factors that ultimately affect the share price and the cost of capital, whether borrowed or invested.

The process in the Investor segment can include these steps:

- *Awareness.* Potential investors must know that your company exists and have a general opinion about what it is, what it does, and how it works. Measure the awareness through traditional awareness surveys.

- *Ratings and Rankings.* Monitor how financial, business, and trade media deal with your company and how they rank you in comparison with other similar companies. If this is not enough, add ratings and rankings questions to your awareness surveys.

- *Investor Satisfaction.* Measure how your owners, investors, shareholders, and lenders appreciate your company, its performance, its reporting, and other key issues. Monitor closely reactions from investors to the information you provide. Support, if necessary, with formal surveys.

- *Investor Loyalty.* Measure how attractive your company is to present investors in terms of their staying with the company through periods of ups and downs. Monitor such factors as shareholder turnover in various categories.

- *Board Commitment.* Measure board performance in corporate governance terms, including board member independence, member attendance, share ownership, and other aspects. Make sure that board members are informed of the expectations the chairperson and the company have for their performance and keep track of individual members to ensure that they meet those expectations.

Public Opinion Segment

Here is another axiom: A company that is known and respected by those who create and influence its public framework finds more support and meets less obstacles than a company that isn't.

In all democracies, companies operate by formal or informal approval of the public opinion. In the Public Opinion segment, the dashboard numbers are based on factors that lead up to an essential strategic goal of most companies, "license to operate" without unnecessary hurdles. The factors stake out the way for the company to deserve its relative independence, in its turn critical to company survival, earnings, and growth.

The public opinion segment includes public policy makers in the company's sphere of interest, local and national (and international) politicians and administrators, industry leaders, regulators, the media, and opinion groups. Acceptance of the company as a good member of the communities where it works, a good "corporate citizen," is a frequent term to cover what needs to be done and is measured in the Public Opinion segment of the dashboard. Successful work helps remove hurdles and paves the way for smooth and mutually beneficial relations between the company and its political and semipolitical environment, ultimately contributing to a higher level of freedom to act.

Case in Point—Ericsson Response

Ericsson is a leading provider in the new telecom world, with communications solutions that combine telecom, datacom, and user mobility. Its products and services combine true global reach with individual human needs. When Ericsson wanted to get serious about corporate citizenship, it was natural for the company to look for an area where global and local communications needs could be met in ways that made social and human impact. The solution was a program called Ericsson Response.

Ericsson Response is a global initiative aimed at developing better and faster response to human suffering caused by natural disasters, especially in developing countries. It builds on Ericsson's previous experience and involvement in numerous disaster response efforts, such as setting up mobile base stations for refugee camps during the Kosovo crisis, reinstalling telecom equipment for earthquake victims in Turkey, and supplying phones to flood victims in Vietnam.

The project has been developed in cooperation between Ericsson, the United Nations, and Red Cross/Red Crescent. Ericsson and its partners emphasize the crucial role of fast and efficient communications, when disasters strike. The project will provide essential long-range initiatives to exchange and develop communications expertise, support faster and more coordinated approaches to disaster response efforts, as well as offer telecom equipment and services as disaster relief. The project can count on fast and effective reactions through the global network of Ericsson subsidiaries. Company resources will be funneled into the project, as well as voluntary efforts from global and local Ericsson specialists and experts.

The Ericsson Response initiative is an example of how companies can direct their expertise to areas of public needs, provide an essential public service, and, as an added benefit, build public confidence and appreciation.

The process in the Public Opinion segment of the SMART Dashboard can be devised in similar ways as the other segments.

- *Awareness.* Those who form public opinion in your target audiences, local and national politicians, educators, media, and other opinion-building groups should have at least basic knowledge about your company, what it is and does, and its overall performance. Measure through awareness surveys, broken down into relevant audience categories.

- *Visions and Strategies.* The next step is that they should know your visions, goals, objectives, and strategies, respect them and, if possible, share them. Add attitude elements to awareness surveys.

- *Issue Management.* This means their appreciation of your ability to handle difficult issues in your fields (e.g. environmental issues, social responsibility, and fair employment and promotion policies). Complement surveys with elements that include those issues that you feel are relevant.

- *Confidence.* If the public have clear and positive views about your company and its management on the above points, they will tend to provide your company with a cushion of confidence, which will improve your freedom to act or "license to operate." Keep a register of political reactions and general attitudes to your company, including media coverage. Complement with formal surveys as necessary.

Leadership

Another axiom states that a company whose management has defined and communicated clear and understandable visions and strategies finds it easier to gain cooperation and support from employees and other stakeholders.

The *leadership* of the company is the single most important segment pointing to ongoing success or failure. The visions and strategies of the leadership, the corporate culture and behavior the leadership encourages, and the level of acceptance and endorsement of basic concepts that the leadership creates are all critical to company performance and results.

The Leadership segment of the dashboard includes the board and top management, down to a selected level, depending on the level of hierarchical structure the company works under. Successful work in the Leadership segment leads to *supportive behavior* from the company's constituents. The recognition and respect the company leaders enjoy, the support they are able to generate from all stakeholders, within and outside of the company, creates the difference between the company's working in a headwind or tailwind climate. It is a situation that affects the support (or lack thereof) that the company gets from all the other segments, the market, employees, the public sector, and the investment community. It is a decisive group of factors that build company survival, earnings, and growth.

Case in Point—General Electric

It is hard to find a more convincing example of excellent leadership in business than John Welch Jr. and his successful period as CEO of General Electric. Having sifted through a broad range of other potential examples, choosing Welch has another benefit: His time in the hot seat is over. It is almost scary to see how many great leadership stories from the last few years have an epilogue where the glory has faded or turned into its opposite.

Natural yardsticks in the Leadership segment include:

- *Awareness.* To what extent are your target audiences, internal and external, in all the segments outlined above, aware of who is in charge of the company, and who its top leaders are?

- *Support for Visions and Strategies.* How well do they know and endorse what visions and strategies the company leadership has, what it and the company tries to accomplish, and what drives them?

- *Support for Basic Values.* To what extent do they know and accept or endorse the ethical and moral norms and guidelines that the company leadership adheres to in the way it runs the company?

- *Confidence and Trust.* What is the level of confidence and trust that key audiences have in the performance of the company and its leadership?

- *Supportive Behavior.* Common sense and research proves that confidence and trust leads to supportive behavior in all essential relations that build a company's success.

The Scales on the Dashboard

A simple way to calibrate a SMART Dashboard:

Segment	Number of Value Drivers	Points for Each Value Driver	Max. Total
Market	5	0–5	25
Employees	6	0–3	18
Investors	5	0–3	15
Public opinion	4	0–3	12
Leadership	5	0–3	15
		Maximum	85

Ideally, the statement includes last year's data for comparability.

A sample SMART dashboard is shown in Exhibit 4.8.

An Advanced Cash Flow Statement — Cash Performance

The purpose of an advanced cash flow statement is to show clearly where the cash comes from, and where it goes *and* how the cash flow relates to company strategies.

Case in Point — The Enron Discrepancy

Consider the discrepancy between Enron's reported results in the first half of 2001: Its "net income" was $810 million. Its cash flow from operations was $1.3 billion, negative, in the red, minus! Without going into the details it is hard to say which figure gives the best general view of where the company was heading. The important thing is that when a discrepancy of that magnitude can occur, it is time to review which data best serve the investing public and all other decision makers that depend on the company's reporting for its decisions. What brings the best chances for fair disclosure?

Market

1. Awareness
   To what extent are potential customers at least aware of our company and its offer?
   0 – 5
2. Brand Position
   How strong is our Brand Position?
   0 – 5
3. Customer Satisfaction
   How high is the customer satisfaction level?
   0 – 5
4. Customer Loyalty
   How many of our customers are regular repurchasers?

   0 – 5
5. "Zero Neglect" or "First Choice"
   To what extent do our customers "shortlist" us at their moment of (re)purchase?
   0 – 5

Total Market Reputation (max. 25)

Employees

1. Awareness
   To what extent are potential employees aware of our company's existence?
   0 – 3
2. Training Investment/Employee
   How does our investment in training per employee compare with business average?
   0 – 3
3. Expertise
   How does the expertise level of our employees rank (in the opinion of our customers)?
   0 – 3
4. Support for Visions etc.
   How well do our employees know and endorse our company's business definition?
   0 – 3
5. Motivation
   Is the motivation level of our employees as high as it should be?
   0 – 3
6. Empowerment
   Do our employees feel that they are encouraged and authorized to take own initiatives in their daily work?
   0 – 3

Total Employee Support (max. 18)

Investors/Finance

1. Awareness
   To what extent do potential investors know about our company and what it does?
   0 – 3
2. Ratings and Rankings
   How do relevant media and ranking institutions rate our company?
   0 – 3
3. Investor Satisfaction
   How satisfied, overall, are our investors?
   0 – 3
4. Investor Loyalty
   How high is our shareholder turnover?
   0 – 3
5. Board Commitment
   How is our board performance in corporate government terms?
   0 – 3

Total Investor Appreciation and Performance (max. 15)

Public Opinion

1. Awareness
   To what extent do public opinion builders in our interest area have at least a general awareness of the company?
   0 – 3
2. Visions, Strategies
   To what extent do they know and respect our visions etc.?
   0 – 3
3. Issue Management
   To what extent do they appreciate our ability to handle difficult issues (ex. race, gender, environment, disasters)?
   0 – 3
4. Confidence
   What general expressions of confidence/ nonconfidence do we experience?
   0 – 3

Total Public Opinion Index (max. 12)

Leadership

1. Awareness
   To what extent do our key audiences know the top names of our company?
   0 – 3
2. Support for visions, strategies
   How well do they know and endorse the main visions and strategies of our leadership?
   0 – 3
3. Support for basic values
   To what extent do they support the moral and ethical norms that guide our leadership?
   0 – 3
4. Confidence, trust
   What level of confidence do they have in our company and its leadership?
   0 – 3
5. Supportive behavior
   How clearly do they express their support for our company and its leadership?
   0 – 3

Total Leadership Index (max. 15)

EXHIBIT 4.9   CASH FLOW STATEMENT RATINGS (A–F)

	Income Statements	Balance Sheets	*Cash Flow Statements*
Relevance	C	F	*A*
Reliability/Credibility	E	D	*B*
All-inclusiveness	D	E	*B*
Adaptability	C	D	*A*
Precision (apparent)	B	C	*B*

The Case for an Advanced Cash Flow Statement

Baseline Reporting prioritizes the cash flow statement[12] over traditional income statements and balance sheets. The reason is that cash flow statements tend to be more reliable and have higher credibility. They are less subjected to "creative accounting" practices than income statements and balance sheets. Cash flow provides fair disclosure in a more intelligent and reliable way than income statements.

Comparing cash flow statements with income statements and balance sheets using the rough rating from A to E that we gave earlier, we feel cash flow comes out significantly better. See Exhibit 4.9.

Cash flow statements provide a better view of the company's strategic and operational situation than income statements, especially if they come with enough details, comments from management, and with sensitivity analyses for each important line. The advanced version of cash flow statements presented below provides unmatched clues both to the process of generation of cash and, more important, to management's strategic use of cash resources.

In a traditional cash flow calculation, the purpose is usually to arrive at the free cash flow, the cash flow available to the owners. Operational costs are deducted to arrive at the generated cash flow, and investments are deducted to arrive at the final cash flow.

Beyond the Cash Flow Statement

A detailed cash flow statement with accompanying "sensitivity analysis" links important items in the cash flow with key factors in the Business Definition, the Business Position, and the SMART Dashboard. The sensitivity analysis gives management a chance to add qualitative comments to the numbers, linking important line items to events, policies, and strategies of importance to the company. An advanced cash flow statement of this kind provides more strategic and operational information than income statements, and is less susceptible to fraud or misrepresentation, intended or not.

Companies with several business units make one cash flow statement for each business unit and then consolidate them. Each relevant line is analyzed and commented by management from a sensitivity perspective. Ideally, statements include last year's data for comparability.

A Traditional Cash Flow Statement Is Good...

Even a basic cash flow statement as shown in Exhibit 4.10 is better than income statements and balance sheets.

...But an Advanced Cash Performance Statement Is Better

Even cash flow statements can be improved further.

The cash flow statement we suggest is slightly different from a traditional cash flow statement. It has a double focus: to show not only how the cash is generated—that is, where it comes from—but also how it is used *in relation to the strategic goals* of the company.

The second part of it, how cash is strategically used, includes the following items:

1. Cash used to improve unfavorable conditions that limit the company's freedom to act.
2. Cash used to protect favorable conditions that support freedom to act.
3. The sum of these cash flows as a share of total cash flows generated by the company.
4. The sum of these cash flows distributed over the business areas, as they were defined in the Business Definition process.
5. Share of total cash, including financial transactions, which has been spent but *not* used for the purpose of protecting freedom to act.
6. Share of total cash, including financial transactions, which has *not* been spent but saved for future actions.

The information we seek has nothing to do with whether a payment is seen as a cost or as an investment in traditional accounting. Steps described above, to obtain or maintain freedom to act, can be of either kind.

Cash flow starts with payments to the company from customers who have bought products or services. The funds are used by the company to pay suppliers, employees, investors, and other stakeholders. Already at this level, management can allocate resources or buy services to deal with strategic issues. They are then included in company operational cash use. Management can also use the cash flow for special efforts of an investment nature to protect the company's freedom to act. Paying off a loan to reduce an unfavorable dependence on a banker or lender can be a strategic act within the scope of the recommended program.

EXHIBIT 4.10   BASIC CASH FLOW STATEMENT

Items	Cash Flow Amount		Sensitivity factors linked to Position and SMART Statements
	Last Year	This Year	
Cash flow from operations			
Revenues (broken down if relevant)			
Changes in operational assets/liabilities			
Other changes in receivables (broken down if relevant)			
Other changes in liabilities (broken down if relevant)			
Taxes paid			
Net cash from operations			
Cash flow from investing			
Changes in financial receivables			
Investment changes (broken down if relevant)			
Net cash from investing			
Cash flow from financing			
Dividends paid			
Options programs (broken down if relevant)			
Changes in other liabilities			
Net cash from financing			
Starting Cash and equivalent			
Net change in cash and equivalent			
End Cash and equivalent			

For each payment, it must be determined whether it aims at improving any of the relationships indicated, and if so to what extent. This question has to be explored further to avoid arbitrary comments, as much as possible.

The guiding principle has to be that management, as a minimum, must keep cash flow, defined as inflow minus outflow, at a level required to keep business at its present level. We call the remaining cash flow TBM (Cash To Be Managed). Company auditors should be involved in establishing this level.

Checking the way management handles TBM gives an indication of the direction management moves. Problem areas prioritized by management show the future focus. Information at this level can be described as *direction*-oriented. A term for the portion of TBM used for strategic action is FSA (Cash For Strategic Action).

Focus and Charge: Two Cash Ratios to Monitor

Dividing FSA by TBM generates an interesting measure, showing how focused management is toward company strategic development. The resulting quotient is named the FOCUS ratio.

A company that uses TBM for purposes other than strategic priorities will get a low FOCUS measure. Using the whole TBM for strategic purposes generates a FOCUS measure of 100. Using more than 100 percent for strategic measures means either a reduction of liquidity or external financing. Measuring the increase of liquidity, including any externally provided means, during the selected period, shows how much cash management has saved for future needs, measured in Cash Available (CA) divided by TBM. The resulting ratio is called CHARGE.

With access to these measurements for a given period of time, the reader can compare the readings with the real development. Has the business idea evolved over the time? Has the strategic business position improved? How successful has management been from an operational perspective? Getting this information from conventional accounting-based systems is hard, not to say impossible.

The process and the key numbers apply irrespective of business, company size, or geographic location. The process is also considerably less subject to manipulation than present reporting systems, and offers substantial improvements in transparency.

SUMMING UP THE BASELINE
REPORTING MODEL

Baseline Reporting defines company success as its ability to survive, grow, and create a surplus. The system provides consistent and relevant measures of four important fundamentals that measurably track the company's progress toward these goals:

1. A systematic and consistent review of the company's business idea, its visions, and its mission statements. (Ultimate check: Business Definition, UBR, and Market Growth estimate.)

2. Assesses the company in its network, showing its dependencies on critical relationships that can help make or break the company. (Ultimate check: Freedom of action, measured in BIZ.)

3. Keeps track of selected perception factors that the company does not own, not even control, but which the company is dependent on for its success, and consolidates these data on a five-segment Reputation Dashboard. (Ultimate check: Stakeholder appreciation, measured in the SMART Index.)

4. Tracks the cash flow, both its sources and its uses, and relates cash performance to company strategies. (Ultimate check: Cash Performance with FOCUS and CHARGE.)

The system does not lean on a traditional numbers analysis of financial details in company accounting. Rather, it reports mainly nonfinancial data, what is essential in the company and its network, presents it, and helps draw conclusions from it. The conclusions, again, are not presented in accounting-based numbers but in data related to their significance for the company, with a focus on relevance rather than precision.

In Chapters 5 through 10 we will go from sounds to things. In Chapter 5 we will explore how companies can and do use Baseline Reporting in one of the most important business processes, business planning and risk assessment, and in Chapters 6 through 10 we will review how it works in other crucial applications, corporate governance, due diligence in mergers and acquisitions, reporting and investor relations, auditing and risk management, and financing/lending/investment processes.

NOTES

1. See Peter F. Drucker, *Managing in the Next Society*, Truman Talley Books, St. Martin's Press, New York, 2002, p. 90: "In a business you have to make sure all the various groups converge to produce the desired result. This is the key to understanding what's ahead."

2. Arie de Geus, *The Living Company: Habits for Survival in a Turbulent Business Environment*, Harvard Business School Press, Boston, 1997 (op. cit.) and Kevin Kelly, *New Rules for the New Economy: Ten Radical Strategies for a Connected World*, Viking, The Penguin Group, New York and other places, 1998.

3. Ronald J. Alsop and Ron Alsop, *The 18 Immutable Laws of Corporate Reputation: Creating, Protecting and Repairing Your Most Valuable Asset*, Simon & Schuster, New York, 2004.

4. Charles J. Fombrun, *Reputation: Realizing Value from the Corporate Image*, Harvard Business School Press, Boston, 1996.

5. Julia Homer, Editor-in-Chief, "Gains and Losses," *CFO*, December 2002. In the same issue, see also a well-documented article by Ronald Fink, with Charles W. Mulford and Michael Ely, *"Tuning in to Cash Flow."*

6. The light touch of baseball terminology may be more familiar to our U.S. and Japanese readers than to some others. It is intended to evoke an image of inter-action, of ongoing process, and a consistent search for measurable, goal-oriented performance. Those unfamiliar with baseball can visualize the four aspects as a four-wheel test, with the company as a four-wheel-drive vehicle. For the company to move forward, the total traction power of the four wheels must be optimal. Each aspect must meet the demands of strong performance in its segments, and they must interact for complete driving results.

7. Please note that this is a different approach to the more often described Unique Selling Proposition (USP). The approach we advocate follows the outside-in pattern, in putting the customer's interests first!

8. Mohanbir Sawhney, quoted in *Fortune*, March 5, 2001.

9. In *Forbes ASAP*, February 26, 1996.

10. For an incisive discussion on this perspective on company success and failure, please see James E. Post, Lee E. Preston, Sybille Sachs, *Redefining the Corporation: Stakeholder Management and Organizational Wealth*, Stanford Business Books, Stanford, CA, 2002.

11. Margaret M. Blair, Steven M.H. Wallman, *Unseen Wealth*, Brookings Institution, Washington, DC, 2001.

12. Please note we are not talking here about imaginary future cash flows, as in discounted cash flow. We are talking about the real cash flow, with the added requirement that each significant item be detailed and commented on by management.

PART TWO

It Can Be Done!

CHAPTER 5

Business Planning in an Unpredictable World

Unpredictable are future calls,
yet, finance rules by crystal balls.

"Give me where to stand, and I will move the earth!" Many board members and CEOs have a great deal of sympathy for Archimedes, when they desperately seek a fixed, reliable starting point for the company planning process. They may find it easier to define where they are going: For a long time now, board work has ultimately aimed at increasing the company value, perhaps expressed as shareholder value. The way to do this, as we have explained in the "Value Mess" segment in Chapter 1, is to increase the company's appreciation in the eyes of significant stakeholders, customers, suppliers, employees, and others. (For measurement aspects on this issue, see Chapter 4.)

However, as *Alice in Wonderland* taught us long ago, if you do not know where you are, it is difficult to know how to get where you want to go. Taking out the company compass direction from a mistaken starting point can lead the company in a totally mistaken direction and expose it to totally unexpected dangers. Defining the starting point, the company position, in meaningful terms is quintessential to any successful planning process.

The problem is real! During the years 1998–2003, no less than 100 of the Fortune 1,000 companies lost 55 percent or more of their market capital within one single month (though not the same month). A common feature seems to be that they had been using the wrong decision parameters. And still, these were major companies with—on the whole—well-functioning boards and management teams in place. Like Archimedes, the executives of these 100 companies may not have felt that old parameters gave them a firm point of departure.

In reality, both the starting point and the goal may be hard to define in specific terms using old parameters. Value, as we explained in Chapter 1, is not a quality, resting in the company itself. It is not the objective fact, expressed in numbers, that traditional, accounting-based management tried to maintain. Instead, supported by many behavioral economists, we have argued that value is based on perceptions, emotions, held by owners, potential owners, and other interested parties. These perceptions of company value, in turn, indicate the potential of the company to survive, grow, and be profitable. Especially the methods described in Chapter 4 make those conditions specific and measurable.

In this chapter we will go into more detail about how to improve your company's planning, starting from a reliable launch pad.

BUSINESS PLANNING AND ENTERPRISE RISK ASSESSMENT

Well-known management guru Peter Drucker suggests an outlook that seems reasonable: "A time of turbulence is a dangerous time, but the greatest danger is a temptation to deny reality."[1] This is why we have emphasized, time and again, that any manager must accept the basic truth that the future is unpredictable, and cut off the siren songs from analysts and other future sellers of all kinds, from the simplest to the most sophisticated. The reality is that the world is always more complicated than we can expect. Forecasting is simply not an acceptable tool in the executive's toolbox.

A cornerstone to justify value-creating perceptions among interested parties is the confidence that stakeholders have in company board and management. Is the leadership capable of making the right decisions to take the company from the present to a future of survival, growth, and profitability? An important question then is: "What is their starting point for decisions about the future?" and "What are their tools for looking forward?" Unfortunately, in more cases than not, the platform is crystal-ball readings about what the future will be like. But the future is genuinely unpredictable! Prognoses, scenarios, and other forms of guesswork are not valid platforms for serious decision making. In fact, prognoses, more often than not, only serve as a treacherous substitute for professional strategic planning. Our news media confirm, on an almost daily basis, the frequency and seriousness of totally unforeseen events that radically change the conditions of individual companies, whole businesses, or—as with the December 2004 tsunami disaster— whole countries or regions.

Against this realistic background, how can a CEO or an analyst make predictions about how an individual company will develop? How reliable are they as a platform for decisions and actions? The purpose of using such predictions as an ingredient in the planning process is not to willfully mislead the actors in the stock market, although that may in reality be the consequence. The reason for those predictions is rather that the CEO, or analyst, knows no alternative and feels comfortable, when a future is described in words and numbers, no matter how useless they are. The forecasting humbug, fed by trend extrapolations and consulting and analyst mumbo-jumbo, thrives on such ignorance, just as astrology and horoscopes do in other fields.

Case in Point—Ericsson "2005"

An example of the application of the scenario method can be found in the annual report for 1996 of the telecom equipment company Ericsson. The heading was "2005: Ericsson Entering the 21st Century." Ericsson explains: "More than 500 of Ericsson's experts and managers have been involved in the activities surrounding '2005,' which became the working name of the study. We also had the help of experts at leading universities, independent research organizations and consultancies. Following two years of intensive work, '2005' has evolved into something more than merely a blueprint for the future. As the most extensive analysis of the telecommunications industry that we know of, '2005' has started a process that is one of the most revolutionary in all of Ericsson's 120-year history."

This must have been a highly motivating exercise for most of the participants! But, to the best of our knowledge, the study does not contain one word about those factors that a few years later forced Ericsson to fire about half of its work force around the globe and sent its previously golden shares to price levels that were below the price of a stamp.

What is the use of spending such enormous resources on a project that you know will end up somewhere else than where the real development ends up?

What Is Wrong with the Traditional Approach?

In drafting this segment we have studied guidelines and instructions from major auditing and consulting companies and a number of financial institutions to try to learn about the procedures they advocate for writing a business plan, either to prepare an investment or simply to plan for the next business year.

One common feature for many of them is an effort to try to (a) identify future events that could influence the company, and then (b) estimate the probability that they will occur. The focus then turns to trying to prevent serious damages with high probability.

In order to identify future events, the guidelines often use scenarios, trend extrapolations, prognoses, and assumptions related to future sales, prices, cost items, market trends, inflation levels, currency changes, interest rates, and so on. For reasons we have exposed in some detail in Chapter 2, such efforts are futile. The traditional approach to risk management includes many of the same components. Increasingly, companies want to combine the two processes to provide efficiency and consistency. This is, however, only possible if the plan components are reasonably reliable. If that is not the case, combining the processes can instead turn out to be a double whammy!

The next step is to assign probability numbers to future trends and events. Unfortunately, they are just as useless as attempts to foresee events, and for the same reasons. Experience shows convincingly that most major events were not even imagined, before they happened, even less could they be assigned a probability number. A simple way to verify this is to go back in company history and study major company turning points. Doing that, one will find that in most cases those major turning points, at the time they happened, could not have been, and were in fact not, predicted. If you wish to extend this approach for further confirmation of reality, look back to the major turning points in your own personal life! Were they, or could they have been, predicted?

High Impact, Low Probability

The problem any CEO faces is that most events that, after the fact, turn out to have major consequences share one common feature: the low before-the-fact probability for those specific events to happen. This has always been true. But today's globalization, fast technology development, and increased interdependence between companies have dramatically increased the number of unexpected, unpredictable events with high impact. Every company today is exposed to a drastically increased number of potential high-impact events, each of them with low probability. The total probability of something dramatic to hit our company has increased, while our ability to predict such events remains practically nonexistent.

In a traditional planning process, all these untenable assumptions are combined into detailed financial worksheets that show future capital needs, future income statements, and balance sheets. Assessing which numbers to allocate to each component for the time period in question is, again, a highly uncertain process, and the uncertainty typically grows by the length of the planning period. Who knows the oil price or the currency exchange rate five years from now? Who knows what customers will like or dislike next year? Who knows what is cooking in competitor labs? What effects will globalization have on wage and cost development in the next couple of years? Where will the next technology breakthrough come? Will there be any major political conflicts in the picture within the planning period? When will an existing trend change and move in a different direction, and if so, in which way?

If every component in the total process is allotted an uncertainty factor, the combined uncertainty grows to a point where the calculations become worse than useless as a decision-making platform, which, of course, is entirely consistent with the laws of nature.

Traditionally, some items in the calculations may have been left constant over time. However, more and more often we can see business experts in media complain that old rules of thumb no longer apply, as a consequence of, among other things, increased interdependence between countries and companies. New technologies suddenly change the whole game and consumer tastes change for inexplicable reasons. Disasters like SARS and mad cow disease, and tsunamis and weather patterns change the conditions for business. Political turmoil, conflicts, and sudden agreements turn old rules and affiliations around.

All these and many more factors make assumptions irrelevant over night, no matter how historically well based they may be. The irrelevant or crashed assumptions bring down with them the traditionally designed business plans. The only thing one knows about the future, with some certainty, is that it will never turn out as predicted.

Some executives draw conclusions from these experiences and argue that it is useless to write a business plan, because conditions change so rapidly that the plan is quickly outdated. While it is certainly true that change is a matter of course, the process of preparing a business plan is at least as important as the plan itself. It forces management to think through the business in detail and to set objectives. It allows benchmarks to be set, against which the company's future performance can be monitored.

This is a frequent way of reasoning among those who defend traditional business planning. They realize that the plan may become useless before it has been completed, but feel, at the same time, that the plan can be a way to set goals in the company and to measure the achievements of managers and staff. This, of course, is a contradiction. Why use company management time and other resources to generate something that gets useless in no time at all? Why measure performance against goals that are irrelevant to the reality at hand? Why use measurements that are no longer valid?

We have (in Chapter 2) compared management in a time of fast change with white-water rafting. When planning a trip down such waters one does not use navigation techniques that are made for sailing in well-charted waters with lighthouses and other resources to serve you.

A friend of the old system may object: If the future is difficult to evaluate, let us increase the historical perspective and study the business for a longer historic period. This, unfortunately, just adds more nonsense to the process. "You can never tell the future by the past!"

A CHANGE OF PERSPECTIVE: PLANNING FOR AN UNKNOWABLE FUTURE

The inescapable lesson in our Age of Discontinuity is that we must learn to deal with the unknown! Do we advocate an easy conclusion that planning is useless since we will never know, anyway, what the future will be like? Do we advocate a passive voice of *Que sera, sera?* Of course not! Decision making about the future is the most significant task that a board and CEO faces, and it has to be done. So what is the solution, if there is one?

The clue, as we see it, is a total change of perspective. We must give up asking ourselves what the future will bring, since that approach leads to a meaningless, never-ending sequence of guesswork. What can we do instead? *We need to learn to define the factors or forces in the environment that have the power to affect the company one way or another.*

This approach has revolutionary benefits. One of the obvious ones is that, while the number of events that can affect the company is endless, the number of factors or forces that the company has a relation to or is dependent on is limited. Furthermore, if we structure the potential factors or forces into logical groups of positive or negative impact on the company, and focus on the single factors in each group that *can impact the company most* (*not* those with the highest estimated probability!), the problem becomes manageable.

Accepting that we must plan for an unknown and unknowable future means that the significance of detailed budgets and other forms of guesswork about the future is drastically reduced. We can save enormous amounts of work that used to go into these processes when we realize the uselessness of detailed, sophisticated budgets. Anyone who thinks a budget could be fun to have may make one, of course, but budgeting as a serious, multidepartment, month-long project is highly unlikely to pay off. Put that process where it belongs, in the dustbins of the planned economies!

The liberation from budget making and its tyranny also includes a reluctance to present and publicize prognoses for the year to come to shareholders and financial markets, while explaining to them why this approach has been selected. Only those who are still stuck in the quagmire of discounted cash flow and similar methods would object to this approach. Legal or stock exchange requirements for companies to present prognoses have to be eliminated.

Surf or Drown: A New Perspective on Planning

The conclusion is that we must leave the traditional planning perspective, the sooner the better. But is there an alternative to traditional planning, a realistic alternative that avoids the pitfalls of trend extrapolation and probability numbers? Yes, there is!

What is called for is to use the concepts presented in the previous chapter or some other method that builds on the same perspective, studying the new fundamentals, and building on a reliable diagnosis of the present situation instead of prognoses of an unpredictable future.

The purpose is to assess the forces that may exercise an influence on the company, measure their potential impact, and then systematically reduce their conceivable power to impact the company. The result of this process is that the company becomes measurably more independent of external forces. Its freedom to act—the most important competitive advantage a company can have—is increased step by step. This process offers a solution to the top management tasks of advanced, reliable business planning and risk management at the same time!

As the company's freedom to act increases, so does its ability to survive, grow, and be profitable. Its survival chances increase, since freedom to act means that no single factor or force can hurt the company. Its growth opportunities increase, since the company has more alternatives in every situation and more opportunities to choose favorable possibilities. Its profitability increases, since, in every situation, it has a better negotiating position. Freedom to act makes the company surf on waves of change rather than drown in them.

The overall goal that owners and other parties traditionally express as "increasing company value" can be translated into an actionable and measurable goal for board and management: to increase freedom of action. *Planning for an uncertain and unknowable future aims at reducing company sensitivity to unpredictable events,* increasing its freedom to act. This is strategic business planning and strategic risk management in a nutshell.

A more specific presentation of the process follows, but first here is a quick review of the differences between strategic and operational planning.

Strategic versus Operational Planning: What Is the Difference?

A simple definition of the outcome of strategic planning is "doing the right things" and of operational planning is "doing things right." In an organization a strategic decision at one level of an organization is normally considered an operational decision at the level above. At the end of this is the fact that the board is responsible for the truly strategic matters of the company and the management for the realization of those plans through the operations.

The Baseline Approach presented in this book aims at helping businesses win strategic success by focusing on freedom to act as the company's primary strategic priority.

The Baseline Planning Method[2]

The method that we advocate starts with accepting the fact that the future is genuinely unpredictable. The method saves work and speeds up the strategic planning process by combining, in one sequence, four essential functions of any business plan:

1. The company analysis of the present situation: "where we stand," Archimedes' fixed point

2. A risk (or uncertainty) analysis

3. A concise action plan to help corporate management as well as the individual business units define, prioritize, and reach overall business objectives

4. An educational platform for internal and external communications

Hitting these birds with one stone also ensures that they will be completely aligned and support each other. Experience of the process shows that it consistently helps create unity in the leadership as to company direction and goals. The process is continuous, just as a ship's course is revised constantly, but may be summarized once a year to form a business plan. The process follows a few logical steps based on the concept that a home run touches all four bases.

Home Base

The Business Definition process aims at defining what benefits the company offers to whom and how this is done. It also describes the competitive situation in which the company works. Each one of the various businesses is described from a market perspective (outside-in). To complete this base in practice, use the 25 questions presented in Chapter 4. Repeat until you have covered at least 80 percent of the total *value added* of the company. (Value added is defined as sold goods and services minus the corresponding purchased goods and services of a business area, i.e., the same as many Europeans know as the basis for Value Added Tax, VAT. Value added is in some cases also called gross profit.)

The result of the process is a number of business areas or business definitions, each of them forming a homogeneous and manageable market segment.

The Next Base

The next step is to define the business conditions both per *business area* and consolidated for the entire company. Factors that control and limit the potential of each business area to survive, grow, and be profitable are identified and assessed. The influence of each business area on the total company is also registered.

To complete this base in practice, use the Business Position process available on the Internet. It identifies which of 31 listed environment groups have a relation to the business area and can possibly influence it. Identify, in each relation, which party is Dominant or Underdog (I win-you win), or if the alliance Competitive (I win-you lose). Identify the strength of each of the relationships on a 1–3 scale: 1 = low impact; 2 = strong impact (one or the other party will suffer if the other party exercises its power); or 3 = a fatal relationship (one or the other party could be killed if the other party exercises its power).

This process ends up defining the company's Business Position and assessing crucial threats and opportunities. Information from this segment is weighed into a diagnosis of the conditions each business area faces in its work toward survival, growth, and earnings. It registers unfavorable conditions, areas where action is required, and favorable conditions, which need to be protected and possibly further reinforced.

The process is available as an Internet service at www.realbizonline.com. The same address also offers a demo online.

When the relations to all relevant environment groups of all business areas are calculated, the results are directly applied to creating an overall business plan. Such a plan contains a list of prioritized actions to improve the situation of the company at large and of the respective business areas. These actions are identified in a systematic way, which defines both necessary corrections and preserving and reinforcing favorable conditions.

Three simple questions applied to each unfavorable aspect help structure the process:

1. How can we eliminate the condition that creates the threat?

2. How can we reduce our sensitivity to the threats?

3. How can we reduce the probability of the threat to materialize?

The answers to these questions form the input to the business plan and make it specific, strategic, and highly operational at the same time. The process of prioritizing between the questions will be dealt with below.

Favorable relations to stakeholders send a signal for us to check how we can consolidate and reinforce such relations, where the system warns that some factors behind the good conditions are not as they should. The way to do this is by using a similar three-step approach as in dealing with the threats.

In the case of "fatal" dependencies, stronger than we can adequately deal with, a priority should be to review how to pull back our exposure in a timely way.

It is important to note that this process is not built on guesswork about an uncertain future but assesses significant relationships at this time.

Second Base

When applicable, the process goes into a review of the Stakeholder Management and Reputation Test for each business area and for the overall company. Progress or other change from last year is reviewed. To do this in practice, review the SMART concept described in Chapter 4 and Exhibit 4.8, and specify necessary priorities for improvement in stakeholder relations as part of the action plans.

Third Base

As a checkup, analyze the Cash Performance situation of each business unit and of the combined company. Focus on deviations from expectations, and review progress or other change from last year.

To link cash flow to strategy, list each priority action from the Business Position and the SMART processes and give each one of them a number for use in the accounting system. It is then possible to register the amount of cash used for each priority action and identify them by type, carrier, and purpose of cost. This becomes a unique way to provide a link between all costs and investments on the one hand, and the strategic ambitions of the company on the other hand, for follow-up through the TBM process described in the Cash Performance part of Chapter 4.

A strictly logical sequence in all four bases creates total comparability, both between the various business units and between results for the same business unit over a period of time.

Overall Business Plan

The results of the "home run," the 4-base diagnosis of the present situation, provide direct, free-of-guesswork input to the overall business plan. Each action is identified in a systematic way, which defines both necessary corrections and steps to preserve and reinforce favorable conditions. Such a plan provides a list of prioritized actions to improve the situation of the company at large and of the respective business areas, as well as a platform for comparisons and follow-up. Strategies and action are linked, as are strategic priorities and cash utilization, for anyone to see, management, board members, employees, and other stakeholders.

Making Priorities

Making priorities among actions is a two-level action. The process starts on an overall level, where priorities are made between the various business areas in the company, and then on a detailed level, setting priorities between action alternatives within individual business units.

The Top Management View

The top management of a (larger) company is most often concerned with questions like: "Should we invest in this business? We have several others that seem interesting." Management needs to rank the existing business areas but also to look out for new possibilities that appear from time to time and to select those that provide the best return to the company.

Such decisions force top management to consider a number of factors. We have already ruled out the simple but false way: to make a prognosis and then choose the line that someone guessed is the best. It may feel like a good solution. Unfortunately, it has the drawback of being just about as safe as throwing dice or tossing coins.

We strongly argue for the selection of the business area that offers the best freedom of action, a well-defined measure of the best conditions for survival, growth, and profitability. If that business is also in a growing market, the board can go ahead and invest with reasonable confidence!

But isn't the assumption of market growth also a prognosis, a guess about the future? This is true! There are two observations to be made:

1. Don't invest so much of your resources that you as an investor become dependent on the development of that market (i.e., maintain your own freedom to act).

2. If the market growth is threatened by a known factor, this shows up as a reduced freedom to act of the company, which then becomes a less attractive investment target.

"MONEY TO GREEN": INVESTING IN FREEDOM TO ACT

What if a business area's freedom to act is reduced considerably due to a problem that can be solved easily at low cost? From a management point of view, that is a better venture than a business area with the same freedom to act where limitations can only be reduced at high costs. What management needs to consider is the costs to bring a business into a "safe" area where no single outside factor can force the business to cease its operations. These costs are called "Money to Green," from the green color originally used to designate the field of high BIZ numbers, high level of freedom to act.

Interdependence among Business Areas

When the ambition is to keep a business-based, rather than an accounting-based perspective, it is of vital importance to have an integrated view of the interrelationships between the different business areas of a company. This, for instance, is necessary to be able to assess which business areas can be sold off or closed in order to generate cash for better development of the remaining business areas, for acquisitions, or for other investments.

Exhibit 5.1 shows some typical decision situations from a group management perspective: "Which business areas should we invest in, and which should we prune off?" It is based on the frequent situation that the main threats come from the market. A business area with little freedom to act and in a nongrowth or shrinking market is not a good investment. The opposite, a good investment, is a business area in a high-growth market with a good freedom to act. The ones in between must be investigated more closely and the "Money to Green,"

EXHIBIT 5.1   PROBLEMS/OPPORTUNITIES GRAPH IN A
MULTI-DIVISION COMPANY

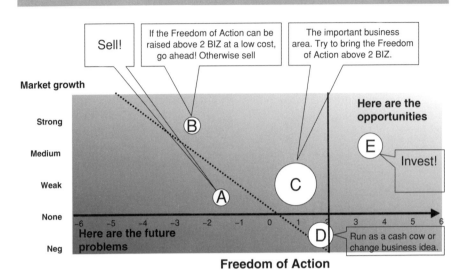

the cost of improving the freedom to act, is a decisive factor for investing or selling off.

In most cases the different business areas are more or less interrelated. From a marketing point of view the company might need a business area with low freedom of action to be able to market products and services from a better business area. The problem is to define how interrelated the company's business areas are.

Then one also has to consider each business area's contribution to the fixed costs of the company (i.e., all costs that are independent of the volume of the business). Some of the fixed costs might be easy to redistribute among the remaining business areas if one is closed or sold off; others are more difficult. Most companies with several business areas have endless internal discussions about the distribution of fixed costs in the company. In situations of selecting what business areas to focus on, it is important to do the allocation correctly in order to avoid surprises, and in agreement, if possible, to avoid unnecessary conflicts in the management team. This is why we describe the method in some detail.

Exhibit 5.2 shows a company with several business areas. Two of them have the same profitability and the same total fixed costs. Given that there is no interrelation in the market place between the two, the first one (*flexible* situation) can easily be pruned off, since its contribution to the true fixed costs is fairly small and those costs can easily be redistributed among the remaining business areas.

EXHIBIT 5.2   WHICH COMPANY WOULD YOU KEEP OR SELL?

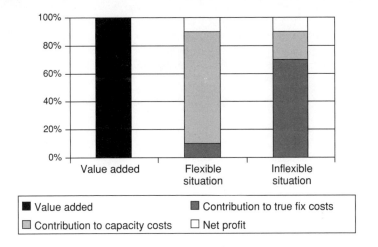

| ■ Value added | ■ Contribution to true fix costs |
| □ Contribution to capacity costs | □ Net profit |

The other one (*inflexible* situation) would be difficult to prune off since its contribution to the true fixed costs is very large.

To decide if business area A can be eliminated one has to calculate the value added it brings to the company to cover its costs and make a profit.

The fixed costs must be split into two categories: *capacity costs* and *true fixed costs*. This split is essential; a wrong approach in this regard can lead to disastrous results. Capacity costs, or costs to maintain a certain capacity, are such fixed costs that vanish in case the business unit is closed or sold off. Employee costs may be an example of capacity costs. True fixed costs remain and have to be redistributed among the remaining business areas. Buildings, in many cases, are examples of true fixed costs.

Then deduct the capacity costs of each business area from its value added and you get the real contribution to the true fixed costs and the profit. That is what must be carried by the remaining business areas if business area A is eliminated.

Case in Point—With Disastrous Consequences

One multibillion-dollar company utilized a single big logistics system to distribute its products. Management ignored the difference between the two types of fixed costs and distributed the total fixed costs of that logistic system according to "best practice," in this case business volume. A business area was considered profitable when its revenues covered the variable costs plus the part of the total fixed costs that had been allocated to it. Instead they should have looked at the contribution from each business area to cover the true fixed costs by subtracting the variable costs and the capacity costs from the revenues. Then they would have known the real contribution that each business area made to the true fixed costs. They made disastrous mistakes when trying to close certain business areas, which did not appear profitable after the best practice distribution of costs, even though they made substantial contributions to cover the true fixed costs of the logistics system.

The Business Unit Management View

The business unit manager wants to make sure that his or her business area can survive, grow, and be profitable. The manager has a number of actions to take in order to improve the situation. The problem is how to prioritize among them.

The simplest way is to calculate the increase of freedom of action (ΔBIZ) per unit of used money. Assume two investments that both would increase the freedom of action of the business area by one BIZ unit. One investment is U.S. $100,000 and the other is U.S. $1,000,000. One should obviously take the first one first.

Quite often some actions coincide in such a way that they solve several problems, sometimes in different business areas. Such actions should be given credit when calculating the improvement of the freedom to act (ΔBIZ) by accomplishing the calculation with the value added from each influenced business area. Since estimating future costs is not an exact science, we propose that the various alternatives for action are classified by powers of 10 in calculating the ΔBIZ per applied amount of money. This is particularly important when you want to compare alternatives between several different business areas. Within each category the preferred action is selected in the business unit(s) that offer the best value added.

Implementation

In this part of the process, the agreed steps are executed in line with what cash flow and other financing permit. It requires familiarity with the company's available Cash to Be Managed (TBM). (See Cash Performance in the Baseline Approach, Chapter 4.)

Only when the company has more cash than needed to pay for all its commitments in due time can it start implementing such activities from the prioritized action list as apply to the whole company. Ideally they should be made in order of priority, but the cash situation may very well force the management to make them in a slightly different order.

Readers may agree that this process is excellently suited for decisions about investments aimed at improving the company's development, but where do operational investments fit in, such as investments in capacity expansion, production equipment, or administrative improvements?

The answer is that these investments get into the planning process when they are called for as solutions to unfavorable circumstances or as defending or improving favorable circumstances. If, for instance, unsatisfactory administrative routines prevent the company from delivering the same or better value for money, compared to the competition, this is a case of unfavorable conditions that need to be eliminated. If they do not play one or the other of these two roles, they should not claim any of the company's limited financial resources.

As a general rule, the strategic initiatives should be given higher priority the less freedom of action the company enjoys. As the freedom of action improves, operational steps play a more significant role.

It is essential to recognize that the planning perspective through the whole process remains outside-in. The company with the best adjustment to its environment has the best chances of survival, growth, and earnings. This is simply an adaptation to the business world of Darwin's basic ground rule "the survival of the fittest."

The Noble Art of Decision Making

Implementation means making decisions. To make a decision is to lose alternatives, since the discarded alternatives are turned down. But if losing alternatives is a way to reduce one's freedom of action, the single most important factor supporting survival, growth, and earnings, should the conclusion be to never make any decisions?

Certainly not! Making no decision is also a decision! How to handle this *Catch-22* situation? The solution is to avoid making big bombastic decisions about things that do not yet need to be decided upon. Try instead to split big decisions into several small ones, sometimes even at the expense of increased costs. The reason, of course, is the same lesson we try to use the whole time: to retain and increase our flexibility. During the time it takes to implement a big decision, the target position at the end of the process may have changed, a situation that causes even bigger costs. The big decision that looked so rational at the initial assessment may in reality turn out to be an expensive relic of planned economy.

What about making a big decision in a go/no-go situation, like investing in a big piece of machinery? Well, then there is only one solution: Make sure you can afford a failure!

Risk Assessment or Risk Management?

As we have shown before in the discussion of risk versus uncertainty, companies do not work under risk, where all potential outcomes are known, such as throwing dice, but under uncertainty, where all potential outcomes are not known.

Once this fact has been accepted, it is obvious that risk assessment is not about scanning the company horizon or making creative scenarios to try to identify risks as possible future events, including their probabilities. Instead, risk assessment is about assessing how well the company is equipped to face an uncertain future. The way to do this is again looking outside-in, identifying factors or forces in the environment that can affect the company, irrespective of how. That is exactly what we do in the business planning process described earlier, especially in the Business Definition and Business Position steps.

Risk management is the task to register these factors, then list the action steps management intends to take to reduce the sensitivity of the company, and finally verify that these steps are properly executed. The consecutive analysis will show the real effect of these steps without a separate risk analysis.

The Business Plan as a Platform
for External and Internal Communication

The information generated in the strategic and operational processes described here creates an excellent platform for consistent and relevant information to all interested parties. What comes out is a consistent and comprehensive picture of:

- The various business areas and business units and the market needs they satisfy
- Their present potential for survival, growth, and earnings, including their interdependence in terms of costs and revenues
- The determinant factors and forces that control and limit the development potential of the respective units
- A prioritized list of action that makes a powerful contribution to the improvement of the company's development potential

EXECUTIVE WEEKEND

All companies need to rethink their strategies now and then, in today's fast-changing business climate more than ever. In many cases this tends to become a long, cumbersome process, perhaps also involving a host of highly paid management consultants. There is an alternative: "Executive Weekend." What is it?

It is a highly focused, intense process, which calls for active involvement from the board and top management, but typically only for three days, an extended weekend or any three consecutive days. The program, as it has been applied in companies of widely different backgrounds, provides a total immersion in the company's critical issues, a mental strategic workout, in which all team members make a highly structured effort to optimize their thinking in a short time. At the end of the third day, the company will typically have a corporate strategic plan worked out in complete partnership with everyone concerned, and consequently with the full endorsement of all involved.

The method applies the same philosophy as companies increasingly use in manufacturing, sales, administration, and in other parts of their business: Cut the slack! A normal management consultant uses weeks for lengthy interviews, intermediate reports, long meetings with separate groups, and then tries to build it all together into a combined approach. In Executive Weekend all those steps are speeded up and welded together into one unified, computer-supported process, with everyone involved, at the same time, under the same roof. The first day is used for the Business Definition process and the first part of a computer-supported and computer-guided interview with the whole team. Normally at noon the second day, the process ends up in a CheckList, summarizing all issues that have been up for discussion, along with the answers and any comments that have been made. In the afternoon, participants get a 40+pages-long computer-generated report, with charts, graphs, tables, and detailed conclusions. This report provides the platform for the discussions the second and third days. Each key factor is given time and attention. Decisions are made and responsibilities are assigned, then and there. At the end of the third day, typically, the team goes back home with a deeply shared feeling of achievement. Every participant can buy into the program, having been part of its creation, and at the same time each has heard the views and priorities of all the others.

The quality of the process is unusual, as is the speed and low cost, and the focus is on business realities and priorities the whole time!

The Executive Weekend approach is a special application of Baseline Reporting. However, even in the normal progress of company life, the Baseline Approach helps boards and management keep their focus on strategies, rather than on day-to-day operational aspects and standard financial reporting.

NOTES

1. Peter F. Drucker, *Managing in Turbulent Times*, Harper & Row, New York, 1980.
2. To avoid unnecessary repetition in this chapter, see Chapter 4 for a broad presentation of the Baseline concept, including the Baseline fundamentals, which are also the essence of the planning process.

CHAPTER 6

"Where Was the Board?"

Governance—the corporate kind
is, like justice, often blind.

Hank Paulson, CEO of Goldman Sachs, stated, "In my lifetime, American business has never been under such scrutiny, and to be blunt, much of it is deserved."1 Public awareness of the crucial role of the boards in running companies has increased, as one of the consequences of the accounting crisis. Corporate governance and strategic management has received more attention from media and the general public in the last few years than many of the actors on the stage may ever have wanted. A question that has come back many times in the discussion of the accounting scandals has been "Where was the board?"

The question seems to be justified in many cases, not only in the sense that the lines of responsibility between boards and management sometimes seemed to have been blurred. Many boards appear to have conceded all their authority and let management run the show on its own. Many of the boards never even seemed to ask tough questions. In later years, however, a "counterrevolution" seems to be on its way among board members. A survey made by McKinsey[2] reported that a majority of board members would like to be more involved in strategy and other long-term issues, but also that they sometimes felt that they lacked the information needed.

An important issue is what material the board gets from management to do its work. In too many cases, boards seemed to have accepted accounting-based information as reliable, relevant, and useful, when in reality it was neither. In this respect, boards unfortunately reflect opinions in society at large. Our experience is that boards enjoy getting more business-related information, rather than finance-related. The material that comes out of Baseline processes gets a high rating from board members.

This is a more serious and far-reaching issue than a few, well, quite a few cases of downright fraudulent reporting. Some have interpreted the accounting scandals as a crisis of capitalism, the free market system, or free enterprise. That is obviously exaggerated. But—and that is a big enough issue to scare many traditionalists—it is a crisis of *accounting* in its self-assumed role as one of the main props of capitalism, the free market system, and free enterprise. If accounting is left in its traditional role as a main pillar on which the credibility of the free market system is built, then this could pose a literally earth-shattering problem. The progress of the world market economy depends on delegating accounting to its original role, as discussed in Chapter 1. At an international conference[3] in the fall of 2002, Dr. Sherman Katz, Scholl Chair in International Business Center for Strategic and International Studies, made a clear distinction between accounting and corporate governance: "Corporate governance is too important to be left to the accountants, lawyers and investment bankers."

This distinction is of crucial importance. Management and business in general have placed an exaggerated amount of trust in reporting based on numbers that have come out of the accounting system. When it suddenly dawns on a broad public in investing and other business functions that accounting was never as strong a hand rail as was widely thought, the confusion may well trigger a strong reaction. The "System Failure" that *Fortune* writes about in the article quoted above is not a matter of minor problems in accounting practices, problems that can be fixed with new rules and stricter supervision. It is, as we see it, and as we have tried to share at the outset of this book, a failure in the accounting system as such, or, more specifically, in the way the output from the accounting system is used. To get more qualified support for advanced decision-making, we need to go beyond accounting. This is a learning process and a challenge that deeply affects the role and work of many boards, corporate governance in a wide sense.

Meanwhile, a development trend has become increasingly visible. Earlier, a great proportion of major and relevant decision influences were, in fact, covered in accounting. Today, decision makers find less and less comfort in accounting numbers. The conclusion is that board and management must find other guidelines than traditional accounting statements. It should for example lead to a shakeup of the old tradition that board meetings must start with a review of company financials.

Much of the discussion about corporate governance in later years has focused on the buildup of the board and on basic board room practices. Other aspects have included board room ethics. Others have stayed on specific issues, such as the role of the board committees (e.g., the audit, nomination, or compensation committees). All these aspects of corporate governance are important,[4] and we will try to make a quick review of them. But we will not stop at these issues. We will move to what we feel is an issue of even higher priority: not only the process but also the contents of board considerations, the factors that reveal or indicate if the company is on its way toward success or failure. And to see signs of success or failure, we must look outside the narrow trail of accounting.

A FIVE-STEP BOARDWALK

Step 1: Board Room Basics

It seems that more than half of what has been published under the headline Corporate Governance has dealt with what we might call Board Room Basics.

We do not want to downplay this discussion. It seems to have been a necessary awakening process, although in the aftermath much of what has been said now seems obvious. We are thinking of the basic demands on board work and board composition, the demands that some of the business media have turned into the beauty contests of boards, their check lists in evaluating good or bad boards. Most of the lists include such items as:

Board Independence

For a board to be useful it must have the guts to take an independent view of the issues on the agenda, and perhaps on the agenda itself. That usually means that all board members, or a strong majority of them, should stay clear of other significant ties with the company than their board directorship. Board members must have the guts, the integrity, and the opportunity to disagree with the CEO, when necessary. The role of the nominating committee in this process is of course essential. The frequent practice in the United States—to combine the roles of chairman and chief executive into one person—as opposed to the European tradition of a clear distinction between the roles, is now being increasingly discussed, and many U.S. experts support a development toward a checks-and-balances system.

Board Competence

The board members must have enough experience and background to be capable of assessing the choices and alternatives the company faces in crossroads situations. That background could be gained through good work in executive positions in other companies, academic merits, or other top positions. Again, the role and independence of the nominating committee is crucial.

Board Time

Board members must be willing and able to take enough time to do their homework between meetings, to study the material they get from company management, and also to get second opinions and alternative views from other contacts and sources other than management.

Board Attendance

Only very strong excuses for missing board meetings should be accepted, and only for very limited numbers of board meetings. Attendance should not only be defined as sitting there; it should also be defined as standing up and contributing to the decisions of the board.

Board Guidelines

Fewer boards than one might think have written down clear guidelines. Even fewer have made sure that board members sign on to them when they are asked to join. Obviously, when such written guidelines are established, they also need to be reviewed from time to time.

Step 2: Board Room Ethics

If Board Room Basics is a first step, Board Room Ethics is a short next step on the Boardwalk. Like Board Room Basics, it ought to be self-evident. Unfortunately, one event after the other has shown that it isn't. Some of the obvious items to be considered in Board Room Ethics include:

Bribery and Corruption

Since 1997, the OECD has a treaty, the Anti-Bribery Convention, in force, and more than 30 countries, including the biggest and most active trading countries in the world, have ratified it. Making sure that the company has adequate policies and checking systems in place to protect against incidences of bribery is certainly a Board Room issue.

Collusion

Board members have been known to get highly profitable deals for themselves through providing well paid consulting, building, air transportation, brokerage, legal, investment banking, and other services. In fact, according to one organization, the Executive Compensation Advisory Services, one company in four is involved in such potential or real conflicts of interest. Other board members have obtained corporate contributions to their favorite political parties, foundations, educational institutions, and other causes. These, and other *related-party transactions*, as they are called in Nasdaq regulations, have often been made without the openness and disclosure that stakeholders could expect.

Responsibility

The overriding ethical issue is perhaps that the board as an entity and individual board members accept that they are ultimately responsible for creating a corporate culture based on ethical guidelines and are also ultimately responsible for creating processes to deal with occurrences of nonethical behavior in the company.

Step 3: Auditing

The board auditing committee, preferably consisting of independent board members, working with independent internal and external auditors, is the primary instrument to ensure that the accounting work of the company is performed according to rules and guidelines, whether GAAP or IAS or FASB or any combination. This, of course, does not guarantee that the accounting data are meaningful or relevant; accounting in itself can not create such guarantees. But it does ensure that the numbers are beyond reproach from tax and legal viewpoints, and that the books give shareholders and other stakeholders a technically correct numbers-based view of the company's past development. As the examples on auditing (Chapter 9) show very clearly, auditors must learn to use tools other than accounting-based tools, such as the Baseline Approach.

Step 4: Compensation

An issue that has gained well-deserved attention lately is the principles and amounts of the compensation that the board sets for itself (although formally approved by the shareholders) and for the top executives. Without going into a lot of details, a few thoughts may be offered:

Principles

The compensation committee is sure to gain credibility if neither the CEO nor other top company executives serve on the committee. One guideline that may be relevant is to prioritize directors' fees in terms of shares and to make out, in principle, all compensation to managers as shares, fees, and/or salaries, and limit other perks to a minimum. The hot issue of options or shares as compensation to executives, and how to expense options, if they are used, has sailed to the forefront in the accounting scandals aftermath. Another issue is loans from the company to its officers—a practice that is either forbidden or closely restricted in many countries.

Amounts

In the early 1980s, U.S. companies paid their CEOs on average 40 times the average salary of the company employees. In the late 1990s that figure had changed to 400 times! The companies hit by the SEC and legal processes after the accounting scandals of the last few years featured CEO salaries that were twice as high as other similar companies! The levels of compensation are certainly an issue for the board to look at, probably at sessions without top management present!

When deciding on compensation levels, the committee should have access to payrolls even for employees that report to the top team, to ensure that the relations are reasonable. Organizations like Directorship and the Conference Board have statistics that may be useful.

Step 5: The Top of the Boardwalk

The board should focus on its top responsibility: *company success.* In the general media debate, it sounds sometimes as if such corporate governance issues as those listed above—Boardwalk items 1 through 4—are the main functions of the work of the board. Of course they are not. These issues, no matter how important they are, are only the framework of how the board is supposed to work. It is not the contents.

The overriding purpose and top responsibility of the board is to support and guide management in its work to lead the company away from failure and toward success. Many board members seem to feel that they are not as involved in these strategic overall processes as they should be. In fact, in a major study of nearly 200 board directors, sponsored by McKinsey,[5] 44 percent expressed concerns that they did "not fully understand key value drivers." In the accounting-driven culture we have had, this has too often meant that board members, even when they have been involved, have spent many long hours poring over endless columns of accounting data, to the detriment of more strategic discussions. Is there an alternative, a way out from the tyranny of what former SEC director Arthur Levitt called "The Numbers Game"?[6]

The accounting perspective is too much rear-view oriented, and too little oriented toward the present, not to mention the future. As we have seen several times in our work with small and big companies, many boards have benefited greatly from a more business-oriented, as opposed to an accounting-oriented, perspective. Such a business-oriented board perspective should be encouraged and facilitated by the board chairperson. One way to do it is to follow the Baseline Approach.

THE BASELINE APPROACH TO CORPORATE GOVERNANCE

The Baseline Approach has been used successfully as a way to support strategic management, crossroads decisions and corporate governance issues. It is a methodic, step-by-step process that helps the board keep a focus on business essentials and away from accounting details.

The four areas identified in the Baseline Approach show where serious threats and potential problems often originate. It helps the board and management to focus their attention on core issues, rather than on meaningless columns of more or less irrelevant numbers.

A first step toward a renaissance in corporate governance, in the sense of a higher sensitivity to strategic priorities, is to rework board meeting agendas. A good way is to start, at least at one meeting per year, with the company's standing on the four Baseline fundamentals (for a more detailed review of the Baseline fundamentals, please see Chapter 4):

1. A review and updating of the company's Business Definition(s), its vision and mission statements, the process by which the Business Definitions have been established, and its level of endorsement by various stakeholders

2. A review and updating of the company's Business Position, changes since the previous meeting, and action taken by management to eliminate or reduce the strategic threats indicated by the dangerous level *A3, C3, D3*, and most certainly *U3* relationships

3. A review and updating of the company's Business Reputation statement, with a special focus on the red flag items, the items where the company either has not made adequate measurements or has received low scores, or where the scores have deteriorated since the previous measurement

4. A review of the detailed Cash Performance Statement, with management comments and feedback on its strategic application of funds, and where the Charge and Focus measures have shown that enough funds are, indeed, being allocated to strategic priority areas

After a strategic process of this kind, at least once a year, the board knows that it has given attention and time to important strategic conditions for company survival, growth, and earnings—the factors and forces that are really the board's primary responsibility. They are, of course, also the primary responsibility of the management, and should consistently be revisited as the fundamentals of relevant reporting and disclosure.

Having dealt with these four fundamentals at the top of the agenda, and given them enough time and attention, the board can proceed to traditional items, such as management reports on financials and operations.

When major strategic crossroads decisions are up for discussion, the board would benefit from a getting a management review of the two or three major alternatives that are being considered, based on the perspectives of these four fundamentals.

In the choice between the alternatives the board is considering,

1. How will the Business Definitions be affected, if we choose alternative A or B?

2. How will the Business Positions come out? Will one or the other of the alternatives influence our relationships and dependencies? Will we come out with a stronger Business Position, if we choose A or B? Or, above all, will we increase or decrease our freedom to act?

3. How will our Business Reputation factors be affected by the alternative action lines?

4. How will the Cash Performance be affected by one or the other of the alternatives?

Chances are that a well structured board discussion along these lines will help the board make a considerably more enlightened decision than if these issues are not considered. One more thing is obvious and proves the point that these issues are not selected arbitrarily: If none of these four factors are affected, then the choice is not really a strategic issue!

Case in Point—A New Insurance Venture

A major insurance group was getting ready to launch a new subsidiary for an entirely new business idea, providing liability insurance to industrial manufacturers with products that could be expected, over their lifetime, to cause environmental concerns, potentially leading to environment-related claims. Companies that were seen as potential clients included refrigerator and car manufacturers.

The project group that prepared the launch of the new subsidiary had followed the strict company manual for due diligence in start-ups. It was ready to go, when it made the last presentation of the business plan to the corporate board. At the presentation, the chief internal auditor wanted to make sure that no stones had been left unturned in the preparation process. He had had previous experience of parts of the Baseline Reporting process, so to make sure that the new company would optimize its chances for success he suggested that the project be exposed to a Business Position analysis.

The result of the analysis showed that the project suffered from seven fatal threats, which had escaped the attention of the project group. The Kite and the Business Position graphs looked like Exhibit 6.1.

The project group realized that a start-up along the lines they had planned would lead to a disaster. They took half a year to reshuffle the cards completely, and came up with a reorientation of the business idea and several of the other parameters. After half a year, a new analysis showed an entirely different picture, as seen in Exhibit 6.2.

The company was launched under the new premises, with a vastly improved outlook for success, although with one fatal threat remaining in the business environment horizon. The venture was successful. After one and a half year in business, a third analysis showed a very strong kite.

EXHIBIT 6.1   NEW INSURANCE COMPANY PROJECT—THE FIRST ANALYSIS

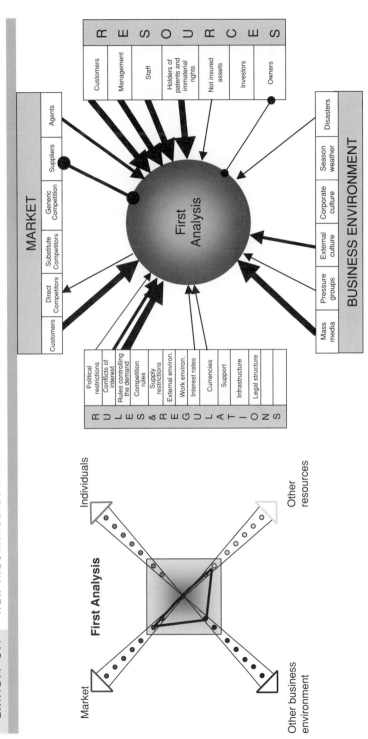

EXHIBIT 6.2 NEW INSURANCE COMPANY PROJECT—THE SECOND ANALYSIS

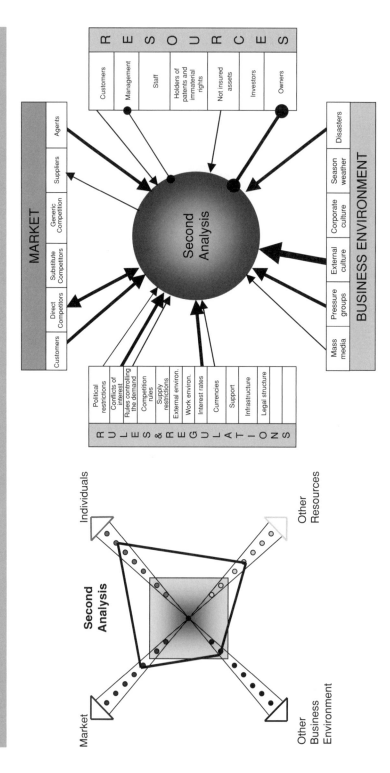

EXHIBIT 6.3   NEW INSURANCE COMPANY PROJECT—
18 MONTHS LATER

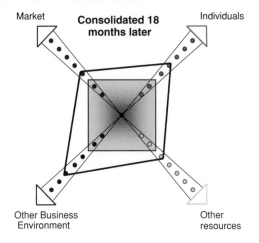

Market   **Consolidated 18 months later**   Individuals

Other Business Environment   Other resources

Management was totally convinced that they had taken all the measures that were consistent with a traditional project approach in their original preparation process. All members of the project team were experienced and had a successful track record from other management positions. They just know that the Baseline Approach in this case opened their eyes to factors that would otherwise have escaped them. Had the project been started without this approach, it would almost certainly have led to a disaster and the whole idea would have died. Today the environmental product liability insurance is a useful and self-sustaining part of the group's program.

To make the picture complete, and as a PS to the story: The final analysis showed that there still was one area that could create problems. The board was fully aware of this risk, when it gave the go-ahead. Two years later, it turned out that this problem area did, indeed, create trouble for the project. Since the analysis had pointed to the problem, management was aware of it and kept it under supervision. As a result of that, the problem, when it came, could be managed properly and without disturbing the whole picture.

The comprehensive Baseline Approach in this case provided great support in a strategic crossroad situation, like the start-up of a new business venture. A Baseline diagnosis and report provided the board with a picture where risks and benefits were illustrated much more clearly than through accounting-based methods.

Case in Point—A Multidivision Company Goes Down the Drain
A major multidivision company, mainly in the transportation business, had a board of which many members had been recruited not for reasons of their knowledge or network in the areas of interest to the company but rather for their past services to support the

interest of the main owner. The books were "cooked": repairs of old equipment had been capitalized and not depreciated as they should have been. As a consequence, the asset side of the balance sheet was strongly exaggerated. However, this was considered necessary to keep equity ratios on a positive level. New equipment was leased.

When a new CEO took over, he wanted to make a complete reorganization of the group. According to the rules for internal auditing set by the board, it was also time for a groupwide internal audit of all parts of the group.

The group entered a program of Baseline analyses for each separate business area, and then consolidated them into a full picture. It completed the whole program, including interviews with the management groups of all business areas, and with full reports with graphs and charts to help the board run its strategic review in a remarkably short time. It reached an entirely new platform of understanding of where the group was, and where it was heading. The process, as in all Baseline analyses, focused on the business parameters, not on financials.

One of the most comprehensive diagrams that came out of the process was a presentation of each business area in a context of size, relation to the core business, position in terms of market growth and size, restrictions and limitations, and opportunities.

When the results, including the diagrams, were presented to the board, it realized that the new information revealed an entirely new situation of the group, a situation that it was not aware of. The presentation of the disastrous business positions of core businesses was simply too much for the board members. They decided not to consider the new information, and went on with their reorganization project. The "messenger," the chief internal auditor who had provided the revealing information, was fired.

A few years later it was no longer possible to keep the group together. The core businesses required a capital injection of MUSD 300 to survive. Most of the subsidiaries were in a financial mess. Parts of the group are presently for sale for next to nothing. (See Exhibit 6.4.)

EXHIBIT 6.4   MULTIDIVISION GROUP FACING RESTRUCTURING NEEDS

Group in need of strategic actions

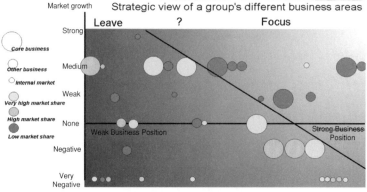

The main goal of corporate governance should be to increase the freedom to act of the company. The case in point above serves as an example of the consequences when that is not the case.

Case in Point—Two Dramatic Lessons in Seven Hours

An old, traditional industrial group called us to get an analysis of its main business area. They just wanted a demo of one business area to see what would come out of the system.

We started with the Business Definition process together with group management. The group had had two main business areas (read: *product lines*) for literally 100 years. The outside-in perspective revealed that in reality they had six business areas. The four "new" business areas had been treated as part of the big ones, during all years. The reason was that they were the same products. However, the products were used for entirely different purposes, by different user groups. The group had lost revenues during all these years by not putting enough resources into the development of these areas.

We continued with the biggest business area, based in London, and the system started to ask questions to group management. Within five hours the Business Definition and the Business Conditions processes were finished. While the system produced the diagnosis and wrote the report there was a short break.

Then we started the Strategic Seminar, where we listed actions to be carried out in order to improve the situation. At the end of the seminar one of the members started to behave strangely. We finally asked what was going on. Management then revealed that the real purpose of the whole activity was to get a second opinion on a more than six-months-long strategic development project. This project had been given to one of the big international consulting groups, based in London, at a cost of more than £1,000,000.

What had happened was that our one-day process had come up with exactly the same problems and actions as the big group had found out in six months, apart from one thing: The other consultants recommended that one large production facility should be sold off. The conclusion of our strategic seminar was the opposite: "Keep it and, if possible, buy more capacity, since this is the only strong foothold you have in the fight with the giants on the market."

About a month later, we were called back to discuss further analyses. We then asked if they had got the final report from the big consultants. If so: "What were the main differences in the conclusions?"

"Yes, we have got it, and there are no main differences," was the answer.

"How come? They recommended you to sell off the production site!"

"Yes, but they changed their minds when they were faced with the result from the strategic seminar with you!"

NOTES

1. In a speech, quoted by *Fortune*, June 24, 2002, in an article called "System Failure."
2. *The McKinsey Quarterly*, March 8, 2005.

3. The conference was organized by the Confederation of Swedish Enterprise, in Stockholm, Sweden, September 5, 2002.

4. For a review of many significant corporate governance issues, and a "rating" of how some companies do on these issues, see *Business Week*, October 7, 2002, "The Best & Worst Boards." *Fortune*, September 2002, also has a good article going into a broad coverage of the trends for improved corporate board work under the title "In Corporate America It's Cleanup Time."

5. The study was reported in an article by Robert F. Felton and Mark Watson, "Change Across the Board," in *The McKinsey Quarterly*, No. 4, 2002.

6. "The Numbers Game" was the title of a speech by Arthur Levitt at New York University, September 1998. It was in many ways a precursor and warning call against the accounting disaster explosion that erupted a few years later. It was also reviewed in Arthur Levitt's book, written with Paula Dwyer, *Take on the Street: What Wall Street and Corporate America Don't Want You to Know. What You Can Do to Fight Back*, Random House, New York, 2002.

CHAPTER 7

Due Diligence or
Undue Negligence?

Diligence that's less than due,
deserves a rough and tough review.

Virtually every serious study done shows that it is
very difficult to bring off a successful merger.
(Business Week *editorial, October 1997*)

THE FINE LINE BETWEEN SUCCESS AND FAILURE IN MERGERS AND ACQUISITIONS

Of all the challenges that boards and management teams face, there is probably no one that is more difficult than to successfully carry through a merger or an acquisition. The dismal track records of failed mergers prove this beyond reasonable doubt. Yet, the urge to merge seems irresistible.

Although with some up and down waves, merger and acquisition (M&A) activity for a long time now has been at high levels, in numbers and values. So have the merger hangovers. The history of corporate mergers is a world of big bubbles bursting and well-inflated balloons suddenly punctured or slowly fizzling. The time span between celebration and hangover is often surprisingly short. Reality has often set in long before the press releases have faded, with their trumpet fanfares about anticipated synergies, increased shareholder value, and global market advances. And reality speaks an entirely different language, one about turf battles, key employees being fired or leaving, plant and office closings, customers and suppliers getting fed up, and disappointed investors losing their savings. "In fact, mergers and acquisitions in recent years have produced a disheartening negative 12 percent return on investment."[1]

Mergers outside the corporate world are not any easier. In the wake of 9/11, the United States announced the merger of more than 100 departments and government agencies with very different functions and cultures among their more than 170,000 employees, combining them under one hat into a department of Homeland Security. No doubt corporate officers, academic experts, and the media will follow this process with much curiosity.

Case in Point—DaimlerChrysler

Few corporate mergers in recent years have gotten more coverage in the media than DaimlerChrysler. Official confidence that it would be a success was sky-high, when the merger was announced, in 1998. When the new company's shares were listed on the New York Stock Exchange, the word from DaimlerChrysler executives was: "Seventy percent of mergers have fallen short of expectations. We don't care about that. We'll be in the 30 percent that succeed."

The size of the merger was remarkable, in dollars and numbers of people affected, even for the M&A-loaded 1990s. Although the difficulties were recognized, conditions seemed favorable. The two merging companies had been successful in terms of growth, earnings, and public approval. Chrysler had gone through ups and downs, but their profits in 1998 were impressive. At the time of the merger, Chrysler had the highest profit per car of any automaker in the world. Its profits were a considerable part, in fact half, of the combined company's profit. The Chrysler Jeep Cherokee was the strongest brand in the fast-growing Sports Utility Vehicle segment.

Daimler Benz as well had an excellent earnings record, and few cars have such a reputation among car buyers as Mercedes, considered by many branding experts to be one of the most well-respected brands in the world, in all categories.

The "merger of equals," as it was officially proclaimed, seemed to many financial and automotive industry writers like a perfect match. It was intended to prove that cross-cultural and cross-national company marriages could succeed. CEOs on both sides painted the picture of a wonderful future. The merger was certainly well researched and analyzed, before the decision was taken. Nobody would accuse high-level German executives of speeding through a business transaction of this magnitude without due process.

And yet, less than a year after the bold statements, the picture had changed dramatically. We all know what happened, of course: Real and predicted profits became huge losses. Share prices plunged by two-thirds, a loss of $40 to $60 billions of investor holdings. Talk about increasing shareholder value! Suppliers revolted, in response to demands of across-the-board price cuts. Investors initiated lawsuits and protests in Germany and in the United States. 25,000 to 30,000 employees, one-fifth of Chrysler's workers, were let go, idling 5 to 10 plants. Top executives were fired. Many of those who were not fired left on their own. Market share and momentum was lost, with unsold inventory piling up. Cultural differences were described as 180 degrees, not quite the announced harmony. Finally, a "recall" was made, of a unique kind even for the automotive industry, renaming the whole transaction from "merger of equals" to a pure takeover.

The DaimlerChrysler acquisition has a chance to go down in history as an alliance that has gone from a higher expectation level than perhaps any other, to a more disappointing outcome than any other, in a shorter period of time than any other.

How could this transaction go so wrong? How could two major companies, with all the resources one could imagine, with lots of due diligence, and both sides basically in the same business, automotive engineering, miss their merger mark by such a wide margin? If these companies went from anticipated success to a near complete failure in such a short period of time, it is no wonder that other companies experience difficulties in mergers or acquisitions.

WANTED: A NEW KIND OF DUE DILIGENCE

What could DaimlerChrysler have done differently? That question, no doubt, will be asked in corporate headquarters and business schools all over the world. What can other companies do differently when they prepare a merger or an acquisition?

What seems obvious is that dealmakers and investors need improved procedures, as shown not only by DaimlerChrysler but also by the high number of other unsuccessful mergers, 70 to 90 percent by many estimates. Something must be very wrong, when there is such a wide spread between the rosy forecasts and the harsh reality, in so many cases. The preparations that go into them are often substantial. Lawyers and financial experts are engaged. Expensive consultants are involved. Professional and dedicated boards and management teams on both sides spend weeks or months going through the books.

The issue is of great importance. Each failed merger is more than just another lost business deal, even if that is serious enough. Most of them involve human tragedies, lost jobs, forced relocations, lost savings, communities losing their employment base, and lost confidence in business and its leaders.

WHY MERGERS FAIL

Why do so many mergers fail? The reasons are probably as many as the mergers. Each new merger seems to offer new potential for failure. After-the-fact reasons (or more correctly excuses) are legion, and they range from accounting gimmicks to corporate culture.

The sad records provide more evidence than anyone needs that traditional due diligence methods are less than perfect. We are not going to present a short check list[2] on how to succeed in mergers and acquisitions. We recognize that M&A is a difficult function, even with the best intentions, and under the best circumstances. What we feel is needed is an entirely new perspective—a nonfinancial perspective. Just as a company is not primarily the financial numbers, it is important to recognize that M&A is not primarily a financial operation! It is a *business* operation, and should be treated as such.

It seems obvious that there is a need for other and better data before the mergers, to support the decision making, and also to handle the integration after the fact. An accounting-based perspective is not the answer. Neither do accounting gimmicks, "pooling of interest," "goodwill" accounting, or discounted cash flow guesswork, or others, save an ill-conceived merger from failure. Accounting-focused M&A processes have had their time. Their records speak for themselves. A company is not the numbers—it is the forces that drive the numbers. A successful merger (unfortunately, the expression has a ring of oxymoron) must be based on the driving forces of the two companies involved, not on the accounting numbers, manipulated or not. Those driving forces of business, not the accounting or legal aspects, must be the main objective of the due diligence. Any other approach risks to be one of the much too frequent cases of undue negligence.

If M&As were mainly financial transactions, then the experts ruling the financial sector should be able to provide a long list of examples of successful mergers. Unfortunately, that is not consistent with the track records of bank mergers and other company alliances in finance. Here are just a few examples of questionable mergers from the financial area:

- Financial services company Conseco Inc. acquired Green Tree Financial in 1998 for close to $8 billion. Debt payments have strained the acquiring company and will force it to sell other business units.

- J.P. Morgan's megamerger with Chase in September 2000 was followed by tough times for the combined superbanking house with venture-capital losses and bad loans, including to Enron, pushing down earnings and stock prices, and pushing out investors and clients. Dozens of executives left the combined company, despite generous retention bonuses.

- Deutsche Bank bought National Discount Brokers in 2000, only to sell it at a loss in 2001.

- Zurich Financial Services Group bought Scudder with "disappointing results."

The conclusion of the less-than-perfect track record of acquisitions, even in the financial arena, is: Successful M&As cannot be built on financial skills.

True, there are exceptions: After much turmoil, it seems that the Citigroup-Travellers merger has hit the ground running (although, in 2005, this high-profile Wall Street marriage, just as its counterparts in Hollywood, seems to be followed by a divorce). The First Union-Wachovia merger is still in its early years.

The whole attitude towards mergers and acquisitions has to change, and different methods need to be developed and applied. A crucial problem is that much of the "due diligence" practiced in preparing mergers and acquisitions is steeped in the molds of legal, financial, and accounting practices and procedures. A "simple" improvement would be to treat mergers and acquisitions more as *business* transactions, not primarily as *financial* transactions. If they were seen with a business focus before, during, and after the event, chances are that (1) many M&As would be halted in time, and (2) those that were pursued would have a better chance of success.

Business Is People

A business perspective, with a focus on people and relationships, rather than a financial perspective, with a focus on numbers, would reveal what accounting never can achieve. Some of the conditions and qualities, as well as risks and threats, of any two companies involved in a merger are simply not visible through traditional accounting-colored glasses.

Here are some basic facts:

- M&As are forward looking—accounting is not.
- M&As must be treated as business transactions—not primarily financial.
- M&As succeed or fail, just like most other business ventures, because of people and relationships—not necessarily the fortes of the accounting and legal specialists.

There Are Better Ways

There are better ways to run an all-inclusive due diligence process. But that requires a new approach, covering important *business fundamentals*.

The four groups of business fundamentals that form the cornerstones of Baseline Reporting offer clues to a successful merger—or warn the boards, when conditions are precarious. The key is the Business Position and the SMART data before and after the merger. Baseline Reporting provides tools to measure this.

It would be preposterous to come up with a post-the-fact prescription for a merger such as DaimlerChrysler's. What we know is that, when the Baseline Approach has been used in preparing and executing mergers and acquisitions, one of two things has happened:

1. Quite frequently, the analysis has resulted in a well-documented recommendation not to pursue the merger plans. (This, incidentally, has happened also in the occasional cases when a CEO has made up his mind in favor of an acquisition in advance of the due process.)

2. In some cases, the analysis has ended in a green light. In those cases the process has given important guidance for a successful execution.

HOW DOES THE BASELINE APPROACH TO DUE DILIGENCE WORK?

A Way to Sharpen Due Diligence Processes

The main reason for its success is that the Baseline Approach does not stop at accounting data. It goes to the core of company life, to the fundamentals of the business situation of the two companies in question.

It starts by comparing and analyzing *each one of the two companies* concerned by the four fundamentals presented in Baseline Reporting (i.e., Business Definition, Business Position, Business Reputation, and Cash Performance). (For details, see Chapter 4.) It then adds *a consolidated review for the potential combined company.* The process includes:

1. A review and updating of the Business Definition of each of the companies, how strong and viable the respective Business Definitions are, and how well they are understood and endorsed

2. A review and updating of the Business Position of each of the companies, with special attention to the strategic threats indicated by level 2 and 3 relationships

3. A review and updating of the SMART Business Reputation diagram of the companies, with a special focus on the red flags, the weak numbers, or the nonexisting measures

4. A review of Cash Performance, with management comments, for each of the companies involved

Having finished that process, when the three reports, Company A, Company B, and Company A+B, are placed next to each other, they reveal clearly and in great detail important similarities and differences between the companies, risks and potential threats, and also strength factors and opportunities. In a positive case, the process will show that the combination increases the competitiveness, the freedom to act, by evening out some weaknesses, so that the combined company, in those regards, comes out stronger than the two separate companies. In other cases, the weak points of the two companies pull in the same direction, so that the combined company comes out more sensitive to some threats than the two companies would be, one by one, reducing their freedom to act. The report becomes a very clear platform for the strategic pre-merger discussion, the price negotiations, and the decision-making process of the two boards and management teams.

This study of the two separate companies, compared with the potentially merged company, also serves as a basis to establish a reasonable price level (please, *not* "value"!). One common reason for many failed mergers is that the price was too high, which resulted in a weakening of the financial viability of the new company.

Case in Point—Saved by the Bell!

A company in the farming machinery industry had set its sights on acquiring a smaller company that was a market leader in one type of farming equipment. All conventional financial and legal due diligence work had been made. The company seemed to be not quite a star but not too bad. It appeared that the combined company had reasonable chances to develop well. Management had made up its mind and had prepared all the material for an upcoming board meeting in a week's time, when they incidentally met with one of the authors of this book and were convinced that they should add a Baseline Reporting analysis to the board material.

The analysis was performed in two days and showed the kite diagram in Exhibit 7.1. With such a weak kite, the company would have required a substantial injection of many kinds of resources—management, marketing, and other—to have a chance of success. The acquiring company stopped its plans immediately. The acquisition target was bought by another company and went bankrupt in 18 months.

EXHIBIT 7.1   M&A CANDIDATE WENT BANKRUPT 18 MONTHS LATER

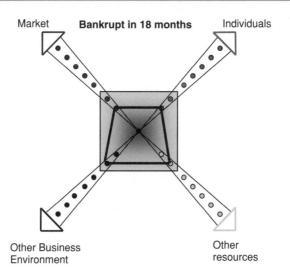

Market   **Bankrupt in 18 months**   Individuals

Other Business Environment

Other resources

Case in Point—The Swiss (Near) Miss

A Swiss company planned to acquire a company in Germany. Most of the due diligence was already finished and the CFO, the company lawyer, and a few others from the top management team visited the German company to finalize the process.

The CEO stayed in the Zurich-based headquarters and had called in a Baseline team to perform an analysis based on the information available that day.

When the management team returned from Germany the following day and presented their findings, they were still very much in favor of the acquisition. The CEO asked them about four serious threats that had come up in the Baseline analysis. It turned out that none of them had surfaced in the months of conventional due diligence. The deal was cut off at the last minute.

A Tough Process, but Surprisingly Fast

Whenever a process of this kind is used, chances are that a number of misguided M&A efforts are aborted at an early stage, saving shareholders big amounts of money, and saving employees, customers, and others affected from big disappointments, losses, and trouble. For those M&A projects that come to fruition, the business-oriented process will increase the success rate substantially. If the decision is made to go ahead with the M&A, the process has also produced an uncompromising blueprint showing the new leadership the strong and weak points of the transaction. This blueprint serves as a background for a post-merger action plan. If, as is frequently the case, the two management groups have been partners in working out the analysis, they feel a great deal of ownership of the outcome, an excellent platform for future cooperation.

Points of strategic importance come out very clearly, making it easy for the board to keep a focus on essentials and to monitor deviations in all four parameters, through frequent follow-up analyses in the first year or so after the transaction. The board can also report on such progress or deviations to all stakeholders concerned, in a clear and consistent manner, with graphs, charts, and data.

As experience shows, traditional accounting data and trend extrapolations are of limited, or in reality of no, help in guiding decision making in mergers, acquisitions, and other alliances, and often give misleading or even disastrous results. The Baseline Approach clearly identifies the strategic benefits of a planned partnership as well as the threats and risks involved in the transaction.

Essential Benefits of a Baseline Due Diligence Process

1. A due diligence process supported by the Baseline Approach does not necessarily replace traditional models, but it adds substance, value, and a clear business focus.

2. Baseline is cost and time effective. After the computer-supported interview in the Business Position segment, which typically takes 5 to 8 hours, the computer-generated report is delivered in a matter of minutes.

3. Baseline is neutral and unbiased.

4. Baseline provides systematic strategic information that is difficult or impossible to obtain through other methods.

5. The Baseline computer-based elements create a convenient way to assess and compare the two companies and to preview the proposed combination.

6. Frequent users such as venture capitalists, consultants, or bankers gain experience that gradually helps them improve criteria and policies for each new due diligence process.

7. The Baseline Approach gives valuable guidance also to the strategic management process in the first period after the fact.

8. The Baseline Approach allows the user to assess if the price of a company is acceptable for the buyer.

What Auditors Say

One experienced director of auditing states: Baseline Reporting provides more valuable information in three days than traditional methods in as many weeks. Another auditing specialist, in one of the Big Four accounting firms, says "the process uniquely defines the conditions that create the framework for the company's business and provides a good platform for assessing threats and risks."

NOTES

1. Don Durfe, "A Question of Value," *CFO*, March 2005.

2. There is plenty of literature available on the subject. One article that is short and to the point was published in fact just before the announcement of the DaimlerChrysler venture. David A. Nadler, "10 Steps to a Happy Merger," *New York Times*, March 15, 1998. It is beyond our knowledge whether it was ever read by the masters of the DaimlerChrysler project.

CHAPTER 8

Fair and Meaningful Disclosure

Why do all rely on books,
when books are cooked by looks and crooks?
Like it or not, nontraditional yardsticks are on their way.[1]

REPORTING AND COMMUNICATING FOR ACCOUNTABILITY, REPUTATION, AND RELEVANCE

Annual reports from many big companies have become thicker and glossier over a long period of time. An increasing number of companies have found that their annual reports and other financial and nonfinancial communications are important instruments in building understanding and appreciation among their various stakeholder groups. This trend is hopefully continuing, as a way to counteract the damage made by accounting trickery and as a way to restore the confidence in the business community.

However, there is a risk in seeing this process too superficially. The corporate communications function has a responsibility, together with other parts of management, to ensure that the reporting and communications work is taken seriously. Substance, timeliness, and openness must guide the process. To achieve this, company reporting must be geared to and based on real business performance, and the conditions for it, not on "the numbers game" of accounting.

In the United States, not only the SEC but also for example *CFO* magazine have long urged companies to adopt a high level of transparency, sometimes called "full disclosure." In the wake of recent accounting disasters, we can expect continued demands for openness and relevant reporting.

Other countries need to review their reporting patterns as well. Several of the continental European countries have reporting traditions that are almost as tight-lipped as the old Soviet KGB. Some Asian and South American countries have even bigger problems. In India, the government is trying to enforce new corporate conduct and reporting codes, which, if followed, would put India in a leadership position among Asian countries.

Rather than lobbying against more openness, national and international business organizations should embrace this development as a much-needed way to rebuild public confidence in business after the last years of accounting scandals.

TRANSPARENCY, DISCLOSURE, AND RELEVANCE

Reporting needs to be reformed in order to adequately respond to two critical needs for companies and other organizations:

1. To provide useful documentation for the strategic governance process of boards and management
2. To give owners, analysts, and other outside stakeholders a realistic picture of company progress, performance, and problems

Internal/External Reporting

Keeping the two purposes closely aligned is important in order to safeguard a company's credibility among employees, investors, lenders, political decision-makers, and the general public, and for the integrity of the internal management decision process.

> #### Case in Point—Internal/External Reporting
> What kind of information did Sunbeam, Cisco, Qwest, Enron, and all the other companies under SEC investigation use as a base for their decision making at their board and management meetings? Did Sunbeam, internally, use the same manipulated data that they released to external stakeholders, thus deceiving even their own inner circle, or did they speak with a forked tongue, using one set of documents for internal and another set for external use? Was that their way to give new meaning to the term *double Italian accounting*?

Honest and relevant internal reporting gives the top team a chance to really take and measure the pulse of the company, to keep the board and management on top of important facts and developments, and to provide accurate guidelines and follow-up instruments. A management style that allows or encourages incomplete, misleading, or otherwise unsatisfactory internal reporting can lead to disasters by destroying the whole decision-making process. Internal reporting may sometimes be more detailed than externally published reports, but in both, realism and honesty are critical to the function of the reports.

Externally, the company has an obligation to keep shareholders, analysts, and other stakeholders, as well as government bodies and regulators, up to date about the company. While these purposes may be different, the various audiences are not separated by watertight compartments, so in all essential respects all reporting from a company should be consistent and give a fair and relevant picture of the company.

Case in Point—USA Networks

One company that decided to eliminate the suspicion of disparity between its internal and external reporting is USA Networks. USA Networks chairman Barry Diller felt that the best set of information to external stakeholders would be the information that the board and top management use for their best practices. USA Networks committed itself to providing the investment community with its actual internal budget material, even broken down by business segments. In the words of Barry Diller, "There is no better way to let the investing community understand our goals and challenges than by bringing the external world inside the company through the disclosure of USA's internal budget."[2]

Sharing with investors and other "outsiders" the full information used for internal decision-making may seem like a very bold move. What about the competition? Won't we be telling them too much? Maybe, but then again, in normal business practice lots of managers realize that, somehow, competitors often seem to know as much about the company as the internal management team. As Mr. Diller seems to acknowledge, why not disarm them by freely sharing internal information with everyone concerned?

External Reporting

At the root of the discussion about external reporting are at least two aspects: (1) Does the board and management *want to* provide relevant information, and (2) has the board and management set up systems to gather and present relevant information?

The issue of how much external disclosure a company should provide is essential. However, the demand for relevance and honesty is equally important, whether reports are used for one purpose or the other.

Reporting that Follows the Rules

If consolidating internal and external reporting would be a first, bold move, the next step toward a meaningful, reliable reporting system, in the minds of many accountants, might be to follow all the rules of FASB, GAAP, IASC, SEC and other regulatory bodies. Even that basic requirement would be a major initiative in many companies. In an article in *Fortune,* August 2, 1999, U.S. Attorney Mary Jo White says that calling it "managed earnings" is too polite. She feels it really should be called an ungarnished "cooked books."

Arthur Levitt, former chairman of the SEC and a supervisor of U.S. company reporting standards, declared war on bad financial reporting. In a speech in September 1998, called "The Numbers Game,"[3] he addressed a group of lawyers, CPAs and academics, blasting out at accounting irregularities, or, as he called them, "accounting hocus-pocus." He focused on the worst kind of irregularities, the intentional misstatements.

When responsible people, like the SEC chairman or a U.S. Attorney, use such strong words as "earnings hocus-pocus" and "cooked books," then there is reason for concern. And these examples and comments are from the United States, which normally praises itself for having stricter standards and more open reporting than most other countries.

When Following the Rules Is Not Enough

The truth is that reporting on the basis of traditional accounting, even following all the rules, tends to give stakeholders very little useful information about the essential choices and the critical strategic and operational issues that affect company success or failure.

One of the dangerous consequences of this situation is that accounting is increasingly removed both from the strategic priorities and from day-to-day operations. Despite the detailed spreadsheets and four-color charts it generates, accounting is largely useless for its proclaimed purposes of supporting decision-making. Both for the internal decision-making process and for decisions by investors and other stakeholders, accounting data are not enough. To dramatize, one could say that today's accountants have created more and more sophisticated systems to measure and report data that are less and less relevant. We need methods to systematically collect other information.

Board members and managers rely less and less on the sheets of endless numbers that accounting generates. They know that accounting data are of little use to help them in their double responsibility, drafting and executing the company's strategies and supervising company performance.

Business and financial analysts try desperately to find useful sources of information outside the official reports. Some of them claim that if they find anything of interest in the reports, it is in the footnotes.

Auditors, external and internal, face the choice of either sticking to the books and being out of touch with business itself, or staying with their responsibility to assess significant aspects of business threats and opportunities, which means they need to go outside the accounting system.

Financial journalists prefer hearsay and insider reporting rather than published data. They know that even many unauthorized sources provide more relevant and reliable information than accounting data.

A MATTER OF RESTORING CONFIDENCE

The first responsibility of the business community today is to restore and maintain a general level of trust in business. Adequate reporting based on timeliness, credibility, and accountability is a must.

Let us assume that from now on, by a mystic movement of an accounting wand, all companies were to follow all the rules. Would that give us meaningful reporting? The Israeloff quote from *CFO* given earlier seems to indicate that it would not solve all problems. Why? Simply because, as we have seen in Chapters 1 and 2, accounting at best reflects only parts of the indicators of company success or failure.

Traditional accounting-based information is not enough. It does not provide the board and management with more than very marginal information for their planning and decision making. Neither does it satisfy investors or other stakeholders. It often excludes some of the most important factors in assessing and evaluating company performance and progress. We need something that goes beyond accounting, as we know it. Except perhaps for tax assessment purposes, a new approach to company reporting is needed to more adequately serve the demands of the readers and provide a better, more transparent, more reliable, and above all, more relevant picture of the company.

Basic Insight: Company Reporting Must Meet Tougher Standards

To be relevant, company reporting must meet new and tougher standards. These standards must consider the realities of the fourth economy, including an appropriate set of nonfinancial yardsticks.

Until national and international standards are developed and agreed upon, it is up to every company to create its own systems and measures.

Honest Reporting: Telling It Like It Is—Today

Many companies do an excellent job in providing their stakeholders with broad and relevant information about their business situation, marketing and technical issues, staff development, and social responsibility initiatives. They try to provide adequate reports, in line with and beyond laws, regulations, and generally accepted business and accounting practices. But what if laws, regulations, and Generally Accepted Accounting Practices are insufficient or misleading? What if reality has changed so much that generally accepted accounting rules are no longer acceptable?[4]

SE&O: Traps in Traditional Reporting

The serious mismatch between the accounting system and business reality became increasingly obvious at the end of the twentieth century, with the dramatic changes in the basic conditions of the global economy. Despite obvious evidence that a new situation had come, many accountants and economists, with a few bright exceptions, have reacted like the caricature of the army sergeant who sternly declares that, if the map and reality disagree, the map rules.

Some of us may recall the letters *SE&O*[5] in auditors' reports and other financial statements. They signified, by and large, a way to escape responsibility.

If honesty and relevance in reporting were serious requirements today, every corporate CFO or accountant would have to put *SE&O* in big letters on every page of an annual report. Our accounting system creates errors and omissions in practically every item presented in a report.

Consequences of the Irrelevance

Corporate financial reporting, which was supposed to present a fair picture of a company's well-being—or the opposite—its indicators of success or failure—is at best irrelevant, at worst misleading. This is why financial regulators, academia, and other key players should go beyond stricter rules and enforcement of present practices to face the challenge of adopting a reporting system for our time, a reporting system that at least has a better chance of providing useful information than what we have today.

Elements of a New or Complementary Reporting System

To initiate such a discussion, we feel that the elements of a new, complementary, or alternative reporting system that we presented in Chapter 4 could be considered. They are based on common sense and sound business practice.

They do not violate any rules of today's system, which means that any company that wishes to try it can go ahead and do so, without fear of rebukes from auditors or regulatory bodies. Yet, they offer substantial improvements in terms of relevance, realism, usefulness, and honesty over today's accounting-centered practices.

THE BASELINE APPROACH TO FAIR DISCLOSURE AND MEANINGFUL CORPORATE REPORTING

In 1994, the American Institute of Certified Public Accountants (AICPA) published its report, "Improving Business Reporting: A Customer Focus, Meeting the Needs of Investors and Creditors." It concluded that "to stay relevant, financial reports must provide more information about business plans, opportunities, risks, and uncertainties, include information on non-financial performance measures; and disclose data previously reported only internally."[6]

One interesting detail in this report is that "relevance" is introduced as a condition for satisfactory reporting, not only meeting formal accounting law requirements.

The Baseline Approach to disclosure and corporate reporting offers a way to improve external reporting, a way that satisfies the demands put forward by AICPA, and makes fair and meaningful disclosure to shareholders and other stakeholders. It provides relevant and logically structured information on crucial issues with a minimum of clutter.

All Annual Report work should include coverage of the following four items, which are what stakeholders have a strong interest in:

1. The company's Business Definition(s), and how well it is (they are) known and endorsed

2. The company's Business Position, changes since the previous report, and action taken by management to eliminate or reduce the strategic threats indicated by level 2 and 3 relationships

3. The company's Business Reputation diagram (SMART), with a special focus on the red flags

4. A detailed Cash Performance Statement, with management comments and related to the company's strategic goals through the FOCUS and CHARGE measures

All items should ideally be reported for each separate business area, and then summed up in a consolidated report.

The information generated in the strategic and operational processes described here creates an excellent platform for consistent and relevant information to all stakeholders.

What comes out is a consistent and comprehensive picture of:

• The various business areas and business units and the market needs that they satisfy

• Their potential for survival, growth, and earnings, including their interdependence in terms of revenues and costs

- The determinant factors and forces that control and limit the development potential of the respective units
- A prioritized list of action that makes a powerful contribution to the improvement of the company's development potential

A reporting system that includes the four fundamentals we suggest provides considerably more strategic information, both for the strategic and operational planning and for follow-up of development and results, than any accounting-based reporting system.

Case in Point—Action Urgently Required!

A company in the fast food business had severe financial problems to the extent that it had even sold its own trademark and leased it back. The two main owners argued about the reasons for the situation and thus about what action should be taken. A team using the Baseline Approach was called in to find out what to do.

The management team, the chairman, and the president participated in the two-day session. The system clearly pointed out the reasons for the troubles but also new threats, not yet realized.

One of the problems was the president, who was fired the following day. The chairman took over and used the analysis material for internal communication and seminars, where the employees were asked to suggest improvements to the situation.

Afterwards the chairman regretted that that they had not made the analysis half a year or a year earlier, when they would have had more leeway to avoid threats that had been identified in the process. Some of these threats materialized only a couple of months after the analysis, further deteriorating the situation of the company.

The board then decided to be frank and open about the situation of the company. Articles were written in newspapers and some reports aired on TV. Another company then realized that they could be a better owner of the company and acquired it, thus stopping the previous owner's bleeding.

NOTES

1. Robert L. Israeloff, chairman of the American Institute of Certified Public Accountants, in the headline of an article in *CFO*, March 1999.
2. From a memo submitted October 24, 2001, by USA Networks chairman Barry Diller to the SEC, quoted by *Fortune* under the headline "Stop the Madness."
3. See also Chapter 6, end note 6.
4. See "Capital Thinking," *Forbes*, August 23, 1999, by Jon Low and Tony Siesfeld, Ernst & Young, and David Larcker, professor of accounting, Wharton School of Economics.
5. Abbreviation of Latin, *Salvo Errore & Omissione*, approximately translatable into "We are not responsible for mistakes and omissions."
6. As reported in *CFO*, December 1994.

CHAPTER 9

Auditing and Risk Management in a New Situation

Numbers are a tricky game,
hide the picture, show the frame.

RISK ANALYSIS AND MANAGEMENT IN UNPREDICTABLE TIMES

Why Is This Area Important?

Auditing has probably never been as much in the public eye as it is today. While some of the reasons for that exposure are deplorable, chances are that some good may come out of it, not least for the role and influence of the auditing profession. This chapter brings out some of the issues and shows how new initiatives can give the profession more than a facelift.

Auditing: An Operational or Strategic Process?

Auditing has widely been seen as a support system for accounting. A strong tradition views auditing as a control function, a way to check whether accounting is run according to GAAP, FASB, IASB, and other standards. If a company's accounting is seen to be in line with these rules, some auditors, external or internal, feel they can put their mark of approval on the books and then go to sleep with a clear conscience.

Recent events suggest that the auditor's role may not be quite as simple as that. The IIA definition of Internal Auditing states that "Internal auditing...helps an organization accomplish its objectives." That definition certainly takes Internal Auditing from a purely operational support system for accounting to a strategic function for the company or organization.

The flow of recent incidents of questionable accounting in big companies has revealed a long list of shortcomings in present practices. Questions have been raised about the roles of independent board directors, the board auditing committee, internal and external auditors, rating agencies, and financial analysts. The reliability of accounting data has been questioned.

In all this turmoil, what is the role of the auditor, internal or external? Is accounting itself beyond reproach? Should the auditor support the role of accounting, even when the accounting system as such is under debate?

HOW SERIOUS IS THE AUDITING CRISIS?

Let us consider five issues that justify an in-depth discussion about the role of accounting and a more independent role for internal and external auditors:

1. *What does "value" mean in accounting?* As we have discussed in some detail in Chapter 1, accounting uses several entirely different meanings of "value," which causes considerable confusion in a basic area of corporate management and asset measurement. In this situation, should the auditor insist on "due process" and demand stricter definitions of "value," or should he or she close his or her eyes and go along with conventions, no matter how irrelevant?

2. *Can we trust accounting?* Where should the auditor draw the line, when accounting gets suspicious: go along with doubtful practices or slam the lid of the cookie jar, even at the risk of. . .?

3. *Is accounting relevant?* Should auditors actively pursue broader standards for reporting on issues that are relevant to company success or failure, even if such standards were to take reporting beyond traditional data?

4. *Are accounting data useful as platforms for decisions?* Should auditors insist on a tougher distinction between the legitimate use of accounting as a method to register transactions, and more creative uses of accounting for advanced decision making?

5. *Does accounting work in our economy?* The world and economy of the twenty-first century is hardly the same as that of the fifteenth! The three characteristics of the fourth economy that we have suggested in Chapter 2 have an impact on the process of auditing as well as on other aspects of the economy.

Auditing and Risk Management

A report[1] created by CFO Research, a unit related to *CFO* magazine, in cooperation with the AON Group, provides interesting views on new trends in risk management and on the role of auditors and the audit committees. It brings up the need for more strategic initiatives to come from the auditing side, not least from the board-appointed audit committees. The study recognizes that many serious risks and threats to a company's well-being are not necessarily financial. Business risks may be graver than financial risks. The report says (p. 9) that CFOs (and presumably others) "want a clear view of all the risks facing their companies to ensure that there isn't a crucial risk lurking unnoticed and unaddressed." It quotes a vice president of enterprise risk for a Texas insurance group, Chris Mandel: "Business risks, *while difficult to quantify* [our emphasis], could potentially be more significant than those that are more easily quantifiable." We assume that Mr. Mandel does not make the rash conclusion that "quantifiable" must be synonymous with dollars and cents.

We seem to need risk management systems that are as all-encompassing as possible to avoid "unnoticed and unaddressed risks." Since all companies do not have such systems in place, there must be barriers. What are they? The report mentions (p. 18) four kinds of barriers: lack of uniform metrics, too time-consuming, incompatibility with corporate culture, and inadequate IT systems.

What if the authors of the report had found out that, indeed, such new, broad risk identification and measurement methods, with appropriate metrics, time-saving and cost-effective, with limited demands on IT systems, are theirs for the asking? They exist, they are well tested, and are even accessible online.

The Role and Responsibilities of the Auditing Committee

Is a more active auditing committee a blessing or a problem for internal auditors? It can no doubt vary much depending on the personalities and corporate setup involved. By and large, though, it is our impression that a more proactive and involved audit committee can offer valuable support to the internal auditors. What if new methods could offer the audit committee and the board a work-saving way to better oversight, and at the same time make auditors more productive in their parts of the process?

Survival, Earnings, and Growth

Auditors could play a significant role in establishing a new system, starting with a strategic focus on the main goals of most companies. In our view, those overall goals can usually be defined as survival, earnings, and growth. Any threat to those goals would be the object of risk analysis.

The four fundamentals or "Baselines" that we work with are presented in detail in Chapter 4. Most business leaders would easily recognize them as significant parameters for business management in the twenty-first century. The unique feature is that they can be identified, defined, and measured in a meaningful way, including well-tested computer-supported systems. How relevant are the four groups of fundamentals for the auditing process?

Business Definition—Why?

Traditionally, the core identity of a company was defined by ownership, a hierarchical structure, or traditions. Today, none of these pillars are as strong as they used to be. Instead, this role has largely been taken over by the *business idea,* if it can be clearly defined and endorsed by all concerned.

Companies with clear, well-conceived and endorsed business ideas or Business Definitions for each business area have a better platform for risk management than other companies. The system proposes a structured process in a number of well-defined steps to create clear Business Definition(s).

Because of the importance of the Business Definitions as benchmarks for company strategies, performance, and risk management, internal auditors should be involved in hammering out relevant Business Definitions for all the business areas of the companies they serve. In the process they will also improve their understanding of the issues that business management grapples with, which will make the auditing work easier and more rewarding for all parties.

Business Position—Why?

No company is an isolated unit. Like any living organism, a company depends for its survival and growth on its relationships with its environment.

The Business Position shows the company's dependencies on outside forces and relationships. How do we measure? We do it through a well-tested computer-supported process, which defines and quantifies significant relations. Ultimately it measures the company's most decisive success factor, its freedom to act.[2]

Internal auditors should be concerned about this strong area of risk and threat, the company's exposure to outside forces, and make the concept "freedom to act" an integrated part of their risk assessment work.

Business Reputation—Why?

In a market economy, company success depends on thousands of decisions made outside the company, far from the board room.

Companies that are known and appreciated by outside decision makers are more successful than other companies. The success of a company is made or broken by decisions made by important stakeholders, such as market/customers, employees, owners/investors, public opinion/media, and leadership. How do we measure? We do it through a Stakeholder Management and Reputation Test process (SMART), keeping close track of stakeholder attitudes and opinions.

Auditors, internal and external, should prioritize the decision climate outside the company itself, and ensure that management gives it appropriate attention and uses reliable measurement methods to keep track of the development.

Cash Performance—Why?

Cash flow statements are more reliable and relevant than other accounting-related instruments. *Advanced cash performance* statements are even better.

Companies that can show how their cash performs in relation to strategic priorities have better chances of success than other companies. The cash performance statement shows how the company uses and manages its cash *in relation to its strategic goals.* How do we measure? We do it through a Cash Performance process, going beyond traditional cash flow.

Auditors should support a development that upgrades cash performance statements, even when this leads to a relative downgrading of the more traditional but less reliable income statements and balance sheets.

THE BASELINE APPROACH TO AUDITING AND RISK MANAGEMENT

A Better System for Auditing, Control, and Risk Management

Traditional control-oriented auditing is a time-consuming process, yet it often allows serious risks to slip through the net. The Baseline Approach to auditing and risk management goes beyond checking and verifying accounting data, and identifies risk or threat issues of strategic significance to corporate management.

Auditing in the Fourth Economy: New Demands and New Solutions

With the arrival of the fourth economy, internal and external auditors have seen the scope of their work modified and their responsibility expanded. Checking the books has never been enough for performing responsible auditing. Today it is less adequate than ever.

There Is No Getaway for the CEO

That does not mean he or she is left alone. There are people, processes, methods, and systems for the CEO to work with and to enlist.

In recent years, the role of the auditors, not least the internal auditors, has started to change. Auditing is invited to take a more strategic role in risk assessment, risk management, and risk prevention.[3] For companies with a strong foothold in the fourth economy, auditing systems should ideally cover most or all of the new fundamentals suggested in Chapter 4.

How does the internal or external auditor meet the challenge of the CEO who invites him or her to become his partner in business risk analysis and business risk management? Can the CEO count on a positive response and professional support?

To help auditors meet these challenges, new systems and concepts have been developed in the United States and abroad. National and international auditing organizations have come up with recommendations. One basic model that seems to have been accepted worldwide is the one presented by the Committee of Sponsoring Organizations of the Treadway Commission (COSO).

Computer-supported auditing systems are a part of the new resources. A wide range of systems have been made available. Ideally, a new system should go beyond traditional software, into knowledge-based systems.

They need to meet some basic requirements including:

1. Recognizing the fact that nonfinancial factors may play a bigger role in today's economy than traditional accounting

2. Have their origin in real business practices, rather than in accounting theory

3. Be independent of company size, business, and nationality, to facilitate comparisons between different companies and business units in a global network of companies

4. Be neutral in terms of user personality, background, and preferences to ensure total objectivity

5. Be comparable over time and between businesses to make it part of day-to-day company routines

6. Integrate the skills and information of top management and operational management with the professional qualities of the auditors

7. Be waterproof, so the system "can't be fooled"

The Big Railroads Company

The Swedish Railroads[4] (SJ) is a multidivision corporation. Some of the divisions are more third economy in their character, while others are far advanced in the direction of the fourth economy. The following example shows how, in the 1990s, SJ approached the issues of auditing and risk management.

Its method is built on a six-step planning model, integrating elements of COSO, Balanced Scorecard, and Baseline Reporting. See Exhibit 9.1.

EXHIBIT 9.1	STRATEGIC AUDITING AND RISK ASSESSMENT PROJECT

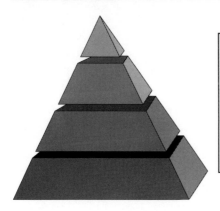

- Identify relevant risks
- Evaluate risks in economic terms
- Identify what causes substantial risks
- Prioritize areas that depend on the quality of Internal Control
- Identify potential weaknesses in the system of Internal Control in prioritized areas
- Establish an auditing plan

For the crucial stage 1, identification of relevant risks, SJ faced a choice of four approaches:

1. Nonsystematic approaches, such as common sense
2. Mathematical matrix models, such as the Deloitte & Touche CSA method
3. Scenario models, such as the CSA methods presented by Tim Leach and Paul McCoach
4. Combined models, which is what they ultimately chose

Traditionally, auditors carry out risk assessment by themselves with no participation from the management. Recognizing that managers are often more knowledgeable of the risks their businesses are exposed to than the auditors, and wanting to involve operations management closely in the auditing process, the auditors of SJ looked for a method that offered a high degree of management participation. The Baseline method uses experience-based software to achieve this, and combines self-assessment with a systematic and consistent approach to risk and internal control, though in a different way compared to the traditional audit approach. The method was developed by Sten Bjelke, CIA, and internal auditors of SJ.

The Assessment Process Runs in Six Steps

1. Preparation

A week or two before the workshop, a brief description of the method and a list of preparations are presented to management.

2. Workshop

During the workshop:

- The financial data entered into the software is checked.
- The business areas of the organization are defined.
- For each business area, all links to stakeholders and other environment factors are defined and potential threats to the business are identified and assessed. The software raises the subjects, one at a time, to be discussed and decided upon.

3. Verification

A CheckList is printed at the end of the workshop. It documents all questions, answers, and notes exactly as they appeared on the screen during the workshop.

4. Analysis and Report

The diagnosis module produces a draft report that is returned to the auditor. Together with the CheckList, the report is a complete documentation of the workshop and the assessment results.

5. Review of Possible Actions

Substantial threats pointed out in the report set priorities for the audit plan. It is vital that discussions about the report and the priorities are held with management and that agreement is reached before the report is finalized. These discussions usually take place within two weeks after the workshop.

6. Action Plan

Actions agreed are spelled out in the action plan.

Summary

With this method, management and internal auditing share a work platform that meets crucial demands from both sides, in a mutually rewarding process, taking all possible aspects into account.

It is based on years of practical work in company assessments, for internal and external auditing applications, in mergers and acquisitions, in preparing IPOs, in credit analysis and new business development, and other applications, with an unfailing track record:

- It has been used successfully for service and product companies, for major corporations, medium-sized companies and small companies, in established industrialized countries, in emerging economies, and in post-communist economies.

- It is independent of subjective preferences and opinions of the facilitator. However, the use of the system requires professionalism to ensure that the management team is well served in the process. An experienced internal auditor can acquire the required skills through training programs provided by the software supplier.

- It creates comparability between various businesses within a company or between companies, and builds bases for comparison over time, to facilitate follow-up and progress reports from one period to the next.

- It uses traditional financial data, but only as a platform for the in-depth analysis that goes beyond accounting into the realities of business position factors that control the company's development.

- It builds a platform between strategic/operational management and internal auditing through the unique computer-supported interview method, where the system decides what questions to ask, phrases them, and provides alternative answers for the user to select from.

- The system then validates the answers to ensure that no contradicting answers have been given, and runs calculations to prepare reports and guide the continued interview.

- It has built-in control modules to protect against misunderstandings, deceptions, and omissions.

- It generates complete and unique reports, with text, summaries, charts, and graphs, for use in management and board presentations, and to create action.

- It is more than a software product—it is a complete process.

Four Immediate Benefits

1. This method saves 75 percent of the internal audit planning process work, time that can be used for professional and strategic input from the internal auditor. The time savings is achieved through careful screening resulting in a focus on priority issues.

2. It identifies the items that should be included in the strategic plan of the company and creates the basis for an activity list to enhance the probability of success.

3. It redefines the input from the internal auditor, to strategic issues that can directly benefit top management and the board of directors.

4. The method is consistent with COSO and other internal auditing guidelines.

NOTES

1. "Strategic Risk Management: New Disciplines, New Opportunities," report prepared by *CFO Research Services*, March 2002. Available online at www.cforesearch.com and www.aon.com.

2. For a detailed view of the analysis system, which provides broad computer-supported coverage of data for an all-inclusive risk management system, check the online version on the web site www.realbizonline.com. The system has been used in practice to improve auditing and risk management in hundreds of businesses of various sizes and industries.

3. See David McNamee and Georges M. Selim, "Risk Management: Changing the Internal Auditor's Paradigm," Institute of Internal Auditors Research Foundation, 1998.

4. The Swedish Railroads (SJ) is a corporation owned by the Swedish Government. Its brief is to work as much as possible as any publicly listed corporation.

CHAPTER 10

"What Are We Lending Against?"

Value now shows many facets,
many more than old-time assets.

FINANCING, LENDING, AND INVESTMENT DECISIONS IN THE FOURTH ECONOMY

Why Is This an Important Issue?

It is important for society and the economy in general that financial resources go to those projects where they can make the maximum contributions or provide the best returns. Even in a world where "minds in interaction" is the primary driving force of value generation, the role of capital must not be neglected. The productivity of financial means is still a basic clue to positive growth and development. Allocation of financial resources still needs to work as well as it possibly can.

Providers of funds, whether in their capacity as bankers, Small Business Administration agencies, lenders, investors, venture capitalists, or in other roles, must have the best possible information on risks, collaterals, and returns when they make decisions on where they put their money into play.

It is finally important to those who apply for investments or other funding that they can trust the financing process to be fair and based on objective, complete, and relevant information. It is also essential to them to fully understand why decisions in their case go one way or the other, so that they can learn from the process and adjust their projects in the best possible way.

In previous economies, with a less intense pace of change, this process may have appeared to be easier than now. While the future has always been unpredictable, the number and impact of potential, unexpected influences that could affect a business project seemed to be less unlimited than they are today.

Also, while mind-based input has always been important in business development, the relative role of physical assets used to be bigger than it is now, when the success or failure of many projects rest almost entirely on mind-based factors. The feeling of security that a lender or investor could experience, rightly or wrongly, in looking at a piece of real estate, machinery, or other hard assets as collateral for his or her funds gave comfort and provided a rationale (not necessarily rational but still with that appearance) for decisions, even when they went against the immediate interests of the applicant. The same feeling of objectivity may seem more difficult to generate and communicate, when looking at the prospect of a new drug, the brand position of a new product, the brain power of a start-up company, or the export potential of a new service, as sources of payback and return on the cash injected in a project. And yet, this is where the overall productivity imperative should lead new money.

In this situation, there are still those who maintain that cash advances of any kind must be secured by "fixed assets," preferably fixed assets listed on that increasingly irrelevant instrument, the balance sheet. If that view were to prevail, as one can easily perceive, it would violate the interests of all three parties outlined above: lenders, borrowers, and society at large. Limited funds would tend to be severely misallocated. It would not be understandable to the borrower, it would not be optimal to the lender or investor, and it certainly would not be beneficial to society.

The problem is that the tool most commonly used to support decision making in most lending processes, accounting, does not know of any other criteria than financial for funds allocation. In most bank lending guidelines, the balance sheet approach still looms high, as if balance sheets were in any positive way related to a project's viability, or as if balance sheets could guarantee return or payback.

Unfortunately, forecasting is equally as useless as balance sheets. In today's unpredictable world, the dynamics of business, technology, the economy, and society preclude such forecasting fads as discounted cash flow, net present value, real options, and similar approaches. They are all part of "corporate astrology."

When balance sheets, other accounting data, and speculative forecasting are out as useful tools, what is left when a potential lender needs to assess the payback ability of business projects?

Are We Stupid?

> We asked ourselves why banks had become such crummy lenders. No other business has done its primary job so badly. Are we stupid? No, but we don't know what we're lending against any more.[1]

Bob Paterson is not the only one who is concerned about the role and performance of banking and other financing and lending operations in the fourth economy. Another very senior banker, who has recognized the same problem, is no one less than the former chairman of Citibank, Walter B. Wriston,[2] considered to be one of the most far-sighted bankers of his time. His comment is legendary: "Flying by faulty instruments is dangerous."

He expanded his thoughts for our benefit:

> We are now in the midst of a huge technological and economic revolution. Yet, we are so accustomed to using the standards of economic and social measurement developed for the industrial age that we seldom stop to consider that the old measures of economic progress and decay, success and failure, are rapidly losing their usefulness. (op. cit. p. 92)

Old balance sheet thinking still seems to prevail. Walter Wriston again:

> Flying by faulty instruments is dangerous. The old instruments may convince us we have failed where we are succeeding or persuade us to turn about in vain pursuit of our past rather than successfully navigating the future. If we are to cope successfully with the "new" economy, *we shall have to develop a new methodology to measure economic success and failure.* (our emphasis) (op. cit. p. 93)

The banks have traditionally been key agents in the process of supporting new companies. Today, banking itself is a business that searches for its new role and identity. The reasons for this are profound, essentially a function of the fourth economy.

Banking, of course, traditionally had a central position in the nineteenth- and twentieth-century economies. In the old industrial economy, capital was king. The banks, as capital dispensers, had a key position of power. When capital was the main resource, the banks were a key to business growth and development. Banks gained a high level of respect in many circles. The local bank manager was a trusted member of the town. This situation is gone, probably forever. Today, the driving forces of company performance and growth are not primarily capital. Furthermore, since financing is still necessary, the banks have shut themselves off to the needs of the new companies, partly because companies in the fourth economy do not provide old-fashioned collaterals. As a result, the surge of new companies in the 1990s has by and large been financed outside the banking system, through various forms of venture capitalism. Banking lost market share to other techniques, such as securitization of trade receivables, as well as to other financial institutions, among them the venture capital (VC) lenders, including bank VC units. Traditional banking had no instruments for assessing companies without traditional balance sheets. The simplistic solution "Just say no!" was obviously not the right answer. Joseph Nocera expressed the fundamental problem of banking this way: "Banking Is Necessary, Banks Are Not."[3] In the same article, banking consultant Edward Furash is quoted as saying that banks used to be at the center of the intermediation process; now they are not.

The railroads in the early twentieth century, and the classical example they provided of difficulties in adapting to new situations, may perhaps offer a relevant comparison with the banks today, with all the similarities and differences that any such comparisons involve.

ACCOUNTABILITY IN LENDING AND FINANCING

Case in Point—Banks as Investors

Consolidations and mergers in the U.S. banking industry have been widespread in the 1990s. Each one of these events has been hailed, when they were launched, as an efficiency measure, aimed at enhancing shareholder value and improving consumer service. Only in exceptional cases have these promises survived more than the first 6 to 12 months. Instead, a fairly consistent pattern has developed: The cost to shareholders, in terms of falling share prices, has been exorbitant, and customer service has gone from bad to worse.

First Union has been one of the most active players in this game. After amalgamating a range of regional banks, closing down offices and "restructuring," that is, reducing customer choice as well as the number of bank employees, First Union ended its 1990s M&A spree by the acquisition of The Money Store in 1998 to begin in the 2000s with the bid for Wachovia.

The Money Store was a lender that had built its reputation, with the help of ad campaigns involving top sports stars, on offering loans to low-income consumers or to consumers with poor credit records. The merger strategy was based on the idea of combining the strong name of The Money Store with the resources and the ensuing low capital costs of big brother First Union. The promise when the merger was announced was that it would result in immediate additions to First Union earnings. The driving force behind the earlier successes of The Money Store was its CEO. Less than a year after First Union's acquisition, the CEO of The Money Store left, apparently in frustration.

What happened to shareholder value and customer service? The promised earnings turned into losses, to the tune of close to $6 billion, made up of a purchase price of more than $2 billion, assumed debts of more than $1 billion, "earnings adjustments" of $100 million, and a final write-off of $2.6 billion. As a result of this and other unsuccessful acquisitions, First Union share prices fell to a three-year low. Customers were turned off. Finally, only two years after the acquisition, The Money Store was closed, and its business idea of providing loans to less privileged customers was shelved forever.

First Union losses are not unique in the history of failed mergers, although the amounts of total losses are at the high end of the league. (See also Chapter 7.) What is embarrassing is that it happened to a bank, a company that is supposed to have unique expertise in assessing other companies, and in this case dealing with a company in their own industry! It appears that the analysis that First Union made of The Money Store was so summary that it was more of undue negligence than due diligence. This is bad for any company and the consultants it hires, but more so for a bank than for any other company.

Is it possible that First Union was so entrenched in old banking procedures and traditions that it made a classic balance sheet analysis of The Money Store and relied on its own lending and financing decision models as a basis for its investment decision?

Old Measures of Success and Failure

The main issue is that banking's chief product, capital, is no longer the all-important resource it was in the industrial age. Mind-based assets—knowledge, motivation, information, loyalty, relationships, and other "soft" factors—tend to replace money and physical assets as the driving force of business.[4] And, while capital is still needed, it is not primarily to finance physical assets. In the new economy, companies want to use capital to build "mind-based resources," knowledge, motivation, marketing, and relationships, expenses that, to the traditional banker, look more like costs than assets. And what do banks get as collateral?

Many leaders in the banking community, as well as other business leaders, have recognized the problem, so well expressed by Walter Wriston: "The old measures of . . . success and failure . . . are rapidly losing their usefulness." It has been harder to find a discussion on solutions, new guidelines, procedures, and tools for practical use in banking and lending.

Much of today's growth "products" are mind-based *services*, health care, tourism, hotels, restaurants, entertainment, information management, financial services, business services, and trade. Disney and Microsoft are bigger exporters from the United States than many traditional manufacturers. Even where products seem to be hard and tangible, their content is more and more *mind-based* and less *hardware-based*. Pharmaceutical products and mobile phones are two good examples. All kinds of machinery, from cars and engineering equipment to robots, have lots of brainpower built into the products. And in traditional industries, service generates more and more of the revenues and profits. Jack Welch, chairman and CEO of General Electric, predicted in 1995 that in 2000, GE would get more than 75 percent of its revenues from services, and 25 percent from manufacturing. Distribution is fast, with instant ordering and delivery systems, low levels of stock, and showroom or pipeline inventory. Dell Computers with its payment-as-you-order policy is a well-known example. Marketing and sales, rather than through wholly owned networks of retailers, tend to be through franchise or reseller arrangements, or direct, on the Internet. The production process itself, even in traditional manufacturing, is restructured to reduce traditional balance sheet assets; outsourcing, IT, JIT, and fast turnover are intended to cut inventories, equipment, and factories, traditional examples of bank collateral.

All this makes traditional balance sheets more meaningless than ever as indicators of success and failure. Add to this the perceived difficulties in evaluating the new assets and it is easy to see the enormous implications of the fourth economy for bank lending and credit management.

Paradoxically, bankers' expertise is still needed, perhaps more than ever! The fourth economy may become a great opportunity for banking, if banking is willing and able to accept the challenge! A banker's professional know-how becomes a more valuable asset the more clients get to appreciate the banker's *expertise* in managing and using money, rather than the "commodity," capital itself. This is a consequence of banking itself moving into the age of nonfinancial performance factors!

Long ago, one of the writers, HJ, worked for a regional bank in a forestry, mining, and manufacturing area of Sweden. As a young banker, he was truly impressed with his older colleagues, the local bank managers. While balance sheet analysis was still the official kingpin of credit processing, these bankers in practice went far beyond that. They were thoroughly familiar with the business situation of the clients they served, sometimes moreso than the clients themselves. Loan processing was typically based on an ongoing dialog between client and banker. The banker's *experience* was the most important value-added part of banking, over and above the *capital* the banker could provide.

One consequence of this was the confidence the client had in the banker. Obviously, if the loan was granted, everybody was happy! But even if the loan was refused, the client had enough confidence in the banker to understand that there was a reason for it. The client knew there were things he (yes, usually it was a *he*) had to do, himself, to be able to come back and get a new hearing.

Can Those Times Come Back?

Not likely. The fourth economy is here to stay, at least until some time in the future when it is succeeded by a fifth economy, about which we know nothing at this time. The future is genuinely unpredictable. A more relevant question is: Can banking adapt itself to the fourth economy? Maybe it can, but it will call for substantial changes of minds, attitudes, procedures, and more. Above all, it will require a new perspective on the lending process, one that focuses on the overall business situation of the client company, not on its balance sheet.

THE BASELINE APPROACH TO LENDING AND FINANCING DECISIONS

Contrary to conventional wisdom, financing, bank lending, and investment decision making get little help from accounting data in today's economy. Many of the challenges apply also to venture capitalists and to bank-like organizations, such as small business agencies, as well as to other investment decision processes. New mindsets and new practical instruments are called for.

The basic challenge is to get away from accounting-based models and focus on the real business situation of the lenders or investment candidates. This is how many bankers in small banks in the 1950s instinctively acted. But in the big-volume banks, often grown oversize by mergers and acquisitions, formal procedures, based on accounting data, took over.

The Baseline Approach: A Way to Restore Financing, Bank Lending, and Investment Decision Making to Real Business

The Baseline Approach to lending and financing restores banking to a process where strategic business information becomes the platform for lending and financing decisions, not increasingly meaningless balance sheet data. It does this in a process that illustrates the lending company's criteria for survival, earnings, and growth—in other words, its payback potential, its business performance. It presents an old-fashioned yet entirely new way for banks to deal successfully with fourth economy companies, a practical, experience-tested yet computer-supported method to reform the credit review and approval process. Far more important than introspective balance sheet analyses in the credit review process, the bank lending process should include careful review of the following items:

1. The company's Business Definition, its endorsement levels, and the strength of its mission and vision

2. The company's Business Position, how it compares with other companies in related businesses, and what action management has taken to eliminate or reduce the strategic threats indicated by level 2 and 3 relationships

3. The company's Business Reputation index, the Stakeholder Management and Reputation Test (SMART), with a special focus on the strong and weak points, its green and red lights

4. A detailed Cash Performance statement with management comments

This process doesn't replace the banker. It uses modern technology to enhance the banker's professional expertise. It helps banks and other lending institutions to tackle the problems and grab the opportunities of the fourth economy. It takes the loan applicant's financial assets into account, but goes beyond them to review the total opportunities and risks of the company. It puts the person-to-person dialog back at the center of customer contacts. It improves the "hit rate" and reduces the risk of credit losses. It supports credit review and approval through an unbiased and objective process appreciated both by the lender and the applicant. Above all, it takes the bank's primary focus away from physical assets collaterals to the client's payback potential.

Case in Point—A Tale of Two Companies

A Small Business Administration Fund got a request for financing from two companies. They were direct competitors and of similar size. Their financial situation, according to their books, was fairly similar. The fund submitted the two companies to a Baseline analysis. The result, according to the 50-page report, which took less than a day to generate, was surprising. In Exhibits 10.1 and 10.2 we reproduce the two kites, which show in graphic form the essence of their strong and weak sides. The bigger the kite, the stronger the business position. As appears, the company to the left, Company A, had a much stronger business position and its survival and payback potential were assessed to be quite satisfactory. The fund granted a loan to Company A, which actually turned out to be a big success.

EXHIBIT 10.1   IF YOU WERE A BANKER, WHICH COMPANY WOULD YOU CHOOSE? COMPANY A?

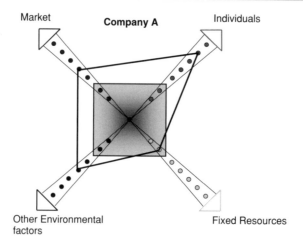

Market   **Company A**   Individuals

Other Environmental factors   Fixed Resources

EXHIBIT 10.2   OR COMPANY B?

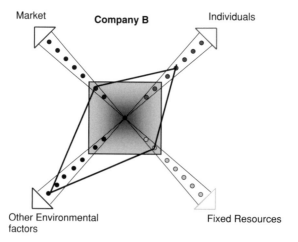

Market   **Company B**   Individuals

Other Environmental factors   Fixed Resources

The Baseline Approach to credit evaluation and analysis can be adapted to policies and practices of individual banks or lending institutions. The Baseline Approach to banking rests on a few basic assumptions:

- Payback potential, not physical collateral, is the primary criterion for granting or refusing a credit application.

- Companies in the twenty-first century depend on other factors for success or failure than those listed on the balance sheet. These other factors are more important in determining a client's payback potential than balance sheet corollary.

- Balance sheets reflect the past. In a world of rapid change, the banker should look for potential for future returns.

- In the fourth economy, the fundamentals do not appear on the balance sheets. Four fundamental conditions for PBP (payback potential) are: a sound Business Definition, a good Business Position (freedom to act), a positive Business Reputation, and strong Cash Performance.

- The critical area in evaluating the threats and future potential of a company is the border line between a company and its environment

Banks use the Baseline Approach to increase their business, reduce their credit losses, provide a valuable service to their clients, improve their lending process, create experience-based credit records and guidelines, and become more competitive.

"The Right Relationship Is Everything"

Checking a client company's relationships and dependencies is obviously one of the crucial tasks in order to determine the credit risks and the loan repayment ability of the company. Banks do themselves and their clients a real service, when they integrate a systematic relationship check into their credit assessment process. Chase hit a jackpot in the 1990s formulating what every bank should have as its business focus, when it adopted the slogan "The Right Relationship Is Everything." It is probably one of the most brilliant tag lines any bank could have today. There is no safer way to evaluate a company's credit application than by examining its relationships, its dependencies, the influences it exercises on crucial stakeholders, and the influences it is subjected to.

Other banks and lending organizations use the Baseline Approach to provide more accurate diagnoses than any balance sheet–based credit analysis can offer, and even under circumstances considerably more difficult than regular, run-of-the-mill company financing.

Cases in Point—Two Extreme Cases

If a credit evaluation process works in making decisions about financing companies in an emerging African country such as Tanzania, would it be worth considering for credit decisions in normal situations in North Carolina or Idaho?

If a credit evaluation process works in granting or denying credit to companies in emerging post-communist countries in the Baltic countries, would it be worth considering for credit decisions in normal situations in Nebraska, France, or Switzerland?

Summary of the Baseline fundamentals, applied to banking and lending operations (for more details, see Chapter 4):

Business Definition

Companies that have a clear perception of where they want to go, in market-defined terms, tend to be better credit risks than companies that do not.

Business Position

Companies that know the significant dependencies and relationships that impact their business are better credit risks than companies that do not.

Business Reputation

Companies that have a clear view and good measurements of the key factors that drive the stakeholders appreciation of the company are a better credit risk than companies that do not.

Cash Performance

Companies that rely on their cash flow statement and use it actively, with a clear sensitivity and strategy analysis, are better credit risks than companies that rely more on income statements and balance sheets.

NOTES

1. Mr. Bob Paterson, senior vice president, Canadian Imperial Bank of Commerce, in *Fortune*, October 1994.
2. In "The Twilight of Sovereignty" (op. cit.).
3. *Fortune*, May 11, 1998.
4. For a broad discussion on these issues, see Peter F. Drucker, *Post-Capitalist Society* (op. cit.), and Frederick F. Reichfeld, *The Loyalty Effect* (op. cit.).

Index

Page references in italics refer to illustrations.